D1515463

The Multinational Corporation in China

Organization and Strategy
Series editors:
John Child and Suzana B. Rodrigues

Published:
Silvia Gherardi
Organizational Knowledge: The Texture of Workplace Learning

Stephen Todd Rudman
The Multinational Corporation in China: Controlling Interests

The Multinational Corporation in China

CONTROLLING INTERESTS

Stephen Todd Rudman

Blackwell Publishing

© 2006 by Stephen Todd Rudman

BLACKWELL PUBLISHING
350 Main Street, Malden, MA 02148-5020, USA
9600 Garsington Road, Oxford OX4 2DQ, UK
550 Swanston Street, Carlton, Victoria 3053, Australia

The right of Stephen Todd Rudman to be identified as the Author of this Work has been
asserted in accordance with the UK Copyright, Designs, and Patents Act 1988.

First published 2006 by Blackwell Publishing Ltd

1   2006

Library of Congress Cataloging-in-Publication Data

Rudman, Stephen Todd.
The multinational corporation in China : controlling interests / Stephen Todd Rudman.
    p.   cm.—(Organization and strategy)
Includes bibliographical references and index.
ISBN-13: 978-1-4051-3369-2 (hardcover : alk. paper)
ISBN-10: 1-4051-3369-4 (hardcover)
1. International business enterprises—China—Management.   2. International business
enterprises—China—Management—Case studies.   3. International business enterprises—
United States—Management.   4. International business enterprises—United States—
Management—Case studies.   I. Title.   II. Series.

HD62.4.R83 2006
658′.0490951—dc22
2005034217

A catalogue record for this title is available from the British Library.

Set in 11/13pt Bembo
by Graphicraft Limited, Hong Kong
Printed and bound in Singapore
by COS Printers Pte Ltd

The publisher's policy is to use permanent paper from mills that operate a sustainable
forestry policy, and which has been manufactured from pulp processed using acid-free
and elementary chlorine-free practices. Furthermore, the publisher ensures that the
text paper and cover board used have met acceptable environmental accreditation
standards.

For further information on
Blackwell Publishing, visit our website:
www.blackwellpublishing.com

This book is dedicated to the memory of my beloved late wife, Cynthia Miriam, of blessed memory. She made this, and so much else, possible.

Contents

Series Editors' Foreword

Blackwell's Organization and Strategy series publishes works of major scholarship based on case studies. It recognizes that case studies offer a unique opportunity to provide an in-depth and holistic understanding of organization and strategy in its context. They offer this contribution through detailed investigation that is longitudinal and/or closely compares key examples. Longitudinal investigation can uncover the dynamics of change, the way that change pervades different levels of organization, and patterns of emergence. Close comparisons between cases can map in detail the nature of variation within a category of organizations. Both types of investigation can also derive lessons from how organizational and strategic innovations have been introduced and their effects.

In this way, case studies address the problem that Andrew Pettigrew noted in his book *The Awakening Giant* (Blackwell, 1985), namely that the lack of a holistic approach, sensitive to both context and history, has seriously limited our understanding of both organizations and their strategies. It is therefore intended that books in this series adopt a holistic perspective which examines the interplay between a range of salient aspects and from several theoretical perspectives. The books should be contextually embedded and, where appropriate, take account of the relevant historical background. They should make an original contribution to theory and offer implications for policy and practice.

Further details on the requirements for manuscripts to be considered for publication in the Organization and Strategy series are available from the Senior Editor, Business & Management, at Blackwell Publishing.

John Child and Suzana B. Rodrigues

Acknowledgments

A work of this nature could not have been completed without the assistance, cooperation and kindness of many people, all of whom I would like to acknowledge.

Professor John Child, my research supervisor, consistently provided a model of leadership, scholarship and humanity which I strive to emulate. I benefited greatly from the help of many people at the Judge Institute of Management Studies: from the faculty, in particular Professors Malcolm Warner, Peter Nolan and Michael Dempster; and from the members of staff, especially Mary Jane Jerkins, who was then personal assistant to Professor Dempster, whose patience and good humor brightened my days.

Research, even in the age of the Internet, depends on the help of librarians. At the Judge Institute I was fortunate to have the assistance of the Librarian, Jane Milburn, and her associates Ruth Newman and Sharon Hicks. In the San Francisco Bay Area I received much help from the library staff of the Haas School of Business, University of California, Berkeley, and from the staff of Golden Gate University Library, San Francisco.

This book literally could not have been done without the invaluable cooperation and assistance of many people within the China-based affiliates of the US multinational corporations portrayed here, as well as their colleagues within the US headquarters of these companies. All of them made time in their demanding schedules to help me, and shared their knowledge freely. Their contributions are acknowledged anonymously, in keeping with the companies' desire for non-disclosure of company or individual identities. I also wish to acknowledge many people in China, Southeast Asia and the US who shared their experiences and insights; since most did so on an "off the record" basis, I regret that I cannot acknowledge them by name.

With all the support and help that I received, however, the customary disclaimer that errors and omissions in this work are my sole responsibility must be added here.

Introduction

Research Objectives, Implementation of Research Objectives, and Importance of This Research

In recognition of the central role that they play in international trade and investment, multinational corporations (MNC)[1] have been the subject of considerable research for decades. Yet within that research comparatively little attention has been devoted to the processes by which MNC are actually managed. Instead, research has involved consideration of organizational structure aspects related to the need to integrate dispersed foreign affiliates into MNC global operations while also allowing these affiliates enough freedom to respond to varying conditions found in different local business environments.

The control of geographically dispersed foreign affiliates has been recognized for many years as the central challenge facing the leaders of global businesses. Yet there have been few studies of the processes by which MNC control and coordinate the activities of foreign affiliates, and even fewer studies that also examine whether MNC control and coordinate their wholly owned subsidiaries (WOS)[2] by different means or in a different manner than they do subsidiaries that are international joint ventures (IJV).[3]

The Multinational Corporation in China addresses the question of *how* multinational corporations actually control and coordinate their worldwide affiliates, focusing on the control and coordination by four large US multinational corporations of their China operations. The empirical research consists of four in–depth case studies as well as comparison and analysis of management control processes across the four companies, emphasizing the functional areas of human resources management (HRM), finance, manufacturing and government relations.

The book is based on the author's research within the China affiliates of the four companies, conducted over a two year period, utilizing a wide range of sources. These include detailed personal interviews with senior managers of the affiliates as well as discussions with consultants, lawyers, government officials, and business managers not associated with the companies being studied and examination of internal as well as publicly available company documentation. Longitudinal perspective was facilitated through review of numerous newspapers and periodicals focusing on business and on China, as well as industry-specific publications, and books and monographs dealing with China and with specific industries and companies.

This book makes several important contributions to the study of the management of multinational corporations as well as to management practice. Among them:

- Unlike previous works it focuses on dynamic management control processes as the units of analysis, rather than on static structures, enabling an understanding of *how* multinational corporations are actually managed.
- It introduces a theory of management control based on precise definitions of control and coordination: definitions that are absent from most earlier research, and which make possible the insight that control and coordination are two different management processes and that it is the interaction of the two processes that enables multinational corporations to manage numerous, globally dispersed affiliates.
- The case analyses and cross-case comparisons demonstrate that the MNC whose affiliates are studied here are able to simultaneously and successfully integrate these affiliates into parent company global operations while also allowing sufficient differentiation of affiliate operations to meet the demands of China's markets. This empirical evidence challenges the argument, raised in earlier works on multinational management, that depicts simultaneous integration and differentiation of MNC affiliates in terms of conflict and lack of operational efficiency.
- The case analyses and cross-case comparisons also provide empirical evidence explaining how simultaneous integration and differentiation are achieved, through an analysis of the "two faces" of MNC management processes. The MNC "internal face" represents the internal management processes of the parent, which are transmitted to and implanted within its affiliates. The MNC "external face" refers to the adaptation, by the parent MNC, of affiliate strategies and organizational structures to enable the affiliates to meet the demands of China's markets. This also represents important empirical evidence of the coexistence of universalist management processes alongside strategies and structures that are contingent upon local business environments.

The Scope of the Inquiry

The Multinational Corporation in China sets out to investigate management control processes in affiliates of multinational corporations through an examination, by means of case studies of management control processes employed by US multinationals within their China affiliates. This examination involves detailed consideration of the following issues:

- Prior theoretical and empirical studies of management control have used the terms "control" and "coordination" interchangeably. Is there a meaningful difference between the two terms, and, if so, what is the significance of the difference for development of a theory of management control?
- What management control processes are used to control and coordinate the operations of the affiliates studied here, and how, if at all, does their use depend on the nature of the control process?
- Do the management control processes employed vary depending on the particular business functional unit within which they are employed?
- Do the parent MNC use the same control processes within their China affiliates as they do within affiliates located in other countries?
- If they do, how are these processes transmitted to and implemented within the China affiliates?
- If they do, then what is the effect of China's institutional and economic environment on the management of the affiliates?
- Does the nature of the management control process employed depend on the ownership of the affiliate, that is, whether the affiliate is wholly owned or a joint venture?
- Do the control processes employed depend on the organizational structure of the parent MNC?

Conducting the Inquiry: Objectives

Studying control through study of control processes

WHAT ARE PROCESSES?

The literature contains many studies that are described as studies of "processes." It is regrettable that the same ambiguity encountered in use of the term "control" in management research (an ambiguity discussed in Chapter 2) also afflicts use of the term "processes."

Beechler (1990, 81) states that the line distinguishing between control processes and control structures "is often extremely fuzzy." This is not accurate.

The distinction has been clearly summarized by Kloot (1997) in one sentence: management control systems can be discussed in terms of process, that is, what they do, and structure, that is, what they are. Processes concern actions by human actors and are dynamic. Structures, by contrast, are static, and are acted upon.

A process refers to a course of action as to how something is done by an individual, group or organization (Nicholson, Schuler and Van de Ven, 1998, 445). The essence of a process is that it is action undertaken by a human actor, or actors. Management processes encompass the way that managers do their jobs – how they make, communicate, implement, monitor and revise decisions (*Harvard Business Review*, 1995).

THE IMPORTANCE OF STUDYING PROCESSES

The call for process-oriented management research, in which factors such as business strategy and organizational structure are treated as outcomes of underlying causal processes, is not new (Lenz, 1981). The concept that organizations are an interrelated set of processes rather than simply an interacting set of organizational units has gained increasing acceptance (Day, 1994).

This concept has influenced international management research, which has increasingly recognized that organizational structure is no longer sufficient to explain the actual management of MNC, and that understanding of underlying processes such as managerial control is now perceived as a necessary line of inquiry (Aharoni, 1996).

The difference between the process of management control and the structure of a control mechanism was clearly expressed by John Kelly, one of MOTORS' senior executives, during my interview with him in Hong Kong:

> *STR*: Again, if I can offer up a general question with respect to joint ventures in China, let me just ask you about a couple of the traditional control mechanisms that US multinationals have used and have your view on the relative effectiveness. One would be insistence on, of course, majority ownership. Is that . . . ?
> *JK*: I will try to summarize where I think you're heading with this. *I don't think it's necessarily ownership. It's the responsibilities associated with having majority ownership. The success or failure, I believe, of any joint venture is in the management of the joint venture. What you get by having majority is the opportunity to control the entity. But that means that you have to be engaged in the control.* That means you have responsibilities for planning; you have responsibilities for controls, financial as well as legal, as well as personnel. You have to implement them and that means you have to really be engaged with the joint venture. *Majority control in China doesn't get you anything unless you exercise it; unless you actually implement what has been successful for your entities worldwide.* (emphasis added)

In international management research, management control has long been recognized as a process (Geringer and Hebert, 1989). The focus of the research here is on understanding management control as a set of processes. The study of processes necessarily involves the study of human actors and their interactions. Thus the methodological orientation of this research is qualitative, using case studies with multiple data sources, that is, triangulating data (Parkhe, 1996).

Studying control processes by means of qualitative methodology using case studies

The focus of this book – management control processes employed by MNC in their China affiliates – determined the methodology employed. Processes are dynamic rather than static (Yan and Gray, 1994) and the focus of qualitative research tends to be on processes, rather than structures, with emphasis on description and explanation, rather than prescription and prediction (Leavy, 1994). While the term "qualitative research" may be, as Leavy states, an "umbrella term" under which several methodologies may be located, qualitative research is characterized by first-hand inspection of organizational life through close-in data gathering activities.

In order to study processes this research employed the qualitative methodology referred to as a multiple case study. Case study methodology is one in which the researcher explores an entity or phenomenon ("the case") bounded by time and activity and collects detailed information using a variety of data collection procedures during a sustained period of time (Cresswell, 1994). Some authors describe this as "clinical field research" to refer to what they see as a more multimethod approach, using not only case studies but also observation and historical analysis (Wright, Beamish and Lane, 1988). The leading text on case method research makes it clear, however, that case studies use a variety of methodologies in order to study contemporary phenomena within their real life context (Yin, 1994, 90–1).

The prevailing emphasis on quantitative over qualitative methodology has rightly been criticized on the grounds that doing business across national borders cannot be studied without understanding the social, cultural and political contexts which companies face in foreign environments; these contexts are beyond the capacity of methodological approaches that demand a narrow, testable focus (Wright, Beamish and Lane, 1988). Recent studies have identified the need for more qualitative research in international management (Yeung, 1997; Wright, 1996; Parkhe, 1996; 1993). A particular need for qualitative research using case method methodology to study management control processes has been identified (Yan, 1998).

Scholars have emphasized the suitability of case studies as the appropriate methodology for use in international management studies. In his seminal 1993 work, Parkhe sees case studies as being able to delve into fundamental questions involving causal events unfolding over the lifespan of an enterprise. According to Parkhe such questions cannot be answered by relying on surveys but must rely on the wider and deeper array of information that only a case study can provide. Dyer and Wilkins (1991) observe that case studies can provide rich descriptions unveiling the dynamics of the phenomenon being studied and can act as clear examples of new relationships or new phenomena that current theoretical perspectives have not captured. Given the current undeveloped state of the theory of management control in MNC, studying management control processes in MNC affiliates by means of case studies is especially appropriate.

Conducting the Inquiry: Methodology

The research sites

This research was conducted at the China offices and factories of affiliates of five US MNC. It must be noted that, due to restrictions on the use of research material imposed by one of the MNC, it was necessary to delete one of the five case studies from the text. Almost all interviews were done in person. In a few cases, identified below, interviews were done by telephone. The companies and the interviewees – all of whom, with one exception are identified only by pseudonyms, in accordance with confidentiality agreements as well as the executive positions held by the interviewees – are listed as follows.

MOTORS

- Both Co-Chief Executives of MOTORS' Asia-Pacific regional organization, Hong Kong.
- Chief Legal Counsel, Asia-Pacific regional organization, Hong Kong.
- Human Resources Director, Asia-Pacific regional organization, Hong Kong.
- General Manager, Shenzhen wholly owned manufacturing affiliate of the MOTORS division, MAYAN.
- General Manager, Shanghai joint venture manufacturing affiliate of the MOTORS division, BRONWYN.
- General Manager, Shanghai joint venture manufacturing affiliate of the MOTORS division, STORMONT, who is also General Manager of that division's China holding company, which itself is administratively separate from the MOTORS Asia-Pacific organization.
- Director of Finance of the Asia-Pacific regional organization of MAYAN, Hong Kong.
- Director of Finance of the Asia-Pacific regional organization of the MOTORS division, CAPWELL, Hong Kong.
- Director of Human Resources of the Asia-Pacific regional organization of CAPWELL.
- Sales Director, China, of CAPWELL.

ELECTRONS

- General Manager of ELECTRONS' largest China subsidiary, a Shanghai-based wholly owned subsidiary which is the company's sole manufacturing facility in China, and its largest single China investment.
- Finance Director (Controller) of the ELECTRONS Shanghai subsidiary.
- Deputy Site Manager for Public Affairs of the Shanghai subsidiary.
- Director of Information Technology Strategic Planning for ELECTRONS' Assembly Test Manufacturing (ATM) Division, of which the Shanghai subsidiary is a part, and who is based in Shanghai.
- Engineering Manager of the Shanghai subsidiary.
- Facilities Construction Manager of the Shanghai subsidiary.
- Design Engineering Manager of the Shanghai subsidiary.

WORLDWIDE

- China National Executive, at China headquarters of WORLDWIDE in Beijing.
- China Public Affairs Manager, at China headquarters, of WORLDWIDE, Beijing.
- General Manager of the China manufacturing organization of WORLDWIDE's largest China business unit, the Medical Equipment (ME) business group, in charge of two joint ventures and one wholly owned subsidiary, at the ME joint venture located outside Beijing.
- Former (now retired) head of WORLDWIDE's Aircraft Components (AC) China business group, a position which he held for 11 years; interviewed several times by telephone at his US residence.

IMIGIS

- Vice President, Human Resources, of both the Greater Asia Region and the Greater China Region, interviewed in person in Shanghai, and subsequently by telephone.
- Legal Counsel, Greater China Region.
- Vice President, Manufacturing, Greater China Region, in charge of three wholly owned subsidiaries and three joint ventures, interviewed by telephone at his Shanghai office.

Use of interview material

A significant part of the expository power of the book rests in the interrelation between the case study chapters and the cross-case comparison chapters. To make it easier for the reader to cross-reference significant points, and for expository purposes, there is some repetition of interview text throughout.

In addition, the phrase "emphasis added" is used where parts of the interview material have been emphasized for the purposes of the context.

Nature of the Research Focus: Senior Management in the Field

The executives interviewed were current (or, in one instance, retired) senior executives. Senior executives were interviewed in order to obtain the point of view of those "responsible for the destiny of the enterprise" (Bartlett and Ghoshal, 1993; Hakanson, 1995; Weber, 1996).

The senior executive perspective permitted data gathering from interviewees who were fully informed about the activities of their respective companies in China and the interrelations among the different China affiliates of their respective companies. Also, almost all of the interviewees had worked in the US as well and so were also familiar with the parent company's management processes and corporate culture.

Research focus: affiliates

I was introduced to the organizational complexity of contemporary US MNC during my business career, and this influenced my decision to conduct this research at the affiliate level. As discussed more fully in Chapter 1, the dyadic "headquarters–subsidiary" construct of MNC management is inadequate to represent the reality of how MNC are organized. Regional organizations are interposed between or in addition to the supposed "direct line" between headquarters and individual foreign affiliates. Few studies, however, explore the effect of regional organizations on management control processes within MNC (Lehrer and Asakawa, 1999; Lord and Ranft, 2000).

Research at the affiliate level also enables employment of a perspective that includes managers who control regional organizations or individual affiliates, and are at the same time subject to control either by the regional organization or by headquarters (Lucente, 1994). It was fortuitous that the companies that granted me research access employ very different organizational designs. These differences are elaborated in both the case studies and the cross-case comparisons.

Research focus: affiliates of US MNC

Studying MNC from a single home country allows concentration on the issues under study rather than diluting attention by the need to consider additional factors relating to differences among national management cultures (Dang, 1977, 41–2; Osland, 1993). My research was greatly facilitated through my familiarity with US management processes from having worked for US companies.

Other Research Issues

Obtaining access to companies

Securing research access proved to be far more difficult and time-consuming than I had originally anticipated and took more than two years in total. The process involved multiple trips throughout the USA and to China involving interviews with companies, professional practices, trade associations and government offices as well as several hundred letters, emails, telephone calls and faxes.

Confidentiality

With regard to each MNC, research access was confirmed based on my executing confidentiality agreements provided by some of the companies; others granted access based on my written representations regarding confidentiality. Both the agreements and the representations provided that the company's identity, as well as the identity of individual executives, would not be disclosed to third parties, with limited exceptions.

Outline of the Contents

Part I: Theory and Context

CHAPTER 1: CONTROL AND COORDINATION WITHIN MULTINATIONAL CORPORATIONS: THE UNDEVELOPED STATE OF THEORY

This chapter reviews the current undeveloped state of the theory of control and coordination within multinational corporations and identifies the reason for this condition, that is, definitional confusion between control and coordination. The chapter introduces the key concept foundational to the analyses that follow, namely that "control" and "coordination" are different processes, and that both control *and* coordination are involved in the management processes of multinational corporations. The author's introduction of precise definitions of "control" and "coordination" remedies a major gap in earlier works, most of which use the terms without definition and interchangeably.

The chapters of Part II and Part III consider the processes of control and coordination and the means by which they are transmitted and implemented in China-based affiliates.

CHAPTER 2: MULTINATIONAL CORPORATIONS IN CHINA: THE INSTITUTIONAL CONTEXT

This chapter provides a focused introduction to the context within which multinational corporations operate in China, and their experience within that context. It introduces concepts used throughout the text. These include the diversity of China's institutional environments, as exemplified by its diverse geography and regional cultures, as well as the political economy of China's "socialist market economy" and its embryonic legal system.

Part II: The Cases

CHAPTER 3: "ACCORDING TO PLAN": CONTROL AND COORDINATION THROUGH THE DISCIPLINE OF PLANNING IN AN AMERICAN MULTINATIONAL CORPORATION IN CHINA

MOTORS is a highly successful US multinational corporation operating globally through many divisions. MOTORS uses the mental discipline required by its rigorous planning system to inculcate a common "thought process" that serves as an integrative process for affiliates operating autonomously in diverse geographic and product markets. This chapter documents the company's planning system and the successful implementation of that system to control and coordinate its numerous China affiliates, all of whom operate through their respective divisional managements. The chapter also analyses MOTORS Asia-Pacific regional organization and its interaction with the divisions and their China affiliates, as well as with MOTORS US headquarters.

CHAPTER 4: "CONTROL AND COORDINATION THROUGH GOALS": THE ROLE OF A PARAMOUNT CORPORATE GOAL IN MANAGING AN AMERICAN MULTINATIONAL CORPORATION IN CHINA

IMIGIS is a US multinational corporation operating globally through six primary business groups. The chapter documents the implementation of IMIGIS' corporate goal of establishing a significant market presence for its businesses in China, and describes the evolution of a strongly focused country organization that operates with significant autonomy from the business groups, a situation unique within the company's global operations. The company's paramount goal of establishing a significant business presence for its subsidiaries and affiliates operating in China serves to control and coordinate activities among the various elements in an organization undergoing concurrent global transformation.

CHAPTER 5: "GLOBAL REPLICATION": COORDINATION THROUGH THE DISCIPLINE OF REPLICATION OF ORGANIZATIONAL PROCESSES IN AN AMERICAN MULTINATIONAL CORPORATION IN CHINA

ELECTRONS is a US multinational corporation that is a leading developer and manufacturer of electronic components. The company's relatively brief history reflects both consistent high profitability and global technological leadership in the information technology industry. The company's operations throughout the world are governed by a process that I call "global replication," in which the company literally replicates its operating and management system at all of its worldwide facilities. This replication is exemplified by the company's manufacturing process known as "Copy Exactly." The case describes the diffusion of the "Copy Exactly" process throughout the global manufacturing operations. It also analyzes the processes that comprise what ELECTRONS' executives refer to as its unique "culture," and how the culture facilitates the interchange and use of knowledge (called "best known methods" or "BKM" in company jargon) throughout the global organization, regardless of geographic origin. The chapter documents how ELECTRONS' operations in China reflect the successful transplantation of the "global replication" process, including "Copy Exactly" and "BKM," to the unique Chinese business environment.

CHAPTER 6: "THE GENETICS OF AN OPERATING SYSTEM":
CONTROL AND COORDINATION THROUGH THE TRANSMISSION
OF SHARED MANAGEMENT PROCESSES IN AN AMERICAN
MULTINATIONAL CORPORATION IN CHINA

WORLDWIDE is a US multinational corporation that is one of the world's largest industrial companies, with more than 100 years of successful operation in diverse product markets throughout the world. The chapter explores the historical record of the evolution of the process by which the company has succeeded in controlling and coordinating its affiliates in many different geographic and product markets. This process is described by the company as its "operating system," or "learning culture in action." The chapter describes how WORLDWIDE's operations in China reflect the transfer of the operating system to the challenging Chinese business environment, and its successful implementation in that environment.

Part III: Comparison and Analysis across the Cases

CHAPTER 7: CROSS-CASE COMPARISON SUMMARY

This chapter integrates the evidence presented in the case studies to explain the manner in which management control processes are used to enable multinational corporations to simultaneously integrate their China affiliates into the parents' global operations, while permitting the affiliates to remain responsive to China's unique economic, political, social and business environments. The roles of both the control processes that prior studies have categorized as "bureaucratic" and which I refer to as management "routines," and the "normative" control processes which I subsume under the rubric "shared values," are documented. Management routines are exemplified by the parents' global management processes, and shared values are exemplified by the parent multinational corporation's corporate culture. Corporate culture is revealed as a significant contributor to the successful implementation of the respective parent's global management processes, without relying on a large staff of expatriate managers. The evidence presented thus challenges the conclusions of prior studies that a mobile expatriate manager force was essential to successful implementation of the parent company corporate culture within geographically dispersed affiliates.

CHAPTER 8: SETTING GOALS, SELECTING STRATEGIES, AND ADOPTING ORGANIZATIONAL FORMS

Chapter 8 expands on the theme developed in the previous chapter: the use of a common corporate culture shared between parents and affiliates to allow the affiliates to concentrate their efforts on development of strategies and organizations that will enable them to achieve designated corporate objectives within China's unique business and institutional environments, without having to simultaneously revise basic management processes. This chapter describes the parents' "market-driven" corporate objectives and the processes by which the affiliates adapt strategies and structures to meet those objectives in China.

CHAPTER 9: CONTROLLING AND COORDINATING PEOPLE: HUMAN RESOURCES MANAGEMENT POLICIES AND PRACTICE

This chapter documents the processes involving the control and coordination of human resources management (HRM). The HRM processes described in this chapter provide clear examples of one of the basic concepts introduced in the text, that is, that the affiliates employ the same internal management processes that their respective parents employ throughout the world (their "internal face"), but that the affiliates simultaneously adapt both strategies and organizational structures (their "external face") to meet the particular needs of doing business in China.

CHAPTER 10: CONTROL AND COORDINATION OF MONEY AND FACTORIES: FINANCE AND MANUFACTURING

This chapter explores the control and coordination of the relatively tangible processes of recording and transmitting financial data and transferring money as well as designing and manufacturing products. Both functions represent a high degree of parent–affiliate integration. This integration is in terms of parental specification of the standards used in the respective processes, whether it is the use of generally accepted accounting principles (GAAP) in the preparation of financial reports, or the employment of Six Sigma, ISO or "Copy Exactly" standards for manufacturing operations. The chapter contrasts the finance function, representing the least degree of differentiation in terms of adapting finance processes to the Chinese environment, with manufacturing. The analysis differentiates between manufacturing process standards, those used by the parent globally (the "internal face"), and manufacturing strategies (the "external face"), exemplified by content localization and product development that are adapted to the demands of China's markets.

CHAPTER 11: CONTROL AND COORDINATION OF RESPONSES TO CHINA'S INSTITUTIONAL ENVIRONMENTS

This chapter discusses the processes of management control and coordination that govern interactions between the multinational corporation affiliates and China's institutional environments. As explained in Chapter 2, "institutional environments" refer to the totality of non-market social structures facing multinational corporations in China. The analysis here is in two parts. First, the focus is on how the scope and nature of the interaction between the affiliates studied here and China's institutional environments are governed by the affiliates' respective globally uniform policies establishing standards for the ethical conduct of business. These policies

are internal standards to which the affiliates' officers and employees must comply
– the "internal face" of control and coordination.

Next, the strategies used by the affiliates for permissible interaction with China's
institutional environments (the "external face") are considered. These are highly
localized, however, as are the executives who bear primary responsibility for daily
interaction with these environments. The chapter concludes with an illustration of
localized strategies, in terms of the affiliates' manner of interacting with *guanxi*, the
untranslatable Chinese phrase that describes networks of mutually dependent social
relationships.

CONCLUSION: INFORMING THE THEORY AND PRACTICE OF CONTROL AND COORDINATION IN THE MULTINATIONAL CORPORATION

The Conclusion integrates the material presented throughout the text to summarize the contributions to the theory and practice of control and coordination
in the multinational corporation. It ends with a short summary of what may and
may not change in both the internal and external faces of multinational corporations in China.

PART I

Theory and Context

Control and Coordination within Multinational Corporations: the Undeveloped State of Theory

Introduction

The case studies and cross-case analyses that begin at Chapter 3 present the results of the research that went into the creation of this book. Before presenting these results, we first review prior research on management control processes in the foreign affiliates of US MNC. From this review it will become clear that the thorough, subsidiary-level examination of the actual employment of management control processes in US MNC affiliates, both wholly owned and joint venture, presented here has not been attempted before. Management control processes within US MNC have been addressed in only a few other studies (Barlow, 1953; Dunning, 1958; Dang, 1977), none of which are contemporary, and none of which made control processes the primary focus.

Undeveloped Theory

In her study of management control of subsidiaries of Japanese MNC operating in Southeast Asia, Beechler (1990, 14) observed that the study of control within MNC had not yet emerged from its infancy. In terms of development of a theory or theories of management control in MNC, it may be better to simply characterize the current stage of theory as "undeveloped."

I use the definition of "theory" provided by Hoover and Donovan (2001, 33), that is, a theory is a set of related propositions that suggest why events occur in the manner that they do. The events under consideration here are those that comprise the processes by which managers of American MNC control and coordinate the activities of their affiliates located in China.

As discussed in the Introduction to this book, there has been a lack of research into the processes by which human actors (managers) manage control processes, as well as a lack of research on the processes through which MNC control subsidiaries located outside the home country of the parent corporation.

With regard to MNC control of foreign subsidiaries, there have been a number of previous works devoted to typifying constructs representing control mechanisms. Other, principally quantitative studies have tried to relate these types to other constructs representing taxonomies of organizational structures that researchers believe they have identified within existing MNC. Attempts have then been made to derive certain conclusions about MNC management control from large scale quantitative surveys that have sought to establish relationships among "structure" variables and "control" variables.

Beechler (1990, 58–60) accurately observes that the concept of management control "remains shrouded in a cloak of ambiguity and confusion." While I fully agree with Beechler's observation, the confusion and ambiguity result from two sources. One, which both she and earlier researchers have noted, is the lack of a generally accepted definition of "control." The second, which has not been fully elucidated previously, is that, while fundamental concepts necessary for understanding control within business organizations, as well as definitions of control, are both present in the literature, these have not been applied in previous studies. This second issue will be addressed first.

Fundamental concepts of management control

The fundamental concepts necessary for an understanding of management control processes were set forth more than 60 years ago by Chester Barnard (1938) in *The Functions of the Executive*. These begin with his identification of the essential elements of any organization: (1) people in communication with each other and (2) willing to contribute their services in order to (3) achieve common objectives (1938, 82).

All of these elements are related to and joined together by what Barnard calls "authority."[4] "Authority" is the character of a communication (that is, an order or a directive) in an organization, by which it is accepted by a member of the organization to govern his/her contribution to the organization (1938, 163). In Barnard's conceptualization, authority requires both communication and acceptance to be effective. Within an organization the communication paths are bidirectional: information flows from the top down and from the bottom up, while acceptance of authority flows upward. The exercise of authority, however, flows from the top down, and in as direct a manner as possible (1938, 176–7).

Management control is the exercise of authority, or, as Mintzberg (1989, 355) put it, to manage is to control. Effective control is exercised on a hierarchical basis. At the same time, control involves a significant volitional element to be effective, and must be derived from consent, as Barnard explained in some detail (1938, 163–5, 171–2n, 173, 174, 181–2). Consideration of this volitional element has been missing from many studies of MNC control, other than those studies focusing on normative control, some examples of which are discussed later in this chapter.

Although the fundamental concepts of management control processes are straight-forward, application of these concepts in research on control processes within MNC has been problematic, particularly so in the quantitative studies. As noted above, such studies especially depend on the creation of variables that must closely approximate the real world phenomena that they seek to describe. Although "control" is what is sought to be measured, there is considerable confusion over the definition or definitions of "control."

Definitions and definitional confusion: the issue of "murky conceptual terrain"

Several factors have slowed the development of a coherent theory to explain the processes by which MNC control their foreign affiliates. These were discussed in the previous chapter in the sections on research methodology. As noted there, the principal factors have been a paucity of qualitative research within organizations on this subject and the inability, due to limitations inherent in the methodology itself, of the more numerous quantitative studies to explore the subject. After these, the factor that has caused the most difficulty in theory development has been the lack of agreed definitions for key concepts:

> At the most elementary level it is almost impossible to do high-quality research that builds the state of knowledge without a set of agreed on definitions. Different authors seem to thrive on coining new terms and expressions that often have vague meanings in a research context.
>
> *(Kinnear, 1999)*

Westney (1993, 66) has pointed out that the debate concerning global integration versus local differentiation in MNC management often takes place in what she calls "murky conceptual terrain." The same conceptual murkiness surrounds the use of the words "control" and "coordination." The literature on management control often uses both in the same work in contexts that indicate differences in meaning, without defining the meaning of either term (e.g. Gittell, 2000).

In the case of control and coordination within MNC, both terms have been used within the same work without definition and interchangeably (e.g. Bartlett and Ghoshal, 1988). Control has also been defined as a means to achieve an end called coordination (Harzing, 1999, 8–11).

Control and coordination: defining and applying the concepts

The respective standard English definitions of the verbs "to control" and "to coordinate" are:

- *to control*: "to order, limit, instruct or rule someone's behavior";
- *to coordinate*: "to make various things work effectively as a whole" (Cambridge University Press, 2002).

When "control" and "coordinate" are used in this study they are used according to the above definitions. Where they are used in citations of other works, they are used in the context of the definitions of the author(s) of the cited works, in those works where definitions are provided.

The precise definitions of "control" and "coordination" employed here represent precision rarely found in discussions of management control. Adherence to these definitions enables us to fully understand the roles of both control and coordination in transference of management processes from parent MNC to their foreign affiliates. This is illustrated by the discussion of US MNC compliance with the US Foreign Corrupt Practices Act, legislation that is described in Chapter 7.

The importance of making a distinction between control and coordination is illustrated by a portion of an interview with MOTORS' Legal Counsel:

> *STR*: Am I being accurate in saying that the standards both of ethical conduct in the marketplace and particularly with respect to relations with foreign governmental authorities are brought directly from MOTORS headquarters?
>
> *JK*: Yes. The standards are brought directly from our chairman at MOTORS headquarters. In addition, without the involvement of senior management all the way to the top it would be impossible, I think, to convey the proper message. Luckily they are strong advocates of a highly ethical company; they have made repeated statements that under no circumstances are we to deviate from those standards. It comes from the top down and it's actually practiced. It makes my job a lot easier to be able to go out and to be able to show that all the way to our chairman level, he believes that philosophy.

The above illustrates that the means through which management processes are transmitted to and implanted within affiliates by the parent company involve *both* control and coordination. Without understanding the difference between the two, one cannot understand the nature of the transmittal processes.

To coordinate the transmission and implementation of ethical standards requires shared values. The shared values, however, are created through both consent and control. People within an organization share values through consent (Barnard, 1938, 82–4). As a former head of Unilever explained, maintaining generally accepted standards of corporate behavior depends as much on everyone in the global organization understanding and accepting them as on formal instruction manuals (Maljers, 1993).

The values that are shared in common by the multiethnic workforce of an MNC operating globally must have some central source and direction. This means that someone must initially set out the values of an organization that its members are expected to share. In other words, someone must "instruct the actions or behavior of others," which is my definition of the verb "to control." This is the control element and it is coextensive with the coordination element. The parent MNC of the affiliates studied both control and coordinate their China affiliates.

To control is to do something different than to coordinate. First, coordination subsumes plural objects, people or actions that need coordinating, while control can be exercised over an individual or groups of individuals, objects or actions. More importantly, while to control something is to do something different than to coordinate it, control and coordination can take place within the same process or activity at the same time. It is important to understand this point because the control processes studied in this book, especially the processes through which the routines and values of the parent MNC are transmitted to and implanted within affiliates by the parent company, involve both control and coordination. Those processes and the means by which they are transmitted and implemented in China-based affiliates will be considered in the case studies and cross-case analyses.

Prior Research on Management Control within MNC

Principal categories of prior research

The following is a summary categorization of major directions taken by research on the control mechanisms employed by MNC, whether US, non-US or both, that are used to direct the corporate affairs of their foreign affiliates. The limitations of these studies will also be noted.

Although not always identified in the studies themselves, most prior research mainly concerns control of wholly owned subsidiaries. Such studies may be grouped under three principal categories.

The first category comprises those studies that focus on typification of what the research refers to as control "mechanisms" employed by MNC. These typifications of mechanisms are intended to apply to MNC control without reference to specific ownership structure, that is, the mechanisms are used to control both wholly owned subsidiaries and joint ventures.

The second category contains two viewpoints of structural taxonomy. One group of studies (Perlmutter, 1969; Stopford and Wells, 1972; Bartlett and Ghoshal, 1987; 1988; 1989) provides taxonomies of parent MNC. The other group (Gupta and Govindarajan, 1991; Birkinshaw and Morrison, 1995) represents taxonomies of foreign subsidiaries themselves, described in relation to the posited functions fulfilled by the subsidiary within the global MNC organization. In the case of MNC taxonomy, Bartlett and Ghoshal's conceptualization has become the accepted paradigm. It is summarized below.

The third category combines elements from the first two. Mechanism typification studies are combined with taxonomies derived from the second category in order to try to relate control mechanism types to certain taxonomies of organizational structures observed or posited within existing MNC.[5] Attempts have then been made to derive certain conclusions about MNC management control from large scale quantitative surveys that have sought to establish relationships involving different variables representing control mechanisms, locus or extent of subsidiary decisional authority, and parent organizational structures (Gupta and Govindarajan, 1991; Roth and Nigh, 1992; Birkinshaw and Morrison, 1995; Harzing, 1999).

Finally, and in contrast to the methodology of the previous category, are studies of "culture" as a control process within MNC. As studies of processes, these works have employed qualitative rather than quantitative methodology. Their significance is examined because of the research findings reported in the case studies and correlated in the cross-case comparisons presented later in this book. The remainder of this chapter discusses these as well as process-based studies of the application of control mechanisms within the foreign affiliates of US MNC.

Before that, however, two issues will be addressed. Specific typifications of control mechanisms and MNC organizational structures will be used throughout this study and these are summarized below.

What is a "control mechanism?"

A 1992 literature review correctly observed that there is no universally accepted conceptualization of control mechanisms (Sundaram and Black, 1992). There are, however, many typifications of MNC control mechanisms to choose from.

The principal works[6] have been Baliga and Jaeger (1984), which itself builds on Child's (1972; 1973) work; Cray (1984); Doz and Prahalad (1984); Kim and Campbell (1997), which builds on Ouchi's (1980) work; Ouchi (1977; 1980); and, most recently, Harzing (2001). Integrating these studies results in the following summary of the principal forms of control mechanisms:

- *Personal* (also called "direct" or "centralized") in which control is exerted by the parent through placement of executives sent from headquarters to supervise and monitor the subsidiary.
- *Bureaucratic* (also called "formalized") in which control over subsidiaries is exerted through detailed written rules, regulations and procedures.
- *Normative* (also called "cultural" control or "control by socialization") in which control is exerted by imbuing managers with the common beliefs and expectations shared by the organization's members. In MNC this depends on the use of a corps of expatriates to occupy most upper-level management positions, where they can act as transmitters of the organization's culture.

Taxonomies of MNC structure

As noted above, the dominant taxonomy is that of Bartlett and Ghoshal (1989). They identify four types of corporate structures used by corporations operating outside their home countries:

- *Multinational.* These are decentralized federations of local firms linked through personal controls, for example, an interchangeable corps of expatriate executives.
- *Global.* Worldwide facilities are centrally managed from the home country. This structure is typically adopted by companies producing standardized products, where foreign operations are considered to be distribution outlets for those products. Headquarters maintains tight control of decisions, resources and information.
- *International.* These are also federations of local firms but, unlike multinationals, they are controlled by a central corporate staff and have detailed formal management systems.
- *Transnational.* Bartlett and Ghoshal's conception of what the global corporation should and will look like. It is a network of specialized units with integrative linkages (relationships and mechanisms) among units and with corporate headquarters, which Bartlett and Ghoshal refer to as "the center."

In the case studies that follow, Bartlett and Ghoshal's taxonomy is compared with the actual organizational structures of the parent MNC of the affiliates studied.

Limitations of Prior Research

We present here some general observations on limitations in prior research on management control within MNC. There are two types of limitations: the first affects quantitative studies, while the second pertains to qualitative studies that focus on management structures rather than management processes.

Limitations of quantitative methodology

Quantitative methodology is inadequate to measure the complexity of one of the units of analysis, that is, the MNC itself, as well as being unable to measure the complexity of the key variable, the "mechanism of control." It is also inadequate to measure the complexities of the relationship among MNC, their affiliates and the processes by which the former exercise control over the latter.

Multiple regression methods are customarily employed in quantitative methodology and are conceptually simple. They posit that the value of one variable (the dependent variable in which the researcher is interested) is determined by the values of the other (independent) variables in the system being studied. Regression equations are then developed to find the relationship between the dependent and the independent variables, to disclose which of the independent variables have the most influence on the dependent variable (Harvey, 1995, 3).

Problems with using quantitative methodology to study processes are inherent in the measurement of variables. Each measure is supposed to do a good job of representing the underlying truth of the abstract concept that the researcher intends to represent through use of a quantified variable (Hoover and Donovan, 2001, 25).

Pettigrew, Woodman and Cameron (2001), however, quoting earlier research, note that, while processes can be encapsulated within variables, a variable about a process is not exactly the same as the process itself. Therefore, processes are closer to the actual behavior than are their encapsulations as variables.

The ineffectiveness of quantitative methodology in the study of managing MNC in China has been recognized by scholars (Osland, 1993; Yan and Gray, 1994). Hamill and Pambos (1996) call large scale postal surveys "a totally inadequate methodology for gaining real insights into the intricacies involved in doing business in China."

Limitations of focus on management structures

The second limitation pertains to studies employing either quantitative or qualitative methods. In essence, it involves generalizing on the basis of concepts that themselves cannot be generalized. Each limitation is discussed in turn.

LIMITED BY COMPLEXITY

In their quantitative study of subsidiary roles within MNC, Birkinshaw and Morrison (1995) raise what they call "the rather delicate question, 'What is a subsidiary?'" The issue that they raise is that a "national subsidiary" within an MNC is sometimes no more than what they characterize as a "legal shell" within which a variety of separate, value-adding operations occur. This observation is correct as far as it goes, but it does not go far enough in recognizing that the dyadic conceptualization of "headquarters–subsidiary" interaction fails to capture the complexity of modern MNC.

The prior chapter's descriptions of the MNC whose affiliates are studied in this book are amplified within the cases involving each affiliate and present a number of variations of relationships between the affiliates and other organizational units within their respective MNC. The variations are described in detail in the respective case studies. In no instance is the relationship between an affiliate and its parent a simple, direct "headquarters–subsidiary" situation. This is especially true of the control relationship.

Many years ago Hymer (1976, 65–6) observed that, in the case of control of affiliates by parent MNC, there is no simple connection between the overt form taken by a foreign affiliate and the underlying relation, and that there were many kinds of control, and many forms which can be used to achieve any of them. Organizations represent a set of relationships among individuals, groups and units, and very different relationship patterns can flourish within the same formal structure (Ghoshal and Nohria, 1993). Even within a simplified "headquarters–subsidiary" conceptualization, these relationships are not identical with respect to individual subsidiaries' relationships with their parent (Ghoshal and Nohria, 1993).

There are a number of recent studies that describe the complexity of organizational relationships among parent MNC, their regional organizations and local affiliates (e.g. Lehrer and Asakawa, 1999; Lord and Ranft, 2000). This complexity cannot be captured in studies focused on a dyadic "headquarters–subsidiary" structural relationship, which explains why some studies explicitly acknowledge that intervening organizational relationships are not examined (e.g. Cray, 1984).

LIMITED BY GENERALIZING FROM CONCEPTS THAT CANNOT BE GENERALIZED

Jaeger (1983) observes that ideal types are never found in pure form in reality, but are useful tools for conceptualization of organizational processes. Usunier (1998, 86), however, cautions that ideal types are both useful and dangerous. Their use, as Jaeger also points out, is that they allow simplification of the conceptualization process and therefore of research design, by providing what he calls "polar reference points" to analyze complex realities. He goes on to observe that the danger is that ideal types will metamorphose into stereotypes due to oversimplification including overemphasis on certain features of the ideal type.

The dominant paradigm of MNC organizational structure is that of Bartlett and Ghoshal, described above, which features the "transnational corporation" (TNC). There are two problems with building theory on management control within the MNC based on the TNC paradigm described by Bartlett and Ghoshal.

First, efforts to generalize the use of a given control mechanism throughout an MNC based on the taxonomical category occupied by the enterprise are contradicted by the extensive research demonstrating that control mechanisms vary not only within the overall structure of an individual MNC, but even within separate business functions of the same company.

Bartlett and Ghoshal (1989, 69–70) observe that the organization that they call the TNC will use a portfolio of different "coordination mechanisms"[7] and that "different parts of the [TNC] organization will be managed differently." These observations are well founded in research that shows that, even within firms that have similar organizational structures, e.g. "M-form" organizations, there are considerable variations in internal management practices among such organizations (Hill and Pickering, 1986).

There is considerable evidence of internal variations within MNC including works by Ghoshal and Nohria (1993), and also Lehrer and Asakawa (1999), as well as evidence of variation in MNC internal treatment of affiliates that are structured as joint ventures (Newberry and Zeira, 1999).

That research confirms earlier findings (Dunning, 1958; Glaister, 1995; Child, 1996) that parent control and subsidiary autonomy may vary between classes of business functions, and within business functions in the same subsidiary. Also, just as MNC employ mixtures of structures and mechanisms, they typically employ a mixture of strategies, rather than trying to implement "one or another" solutions (Taggert, 1998), or "doing everything the same way everywhere" (Kanter and Dretler, 1998).

Finally, generalizations ignore the likelihood that differences in the respective institutional environments of individual host countries will influence the choice of processes that an MNC may employ to control local affiliates, even where those affiliates are wholly owned (Sundaram and Black, 1992; Hamilton, Taylor and Kashlak, 1996).

Prior research also suggests that a truly "heterarchical" organizational structure equivalent to that posited for the TNC cannot exist within MNC. In their comprehensive and balanced review of Nordic international business research, Bjorkman and Forsgren (2000) observe that there is a paradox in the conceptualization of management of heterarchic or transnational firms. On the one hand, such firms are said to rely on different forms of lateral information processes, involving cross-functional groups such as teams and task forces; these firms are also characterized by normative control mechanisms, e.g. a common corporate culture to break down barriers between units. On the other hand, such an organization presumes the existence of an extremely skillful and powerful top management to orchestrate these various activities.

In other words, even a "heterarchy" requires someone at the top to exercise authority. Ultimate decision making authority must reside in the parent MNC's top management, who exercise that authority through a hierarchic process. For example:

> Centralization was the most constantly practiced form of coordination we observed [in their case studies of a number of MNC]. In every company, top management, including the board [of directors], especially reserved the right to decide on major capital requests and key personnel appointments.
>
> *(Bartlett and Ghoshal, 1989, 170)*

While the TNC conceptualization presupposes that foreign affiliates operate with considerable autonomy, autonomy is something that is conferred by the parent (Garnier, Osborn, Galicia and Lecon, 1979; Garnier, 1982). Changes in subsidiary roles are also driven by the parent (Birkinshaw and Hood, 1998). Not only does the parent determine subsidiary autonomy and strategy, but top management also has another powerful control mechanism at its disposal. If the parent is dissatisfied with subsidiary management, it has the authority and ability to replace that management (Doz, 1986, 207). A recent study confirmed earlier research showing that, within US MNC, the autonomy of managers of foreign subsidiaries is on the decline (Lehrer and Asakawa, 1999).

Prior Research on Management Control Processes and Management Control

There is a body of research that treats management control within MNC as a process, including studies of management control and control processes specifically within IJV. These are the subject of the remainder of this chapter because they move closer to the topic of this work.

Process-based research began with studies of overall management processes within the foreign affiliate, and included within their scope both wholly owned and joint venture affiliates. This approach was taken by Barlow's (1953) study of the Mexican affiliates of US manufacturing MNC, Dunning's (1958) study of the British affiliates of US manufacturing MNC, and Dang's (1977) study of the Philippine and Taiwanese affiliates of US manufacturing MNC. The 1979 study by Garnier and his associates of Mexican affiliates of US MNC, and Garnier's (1982) study of both Mexican and French affiliates of US MNC, also treated the foreign affiliate, whether wholly or jointly owned, as the unit of analysis, but, unlike the earlier studies, focused only on the question of affiliate autonomy – autonomy being measured solely in terms of locus of decisional authority in the affiliate versus the parent. Hulbert and Brandt's (1980) study of MNC affiliates in Brazil included a number of US MNC, and considered a full range of management processes, including control processes.

In the 1980s, research on management control processes within MNC affiliates became bifurcated. The increased emphasis on joint ventures as a separate category of research mirrored the increased use of this organizational form by MNC.

Some studies of control processes within joint ventures have focused on more formal control processes, and particular attention has been shown to the question of the relationship between a joint venture partner's extent of ownership and that partner's ability to exercise control over management of the joint venture.

In contrast, studies of management control processes within wholly owned affiliates have tended to focus on normative control processes. The emphasis on informal rather than formal control processes may reflect the fact that in a wholly owned affiliate, the extent of control is not an issue.[8]

Finally, mirroring the change within management research in general (Rumelt, Schendel and Teece, 1991), the nature of the investigation of both wholly and jointly owned affiliates has changed. Studies of IJV have concentrated on predications or explanations of why a particular organizational form is chosen, relying on explanations from economic theory. Studies of management control processes in wholly owned subsidiaries have emphasized normative or social control processes.

There has, however, been much less investigation through studies, such as Barlow (1953), as to how the foreign affiliate is actually managed once it is established (Yan and Gray, 1992), although the need for such a study has been identified (Baran, Pan and Kaynak, 1996). This work aims to fulfill that need.

This chapter has summarized prior research on management control in multinational corporations, and has called attention to limitations in prior research. Before considering the case studies and cross-case comparisons, we will turn our attention to the unique institutional contexts of the Chinese business environment.

CHAPTER TWO

Multinational Corporations in China: the Institutional Context

Introduction

China presents multinational corporations with a variety of institutional environments that are unique in terms of what these companies have encountered in prior operations in either developed or developing countries. This chapter provides an introduction to those environments by describing the environmental contexts within which foreign businesses in China must operate. "Institutions" are social, economic and political bodies that articulate and maintain widely observed norms and rules (Child and Tse, 2001). "Institutional environments" encompass the social norms, laws, rules and requirements to which an organization must conform in order to receive legitimacy (Yan, 1998), as well as the institutions which articulate and maintain these norms, laws, rules and requirements.

China *is* unique, both for its institutional complexity and in terms of its importance for global business, and these factors present both challenges and opportunities for MNC. China is the leading destination for foreign direct investment (FDI), having surpassed the US in this category in 2004 (Agence France-Press, 2004). China's role as "manufacturer to the world" is well known. In 2003 exports amounted to US$438 billion, but perhaps less well known is that 2003 imports amounted to US$413 billion (*AmChat*, 2004). MNC play a major role in China's foreign trade and, with China's accession to the World Trade Organization (WTO), seek to play an equally important role in China's domestic markets.

China's importance to MNC and the unique challenges that operations in China pose for MNC make it a particularly well-suited venue in which to study how MNC meet the challenge of managing their Chinese affiliates in ways that allow the affiliates' activities to be integrated into the parent's global operations while at the same time permitting the affiliates enough flexibility so that they can respond to China's unique institutions and markets (Legewie, 2002). This chapter provides the contextual background for further discussion of the processes through which the China affiliates of US MNC conduct their businesses in these unique environments.[9] It is appropriate to use the plural "institutional environments" because, as we shall see, Chinese geography and history as well as its political and economic structures have rendered unworkable such concepts as a single "Chinese government" or "Chinese market."

This chapter does not attempt to do more than very briefly summarize the continuities as well as great changes that have taken place within some of these environments since 1978.[10] It does identify and analyze certain aspects of the Chinese institutional environments that are particularly problematic for MNC operating in China. The analysis is definitely selective, and omits a number of issues, among them intellectual property protection, customs administration and taxation. This is *not* because these issues are unimportant to MNC operating in China but rather because their resolution depends, in my judgment, on the resolution of issues that *are* discussed here. These issues include the continuing political and economic domination exercised by the combined Communist Party and Chinese state structure (party-state), the Balkanization of China's markets due to unchecked local protectionism, and the absence of the rule of law.

We begin with some basic statistical facts that emphasize the physical and economic magnitude as well as the fundamental divisions of contemporary China. This is followed by consideration of the monopoly on political and economic power currently exercised by the party-state, and how certain aspects of the exercise of this monopoly have been devolved to subordinate political units. Both the power and its devolution have had considerable effects on China's many different markets, and these are then considered, followed by an examination of China's legal system and the cultural system of *guanxi* which functions alongside as well as in place of the legal system. We conclude with an examination of what MNC hope to obtain from China's accession to the WTO, and to what degree those hopes are currently being realized.

Before going further, it is important to consider the words of a noted Chinese-born American historian of China. Speaking of contemporary China, Ray Huang noted that "China's problem in modern times, tracing its origin back hundreds or even thousands of years, is not something that can be easily characterized by labels developed from the Western experience" (1997, 286). Here, I have tried to use the English language translations of the Chinese expressions "the Four Modernizations" and "the Open Policy," rather than the single, imprecise word "reforms," to refer to the dramatic changes in China that have occurred since the 1970s. These changes have resulted in significant gains for China in measures of national income, agricultural and industrial production, exports, imports and education, leading to tremendous improvements in living standards for many Chinese. At the same time, however, the ways in which Chinese society is organized and governed have not, in my opinion, undergone changes of similar magnitude, and to say that the organizations and mechanisms of governance have been "reformed" is, in my opinion, not accurate.

China as Unique: Geographic and Economic Magnitude

China is the world's most populous nation and, after Russia and Canada, the most extensive in land area. Its climate and topography encompass everything from jungle, grassland and alluvial plain up to high mountain ranges. Overall, the topography is rugged, with limited arable land. In consequence the large population is unevenly distributed. In total, 75 percent of the population live on only 15 percent of the land. Ninety percent of the population occupy the eastern one-half of the nation, while the remaining 10 percent occupy the western one-half (Starr, 2001, 26; Lieberthal, 1997).

"China" refers to a nation-state in which an ethnically identifiable population (the Han) has occupied a contiguous land mass for several thousand years. This land mass has been centrally governed since *circa* 221 BCE, using a common written language which has enabled creation and maintenance of a continuous, recorded history dating back more than 2,500 years. In his monumental study of Chinese economic history Elvin referred to China as the "the world's largest enduring state" (1973, foreword to Part One), a fitting description.

The sheer magnitude of contemporary China's economy is equally impressive. China's gross domestic product (GDP) *quadrupled* between 1983 and 2003. The most recent year-to-year comparison shows China's economy growing at an annual rate of 9.1 percent, and, in terms of GDP expressed in purchasing power parity, it is the world's sixth largest economy (World Bank, 2004).[11] With due regard for the difficulties in comparing Chinese economic measurements with those generated by other economies, this extraordinary growth seems to have been driven by an equally extraordinary manufacturing cost advantage. Information developed by the US Labor Department indicates that, in US dollar terms, China's average manufacturing wage was 64 cents an hour in 2002 (Coy, 2004) and overall Chinese manufacturing costs are approximately 80 percent lower than comparable US costs (Stein, 2005).

China as Unique: Diversity and Division within Unity

As noted above, Chinese geography creates substantial regional diversity. A major division is along an agricultural/climatologic line dividing north (wheat) and south (rice) growing areas. Economic differences between regions are much more striking and more problematic, for both China and for MNC operating in China.

Differentiation in relative wealth between different geographic areas within the same country is a condition that is not unique to China. At the same time, the magnitude of China's economic growth has put these differences into sharper focus. Further, the economic divisions that exist between the relatively prosperous coastal urban areas and the poorer rural interior areas have not yet been ameliorated by China's rapid economic development (Crook, 1990; Wright, 1999). A few statistics illustrate that the differences are both profound and continuing.

As discussed in more detail below, Chinese economic development has been heavily concentrated in its coastal provinces since 1978. A 1999 study showed that a single coastal province, Guangdong, accounted for 10 percent of Chinese GDP, 40 percent of its exports, and 30 percent of its incoming foreign investment (Liao, 1999). Chinese residing in the coastal provinces have per capita incomes 75 percent higher than the national average and the coastal provinces typically attract at least 70 percent of annual inbound FDI (Pei, 2002).

Clearly, inbound FDI does have a substantial influence on relative provincial prosperity (W. Zhang, 2001). Yet, a study of interprovincial disparities in output and consumption between 1952 and 1987 found that, during this period, the poorer provinces did not narrow the gaps that separated them from the more prosperous provinces which were ahead in the 1950s (Lyons, 1991). There are also marked disparities in per capita income between urban and rural populations. In 2000, the annual per capita income of a Chinese urban resident was 6,280 renminbi (RMB), while the same figure for a rural resident was RMB 2,253, only slightly more than one-third of the urban resident's income. By 2004 the gap had widened, both in actual terms and in the proportional disparity. The comparable figures were RMB 9,422 for an urban resident, and RMB 2,936 for rural residents (US–China Business Council, 2005, quoting official Chinese statistics).

These disparities in provincial prosperity provide evidence that the concept of a unitary "Chinese market" is highly inaccurate. Interregional trade has a long history in China, although both the volume and the continuity were influenced by recurring periods of political instability and infrastructure degradation (Elvin, 1973, 150–6, 213–15). Nonetheless, Pei's (2002) observation that China historically never enjoyed an integrated national market is still valid.[12] One of the consequences of the absence of such a market was that large business enterprises that would have been capable of challenging the authority of the unitary state never developed. The unitary state maintains its dominance to this day.

China as Unique: Control by a Unitary Party-State

In the introduction to his final book, the great historian of China John King Fairbank observed that in contemporary China, democratic market economies (as exemplified by the US) confronted the last communist dictatorship, yet behind Chinese communism is the world's longest tradition of successful autocracy (Fairbank, in Fairbank and Goldman, 1998, 1).

That traditional autocracy was succinctly described by Jenner:

> The central bureaucracies made and interpreted laws in the name of maintaining the social, political and cosmic order. This left no room for outsiders, such as priests, to challenge the emperor's law by reference to a higher, divine law – the emperor's law embodied the highest principles. Nor did it allow interest groups and other representatives of the subject to agitate for changes in legislation or to demand the right to vote on new or existing laws, or to argue that laws made by the emperor without

their consent had no moral validity. There was no assembly, no senate, no Magna
Carta, no social contract, no immemorial right of the freeborn subject, no constitution,
nothing requiring any of the people to take part in the legislative process.

(1994, 141–2)

China has never had, and does not now have, a pluralistic system in which power
is diffused beyond the apparatus of the state to other power centers, such as
business, organized religious bodies, or non-governmental organizations such as the
professions. Such a pluralistic system, generally described by the term *civil society*, is
one in which state power is controlled through a dynamic system of checks and
balances. These checks and balances are exercised by plural power centers whose
activities are mediated by an independent legal system. In contrast, in hierarchical,
authoritarian systems, command authority is structured within a single hierarchy, and
the supreme entity is the one at the top of the hierarchy (Gordon, 1999, 16–17).
China is such a hierarchical system, and at the top of the Chinese hierarchy is the
Communist Party.

In the terminology of political science, a state in which one party holds either
a *de jure* or a *de facto* monopoly on political activity is called a "one-party state"
(McLean and McMillan, 2003, 383). China is a one-party state, and while the
Communist Party (the Party), the government and the military establishment are
organizationally separate on paper, in fact they are inseparable, by virtue of the
overarching authority of the Party. The Party, through the Politburo Standing
Committee (PBSC), makes all national policy in every sphere of China's life; and
the state, through its civil arm, headed by the State Council, and its military arm,
headed by the Central Military Commission, carries out that policy (Nathan and
Gilley, 2003, 6–10).

While the Chinese system is clearly authoritarian, some scholars regard it as
representing "authoritarian pluralism," that is, a system of authoritarianism with
some flexibility (Scalapino, 1999). Another term used is "fragmented authoritarianism," describing an organizational structure in which officials at various organizational levels have several bosses (Lieberthal, 1995, 163). The strongest evidence of
such fragmentation is represented by actions of the party-state itself: the devolution
of certain aspects of the exercise of its authoritarian power to subordinate geographic political units. This is considered below. Otherwise, genuine pluralism is
difficult to identify, either within or outside the party-state structure.

The Chinese military establishment, the People's Liberation Army (PLA),[13] has
been able to exert considerable political influence at times during the past, and
has also played an important role in the economy, through PLA-owned companies.
Recently, however, the military's capacity to act as a possible independent political force has been curtailed by several factors. The party-state has successfully
enforced a ban on PLA business activities and has established major army units that
operate under the direction of the Central Military Commission in Beijing, rather
than under regional military commanders. Further, the selection, assignment and
reassignment of regional military commanders is under the control of the Central
Military Commission, just as personnel rotation of the leadership of provincial

and local governments remains the prerogative of the central political leadership (Li, 2002).

China does have a national legislature, the National People's Congress (NPC). Made up of over 3,000 delegates, it meets once a year for a session lasting two or three weeks. As Cabestan (2001) observed, the NPC, unlike even the weakest Western parliament, is not an independent institution but is rather an arm of the party-state, charged with carrying out decisions made by the Party leadership. Members of the NPC are chosen not through universal suffrage, but rather by the Party apparatus.

Although China has many thousands of professional societies, civic organizations, community groups and social service organizations, these cannot be considered as autonomous from the party-state. All such voluntary organizations must be sponsored by a government organization and registered with and approved by the government (Li, 2002). While China currently has over 150,000 lawyers and over 8,000 law firms, most all of the law firms are state run (Lubman, 2000).

Thus, Fairbank's characterization of the contemporary Chinese party-state as the current manifestation of the world's longest tradition of successful autocracy remains accurate. The Chinese economy, however, due to the actions of the party-state, has undergone substantial changes since 1978. While these changes have been substantial, they have not displaced the party-state from its role of economic dominance.

China as Unique: the Party-State as Economically Dominant

The Chinese party-state based on a Leninist model has ruled China since 1949. The party-state initially organized a society resembling that of Soviet Russia. This combined authoritarian politics and a command and control economy. While the authoritarian political system remains intact, there have been dramatic changes in China's economy and economic policies. These changes were initiated by the party-state itself, in the Plenary Session of the Party's Central Committee in 1978, where the fundamental objective of the party-state was changed from Marxist-Leninist political struggle to economic development. This change led Chinese economic policy away from exclusive state ownership of the means of production to a policy of permitting more diversity in ownership formats.

These changes have resulted in the evolution of the pre-1978 command economy into another economy that, in addition to state-owned enterprises (SOE), is made up of local private companies and foreign-invested private enterprises (FIE), as well as township and village enterprises (TVE). This was brought about by implementation of the Four Modernizations, along with the Open Policy.

The modernization of agriculture was the first of the Four Modernizations undertaken after 1978 as Deng built support for his modernizing policies at the "grass roots" level, both literally and figuratively. Replacing agricultural collectivization with the Household Responsibility System and its monetary incentives resulted in impressive initial gains in agricultural production. Gains in income in agricultural areas were followed by growth of local industrial enterprises organized as cooperatives called township and village enterprises. The share of Chinese industrial production attributed to TVE grew from 22 percent in 1978 to 35 percent in 1999 (Anderson, Li, Harrison and Robson, 2003, citing statistics from the central government's China Statistics Bureau).

Following implementation of modernization policies in the agricultural sector, the party-state turned its attention to industry. Part of implementing the Four Modernizations in industry and technology was the Open Policy, which encouraged foreign investment. This investment was facilitated by enactment of the Joint Venture Law in 1979, which provided the necessary legal framework within which foreign investors were able to operate.

Sino-foreign joint ventures did not represent a new concept to the Chinese. Joint ventures between Chinese SOE and state enterprises from the Soviet Union had been commonplace prior to the Sino-Soviet split. The 1979 law was revolutionary, however, because it permitted joint ventures between SOE and foreign *private* companies.[14] The effect was to legally sanction the business operations of foreign capitalists in the People's Republic of China for the first time since 1949, and to create a new sector in the Chinese economy, the sector composed of foreign-invested enterprises (FIE). Foreign capitalists were allowed even greater inroads during the 1980s, when foreign investors were permitted to operate wholly owned affiliates in China. These are known as WFOE, the acronym for the English translation of the Chinese term "wholly foreign-owned enterprise".[15]

With foreign capitalists now legally operating in what is still ostensibly a socialist economy, the Party has modified its economic philosophy to accord with the changes in economic policy that it had already adopted. In 1993 the Party adopted a 50 point program for establishing a "socialist market economy"[16] featuring enterprise reform. This was followed in 1997 by the Fifteenth Party Congress' recognition of the "mixed economy model": an economy made up of state-owned, cooperatively owned and privately owned enterprises. Finally, in 1999 the constitution of the People's Republic of China was amended to specifically acknowledge that individual, private and other non-public economies were components of the socialist market economy (Dorn, 2001). Most recently, the *de facto* ownership of private property has now been given legal status, while the state has undertaken a major program to sell equity shares in thousands of SOE to local and foreign private investors.

Many commentators have pointed to these developments as demonstrating that the role of the state in the Chinese economy is diminishing. Nevertheless, the full evidentiary record suggests that the state remains *the* major force in China's economy.

The Market Power of the Party-State

Market power is defined in economics texts and dictionaries as the degree to which a firm exercises influence over the price and output in a particular market (Bannock et al., 1998, 263). To Chinese economists, however, market power occurs when rivals, either independently or in coordination, use market power *or* "administrative power" to control or dominate the market and preclude competition. Administrative power is exercised through *administrative monopolies*, which result from legislation or government administrative action; these administrative monopolies act to preclude competition (J. Yang, 2002). The party-state exercises market power over output and prices in the Chinese economy through administrative monopolies, even though it may no longer be the exclusive owner of the means of production within China's economy.

The market power of the party-state: statistical evidence

In terms of monopolization of the means of production, the party-state's pre-1978 monopoly no longer exists. In 1978, enterprises wholly owned by the party-state (the SOE) accounted for almost 78 percent of industrial production, the remainder representing production by collectively owned companies, largely composed of TVE; there was no production by privately owned enterprises, whether domestic or foreign (Anderson, Li, Harrison and Robson, 2003, quoting official Chinese statistics).

By 1999, SOE accounted for slightly more than 28 percent of production; domestic private companies accounted for 18 percent; "other ownership enterprises," primarily FIE, accounted for 26 percent; and collectively owned enterprises (TVE) accounted for more than 35 percent (ibid.). According to the Anderson et al. study, production by domestic private enterprises may be understated, as some private entrepreneurs may have tried to have their businesses identified as TVE.

Nonetheless, judging the role of SOE in the Chinese economy only by their percentage of production does not give an accurate picture of their still-dominant role. The 1999 statistics cited in the Anderson et al. study also showed that, while SOE share of production has steadily fallen, employment in SOE grew dramatically, almost *tripling* between 1990 and 1999 and representing 44 percent of urban employment (*The Economist*, 2000). The size of the party-state bureaucracy has grown as well; in the 1978–99 period the number of officials also tripled (Pei, 2003).

In terms of investment in fixed assets, in 1999 SOE still represented slightly over half of total fixed asset investment, and were concentrated in relatively few companies; in that year SOE represented less than 1 percent of the total number of Chinese enterprises (J. Yang, 2002). The concentration of economic power in SOE is also illustrated by examining the 500 largest Chinese enterprises; of these SOE account for 96 percent of the assets of the "China 500" and 85 percent of the profits (Goodman, 2004).

The market power of the party-state: control over investment

Reflecting their economic dominance and their preferred access to capital, SOE continue to attract a disproportionate share of investment. In 2004, 58 percent of total fixed asset investment was in the SOE sector (US–China Business Council,

2005). This reflects the party-state's continued control over allocation of capital in the Chinese economy.

The People's Bank of China (PBOC) no longer monopolizes banking in China, as it had prior to 1984. Instead it has evolved into the national central bank. At the same time, the party-state continues to exercise a near-monopoly on domestic banking through the "Big Four" banks, which are all SOE.[17] These banks hold around 70 percent of the banking system's total deposits, and account for over 90 percent of banking business in China (Saez, 2001).

Beneath the Big Four are a second group of 19 SOE banks. One of these, the Xiamen International Bank, is China's first IJV bank. A Japanese bank, the Asian Development Bank, and American private investors hold a total of 25 percent equity interest in this institution (*Wall Street Journal*, 1991).

The presence of privately owned domestic banks in China is minimal, although share issuance by some of the second tier of SOE banks has taken place. Domestic operations by foreign banks in China are presently restricted as to both geographic and product markets. These restrictions are scheduled to gradually end within five years of China's accession to the WTO.

Because all of China's commercial banks essentially remain SOE, they are directly controlled by the party-state on a nationwide basis. In the words of the Deputy Governor of the PBOC, the government has a "high monopoly on funds allocation" (Wu, 2005). Lending decisions are still largely governed by the party-state's national economic policy objectives, rather than by commercial credit-granting standards. Loans to industrial SOE are typically made on the basis of implementing these policies; these loans are referred to as "policy loans" (Fung, 1999).[18] This has created a serious non-performing loan problem for the SOE banks and, given their dominant position in the banking system, this problem is most severe within the Big Four.[19]

Problems with China's banks, and with the Big Four in particular, go far beyond non-performing loans. Even foreign media now routinely carry stories of corruption in the banking system; some of the stories quote reports issued by the party-state itself. One such story from early 2005 quoted a government report that 58,000 people had been punished for misappropriating money or making unauthorized loans at two of the Big Four banks (Barboza, 2005).[20]

In addition to implementing specific national economic objectives, the SOE banks also facilitate provincial economic expansion timed to coincide with convening of the Party's National Congress. Pei (2004) correlated "significantly higher" economic growth with years in which the Party holds its National Congress. These "Congress years," as he calls them, occur every five years. According to Pei, new provincial leaders chosen in the Party Congress are eager to demonstrate their ability to deliver economic growth. Provincial politicians are able to influence local lending decisions by the Big Four through the politicians' control over provincial bank branch managers.

Insuring that industrial SOE have full access to capital is equally important to both the central and the provincial governments. SOE provide approximately 70 percent of total government revenues in China (*The Economist*, 2000).

The market power of the party-state: political control over SOE

Political control is directly exercised over SOE by national, provincial and local levels of government, as well as within individual enterprises. *The Economist* (2000) refers to this as the *popo* problem, using the Mandarin expression for mother-in-law. "Mothers-in-law" exist for SOE at the enterprise level, in terms of the local Party cadre, as well as at the local, provincial and central government levels. Political direction of SOE continues even in the party-state agency that has been created to overhaul the SOE.

The State Asset Supervision and Administration Commission (SASAC), established in 2003, is the government agency charged with implementing the party-state's plan to shut down or sell off most SOE and convert those retained under party-state ownership to profit-making operation. SASAC's operations thus far, however, illustrate that the party-state is interested in increasing rather than decreasing its role in the economy.

In terms of number of enterprises in the SOE sector, from 1998 through 2003 the party-state sold off or shut down over 88,000 SOE, reducing the number of small and medium SOE from 238,000 to 150,000 (Buckley, 2005). Yet at the same time, SASAC has tightened actual operating control over the 196 largest SOE. This has involved disciplining or removing SOE executives and attempting to recruit foreign, private sector company executives for top posts in the largest SOE.

SASAC actions such as these pose a direct challenge to provincial government authorities with vested economic and political interests in the management of local SOE. As will be discussed below, provincial authorities have long been involved in symbiotic relationships with local businesspeople, whether from SOE, TVE or private enterprises.

Administrative monopolies and the market power of the party-state

J. Yang's (2002) study describes administrative monopolies in China in these terms: in China, administrative monopolies are exercised by state-owned or state-directed holding companies, either managed by the state directly or controlled by the state through appointment of managers. Such enterprises exercise market power through statutory or administrative legitimacy. Yang identifies three kinds of administrative monopolies in contemporary China: public utilities, sector monopolies and regional monopolies.

The first type, *public utilities*, represent a familiar concept in economics, that of a natural monopoly. So-called "natural monopolies" occur where technology precludes provision of service by more than one producer; common examples would be the delivery of water, electric power or natural gas.

Sector monopolies occur where large enterprise groups combine business, administrative and regulatory functions within an industry sector. These include, but are not limited to, enterprises that are directly affiliated with government ministries or departments. Yang lists, among other sectors, shipbuilding, tobacco, freight transport, electronics, and print and electronic media as characterized by administrative monopolies.

Although not specifically identified as such by Yang, the banking industry clearly fits the description of an administrative monopoly. Through a state-endowed monopoly on the granting of credit, the industry functions as a means whereby the party-state is able to achieve its economic policy objectives by administrative fiat. Because it fulfills this crucial role, one which influences every sector of Chinese industry, the banking industry is a very significant administrative monopoly, and not only for Chinese companies.

Unlike Chinese domestic enterprises, MNC affiliates in China do have some access to foreign capital, from their parent companies.[21] Still, the administrative monopoly of the banking industry seriously affects MNC operations in China. Chinese manufacturers that are either directly owned by or supported by provincial or local governments have a much lower cost of capital than the China affiliates of MNC. This is due to the domestic companies being able to obtain low-cost financing for new factories from the SOE banks, enhancing the ability of the local companies to compete with MNC (Bradsher, 2004a). As important as the banking monopoly is, even more critical monopolies for MNC to deal with are the regional monopolies.

In J. Yang's (2002) typology *regional monopolies* arise from trade barriers created by administrative regions, whether local or provincial. The trade barriers imposed by local or provincial authorities act to block the free interchange of goods and services between different geographic regions in order to protect local businesses. According to Yang, this regional protectionism has reached a level never known before in China.

Regional protectionism has effectively "Balkanized" China's economy. This "Balkanization"[22] is the most difficult institutional environment confronting MNC in China. In the remainder of this chapter we will examine how Balkanization arose and illustrate some of the difficulties that MNC face in dealing with Balkanization. The chapter concludes with a discussion of China's legal system and China's implementation of its WTO obligations.

The Balkanization of China's Economic Structure

Balkanization is a term used in political science to describe a situation whereby the strength of a unified country is diluted by the creation of internal divisions (McLean and McMillan, 2003, 36). The Balkanization of China's economic structure is noteworthy because, rather than being imposed on the party-state by outside forces, it is the intended result of past policies pursued by the party-state itself. These policies underscore the continuing significance of China's provinces to MNC operations.

Individual provinces of China are comparable to large European countries, such as Germany, in term of land area and population, and many provinces have their own dialects[23] and cultural traditions (Fairbank and Goldman, 1998, 11). Fairbank and Goldman are literally correct that provinces are political subdivisions of the central government in Beijing. The intergovernmental relationships between the central government and the local, provincial and regional subdivisions are quite different, however, from similar relationships within other large nation-states. These differences underlie many of the challenges that foreign businesses face in coping with Chinese institutional environments.

Origins of Balkanization

The views of Mao Zedong on organizing the post-1949 Chinese economy have been aptly summarized by Goldman in one sentence: Mao wanted central control, but not central management (Goldman, in Fairbank and Goldman, 1998, 398). The party-state's imperial predecessors had, whenever possible, barred local political autonomy, as posing a threat to the exercise of power by the imperial center (Jenner, 1994, 246; Huang, 1997, 109). Instead, imperial policy, particularly during Manchu rule, emphasized fragmentation of the management of the state apparatus, in order to insure that no independent power centers could arise that would challenge central imperial control (Jenner, 1994, 30–2). After 1949, Mao adopted a variant of the imperial policy in respect to the management of China's economy. Management, as distinct from control, of the economy was increasingly delegated to economic organizations that were part of provincial or local governments. Further, the provinces themselves were encouraged to develop economic independence through autarchy (Tanzer, 2001).

This autarchic decentralization involved both the physical location and the management control of SOE. It has been noted that decentralization may have simply involved making a virtue out of a necessity. That is, Mao recognized that China's economy was too large and diverse to be managed solely from Beijing (Starr, 2001, 150). Physical dispersal of manufacturing also reflected Mao's concerns about military action by Russia, acting either alone or with America, in the aftermath of the Sino-Soviet split that developed during 1959–61. The resulting massive industrial relocation, known as "the Third Front," was implemented through the transfer of hundreds of factories and an estimated 16 million people from urban industrial areas to remote mountain locations (Clissold, 2004, 52–4). At the same time, decentralization was pursued for non-military reasons as well, and local government units were given increasing authority to establish industrial facilities outside the centrally controlled manufacturing economy (Fairbank and Goldman, 1998, 398–9).

The decentralization of industry discussed above endowed some provinces with substantial economic autonomy. Since the party-state directed all aspects of China's economy, the local representatives of the party-state (the provinces) acquired a degree of autonomy to direct the local economy. Some decentralization of political authority was thus an unavoidable consequence of the decentralization of economic management. This enabled the Open Policy to be initially implemented on a province-by-province basis.

Balkanization's benefits: implementation of the Open Policy

For several reasons, the coastal provinces, beginning with Guangdong and Fujian, were the first provinces to be opened to FIE, followed by 14 coastal cities including Shanghai. These areas had long traditions of involvement in foreign trade. Access to ocean shipping meant that FIE would not have to rely on the underdeveloped Chinese internal rail and highway system to begin operations. Even more important was their relative proximity to potential foreign investors.

Guangdong is located very near to Hong Kong, and Fujian sits across the Taiwan Straits from Taiwan. The capitalist economies of Hong Kong and Taiwan had and have capitalists with money to invest in China, and many Hong Kong and Taiwanese investors in China originally came from Guangdong or Fujian. It is estimated that around 80 percent of FDI in China in the post-1978 period has been provided by overseas Chinese (Fairbank and Goldman, 1998, 413). The most recent data, from 2004, show that Hong Kong, Taiwan and Singapore still provide 40 percent of identifiable FDI (US–China Business Council, 2005).

Portfolio investment was soon followed by physical relocation of manufacturing. This happened first in the Pearl River delta as Hong Kong factories were removed to Guangdong, especially to the Special Economic Zones[24] created around Shenzhen (near Hong Kong), Shantou and Zuhai (near Macao). Taiwanese industry began relocating to Fujian soon thereafter.

In addition to the financial and economic reasons just described, there was another compelling reason for initially implementing the Open Policy in southern coastal cities and provinces. These areas were geographically far from the party-state's Beijing headquarters. Deng Xiaoping and his colleagues were able to implement their policies without facing day-to-day interference from the more doctrinaire Marxist-Leninist members of the Politburo. At the same time, the more doctrinaire members could be satisfied that capitalist encroachments were being confined to coastal areas, rather than being allowed to immediately spread to the interior.

The statistics cited earlier describe the results of implementing the Open Policy in the southern coastal provinces first. These provinces became very prosperous. Deng and his colleagues did believe that coastal prosperity would serve as an engine for economic development of the relatively poorer interior provinces, but, so far, this has not happened to the extent hoped for. Furthermore, the localized implementation of the Open Policy has resulted in local variations in the treatment of foreign investors.

Balkanization as a two-edged sword: the central government, local governments and foreign investors

A number of studies have pointed out that the differences between the central government on the one hand, and the provincial and autonomous regional governments on the other, towards foreign-invested enterprises have been a continuing concern to foreign businesses (Stoever, 1994; Child and Stewart, 1998; Osland and Bjorkman, 1998).

Child and Stewart (1998) concluded that the foreign partner in a joint venture was likely to find the most flexibility and greatest opportunity for exerting management influence within joint ventures located in Guangdong province (Guangzhou and Shenzhen) compared with either Shanghai or Beijing. As mentioned earlier, Guangdong is geographically very far from the national capital, illustrating the continuing applicability of the Chinese saying "Heaven is high, and the emperor is far away."

The relative independence of local or regional governments can work for or against foreign investors. Stoever's (1994) study described foreign investors as "caught between" the central and provincial governments. A more recent study emphasized that provincial and local governments are more likely to be sympathetic to foreign investors who can generate economic benefits for local jurisdictions than the central government would be (Peng, 2000). At the same time, however, such sympathies can be sharply limited by local protectionism.

A 1998 study reported the opinion of MNC executives that local governments would be less likely to apply the "non-discrimination" principles that are part of the WTO, due to interest in protecting local enterprises (Osland and Bjorkman, 1998). This has subsequently proven to be the case.

The annual *White Paper* published by the American Chambers of Commerce in Beijing and Shanghai reports the results of a survey of the Chambers' combined membership of 1,800 US and foreign MNC on China business conditions. The 2004 survey reported members' views that one of the most important continuing challenges for the Chinese government in implementing the WTO is to insure that local and provincial governments do not thwart WTO market access commitments made at the national level (American Chambers of Commerce, 2004, 4). This view is echoed in the scholarly research on local governments and the WTO in China (Lai, 2003).

Problems for foreign businesses arising from the substantial autonomy of local and regional governments are not confined to governmental relations issues. In order to maintain or obtain comparative economic advantage, all of the provinces take action to protect their local industries, made up primarily of companies owned by local and provincial governments, from competition by products and businesses from outside the province. The internal trade barriers that resulted from this protectionism continue to have a significant effect on the operations of MNC in China.

Internal Trade Barriers: the Great Walls within China

The internal trade barriers erected by provincial and local governments are implemented through three principal means: discriminatory licensing, preferential purchasing, and outright restrictions on interprovincial business operations.

Discriminatory licensing involves requiring products and businesses from outside the province or municipality to meet different standards than local products or businesses. A common example relates to protection of local brewers and food processors by imposing much higher "health and sanitation" requirements on products of non-local origin. This occurs frequently, even though the central government has its own system for regulating the health and safety of foods and beverages (Huffman, 2003). Discriminatory licensing is also applied to service industries, such as hotels (Pine and Qi, 2004).

Allied with this type of practice is the "buy local" requirement, often requiring tobacco and alcoholic beverage wholesalers to purchase locally produced products. Provinces use both discriminatory licensing and "buy local" requirements as competitive tools against each other. In order to protect the Shanghai taxicab market for the locally produced Volkswagen Santana automobiles, the Shanghai municipal government imposed discriminatory license fees on Citroën automobiles imported from nearby Hubei province. The Hubei provincial government then instituted a "buy local" program for all government units to retaliate against products from Shanghai (Tanzer, 2001).

Development of nationwide product markets depends on nationwide distribution systems. In turn, these systems depend on nationwide logistics networks. Business logistics in China are seriously hampered by the third type of trade barrier, restriction on transportation of goods between provinces. Road transport companies, for example, are licensed on a provincial rather than national basis. Cargo vehicles trying to bring freight to provinces outside their "home" province are often subject to prohibitive tolls at provincial borders (Huffman, 2003). This means that vehicles may have to be unloaded at provincial borders and their cargoes transferred to local road hauliers. This imposes huge additional costs on transporting cargo between provinces, and frustrates the development of cost-effective nationwide logistics networks.

Internal "walls" and the non-existence of a "China market"

The head of a prominent US-based trade association expressed his members' views about China in these words: "Everybody and his brother wants to go to China. There are 1.2 billion consumers over there" (quoted in Kessler, 2004). The executives with whom I spoke in China do not agree with this market analysis.

A different, more accurate view was offered by a China-based MOTORS executive who told me that the problem with the typical US company looking at a foreign market was in thinking that "population equals market." He was emphatic that this definitely was not true in China.

In terms of the traditional "four Ps" of marketing[25] China is a long way from the Levitt (1983) concept of undifferentiated "global" markets for standardized "global" products (Sun and Wu, 2004). The concept that there is one "Chinese market" is highly inaccurate. In part, this is due to the great disparities in disposable income and consumption between wealthy, urbanized provinces and the poorer, predominantly rural provinces (ibid.). Some analysts speak of "two Chinas" existing within the borders of the People's Republic. One such "China" comprises the urban coastal areas and immediately adjacent hinterlands, with a population of around 400 million people, and enjoying per capita annual incomes of US$1,000; the other is the interior remainder, with a population of 900 million and much lower per capita income (Jiang and Prater, 2002).

When analyzed in terms of the per capita income required to consume particular products, actual market size shrinks dramatically. One study estimated the actual Chinese market for imported luxury consumer non-durable products (cosmetics and toiletries) to be around 60 million people, which is a population equivalent to that of France (Zakreskie and He, 2001). While 60 million consumers are still a substantial number of consumers, that number is considerably less than 1.2 billion.

The relatively small number of Chinese who can afford foreign products also affects those MNC who manufacture consumer electric and electronic products in China for local consumption. In a recent year Whirlpool, the large US-based manufacturer of electric washers, sold over half of its products in only four markets, the cities of Beijing, Chengdu and Shanghai, and Guangdong province (Dolven, 2003). This market focus is likely to continue. Due to competition in China from local manufacturers, Whirlpool has concentrated on manufacturing the more expensive models of home appliances, where it enjoys both higher margins and higher market share (Drickhamer, 2004). Another major factor preventing development of a unitary "China market" is the presence of physical and administrative barriers that prevent free nationwide movement of products within China.

Tangible and intangible barriers to nationwide markets

The most tangible barrier to development of nationwide markets in China is the nation's transportation infrastructure. The infrastructure displays a duality that is just as marked as the urban–rural dualities of income and consumption. The infrastructure duality, however, relates to the differences between the infrastructure used for import-export cargo, and the infrastructure used to move domestic-origin materials and products within China.

As discussed above, companies in many sectors of Chinese industry enjoy considerable manufacturing cost advantages. It is also true, however, that internal transportation costs can be up to 50 percent higher than in North America,

Europe or Japan, and overall logistics costs (including warehousing, distribution, inventory carrying costs and order processing costs) can amount to 20 percent of a company's gross revenues, two to three times the comparable figure for companies in developed countries (Kerr, 2002).

Part of the relatively high logistics costs can be attributed to a transportation physical infrastructure that simply cannot keep up with the dramatic economic expansion (Goh and Ling, 2003). This infrastructure serves a land area the size of the US, but an area that has a more rugged topography. While the volume of cargo moved by rail, road and water transport within China has grown tremendously, the transportation system is best able to handle import-export traffic, and relatively less able to handle Chinese domestic traffic. This is especially true of *intermodal* transportation – the interchange of cargo in containers between two or more transportation modes in order to facilitate rapid delivery. In international transportation, intermodal transportation usually involves intercontinental movement of cargo containers by water, with prior and/or subsequent movement by rail, road or both.

China's extensive rail system offers one considerable advantage over road and water transport. The railroads are subject to one regulatory authority, the national Ministry of Railroads (MOR), and therefore rail is the mode least susceptible to interference from provincial and local governments. This advantage must be weighed against several disadvantages.

The railroad system focuses on the transportation of bulk commodities such as coal and grains rather than manufactured goods or processed foods. Railroad service is slow, with 30 day transit times for cross-China traffic not uncommon; and cargo theft, in the words of a US government report, "is an endemic problem" (Wu, 2003).

Foreign investment in the rail freight system is increasing and remaining restrictions on such investment are scheduled to expire in 2006 under WTO commitments. The most significant foreign investments have been undertaken by major international containership operators and their Chinese joint venture partners. These investments are focused on speeding the movement of export-import cargo between the interior and coastal ports through use of "double stack" freight trains that carry only ocean containers exclusively to and from the ports (Kerr, 2002).

China has undertaken an ambitious program of highway construction and modernization, but the quality of highways varies greatly depending on location. Excellent highway networks connect major cities such as Beijing, Guangzhou, and Shanghai with surrounding areas. Local road transport services within these areas tend to be high quality, and focused on moving cargo between local industries and transportation facilities. Interior highway networks are less well developed. Although China has an estimated 2.7 million companies offering road transport services, only 20 percent of the road transport fleet is capable of handling containers (Wu, 2003). This restricts the ability of road transport companies to handle intermodal cargo. As with the railroads, this sector is being opened to increased foreign investment.

China has an extensive network of rivers and canals that permit heavy reliance on domestic waterborne carriage, primarily for the movement of commodities in bulk. Yet waterborne commerce, especially on the Yangtze and Yellow Rivers, can be seasonally limited by climate, either flooding or drought.[26]

Further complicating transportation within China is the complex regulatory regime, which acts as an intangible barrier to development of a nationwide market. As we have already seen, provincial and local governments can impose their own regulations even when the central government has promulgated regulations that are intended to have nationwide effect. The same problem is present in the transportation system, with a further complication. In addition to varying national, provincial and local regulations, the national regulatory system itself is fragmented.

As noted earlier, the Ministry of Railroads has jurisdiction over the national railroad system. The Ministry of Communications regulates road and waterway transportation, while the Civil Aviation Authority of China (CAAC) regulates domestic air transportation of passengers and freight. International surface freight forwarding is under the authority of the Ministry of Foreign Trade and Economic Cooperation (MOFTEC), while international air freight forwarding is subject to both MOFTEC and CAAC (Kerr, 2002; Wu, 2003).

The uncertainties that MNC face due to conflicts between national and local government, and within those governments, might be removed if the party-state and its components operated as a system governed by rule of law, but such a system does not yet exist.[27]

"Law Blindness": the Chinese Legal System without the Rule of Law

There is a common misconception that China has lacked a legal system during most of its history. This is incorrect. What China has not had and does not now have is a legal system that operates under the rule of law.

Van Kemenade opines that "law blindness" (*fa-mang*) is a "typically Chinese trait, rooted in a moralistic culture lacking a strong legalistic tradition" (1998, 18). Coming, as this statement does, from a knowledgeable and experienced observer of China, it is an all the more noteworthy misinterpretation. China has had a highly developed legal system throughout its recorded history, complete with law codes, bureaucratic legal specialists and a law enforcement system, including courts, to enforce obedience to those codes (Jenner, 1994, 137–40).

Nonetheless, Fairbank and Goldman's (1998, 185) observation that the law basically has functioned as a tool of state administration is historically accurate. Public law, and criminal law in particular, was highly developed in order to enforce the social order and Imperial rule, but law relating to disputes between private litigants was not (ibid.). Commercial law was notable for its underdevelopment, and contracts were intended to be self-enforcing to the maximum extent possible (Huang, 1997, 197; Jenner, 1994, 139–40).

Death, rebirth and expansion of the legal system

The party-state organized its legal system, which included courts and a written constitution, along Soviet lines after 1949. By 1957, however, the legal profession had been abolished, and the remainder of the system was effectively wrecked by the Cultural Revolution, which included targeted deportations of lawyers and judges (Lubman, 2000; Fung, 2003).

Following 1978 the system began to regenerate. The legal profession was re-established in 1980 although there were then only 1,000 lawyers left in China (Van Kemenade, 1998, 18). The growth of the legal profession since then has been remarkable. From 1,000 lawyers in 1980 the legal profession has grown to over 180,000, and a Lawyers' Law has been enacted to redefine the role of the profession from service to the party-state to service to clients (Fung, 2003). An examination system has been instituted for both current and aspiring judges, prosecutors and lawyers; in 2002, over 238,000 people sat for the examination (ibid.). The expansion of the court system and the growth in the number of cases handled by the judiciary have shown comparable growth.

Even more remarkable than the explosive growth of the legal profession is the veritable explosion of laws. Since the passage of the Joint Venture Law in 1979 the party-state has enacted thousands of laws, creating an entire legal infrastructure for a modern, industrialized nation. These include laws establishing health and safety requirements both for the workplace and in the manufacture of consumer goods; environmental regulatory laws; and laws regulating securities issuance, foreign trade and investment, banking transactions, land transfer and development, business organizations and their internal governance as well as public and private sector financial transactions. In slightly more than 25 years, China enacted a body of laws that evolved in the US over a period of 225 years.

The missing element: rule of law

In the words of a noted legal scholar and student of Chinese law, "Rule of law is one of those concepts, such as democracy, that challenges academics and practitioners to agree on a clear definition" (Horsley, 2004). Here, I use the expression *rule of law* as de Tocqueville (2002, 111–14) did, to describe the institution under which an independent judiciary has the power to review and correct the actions of government officers.

Although the Chinese constitution was amended in 1999 to specifically recognize the concept of a state based on rule of law, Horsley (2004) observes that Chinese officials regard the concept as a "Trojan horse" for introducing Western liberal democracy to China. Both the current and former Presidents of the Supreme People's Court have stated that China would not implement Western concepts such as judicial supremacy and separation of powers (Yang, 1999). Neither of these concepts, however, is necessarily coextensive with operation of the rule of law.

England's government has operated under the rule of law since at least 1688. English courts, however, unlike their American counterparts, cannot exercise judicial supremacy; they lack the authority to declare laws passed by the legislature (parliament) to be "unconstitutional." Thus English courts, while a separate, independent branch of government, are not a separate and *equal* branch of government, which they would be if, as in the US, the courts enjoyed powers equal to those of the legislative and executive branches. Most modern governments operate under the English version of "separation of powers," that is, on the basis of some clear demarcation of the respective authorities of the branches of government at national and state levels, without equality of power between the branches. Adoption of the rule of law by China would not require adoption of American concepts of either judicial supremacy or separation of powers.

The rule of law, however, *is* an essential component of a civil society. It is equally important as the means of adjudicating disputes between the government and the governed, as well as disputes between different components of the government. China does not now and has never operated under a rule of law. In the unitary party-state there can be no "separation of powers," that is, a clear, legally enforceable delineation of the authority of the different government components, nor can the acts of officers of the party-state be subject to review by independent judges.

The consequences of the absence of rule of law

A noted Chinese scholar of China's politics has observed that the most serious problem facing China is *not* that it does not have democracy, but that it does not have federalism. By that, Minxin Pei (1999) meant that China has no functioning institutions that might resolve conflicts among the various components of the party-state. Under China's constitution, municipal, county and provincial governments all derive their powers from the central government, but the Organic Law of Local People's Congresses and Local People's Government permits enactment of laws by local governments "according to concrete local conditions and actual needs" (Blackman, 2001).

This "legal Balkanization" is further aggravated because local as well as national party-state administrative agencies can both promulgate laws, and create the regulations that interpret those laws, without judicial review of either (Lubman, 2000). As Lubman notes, most laws originate in administrative bureaucracies rather than legislative bodies, and even when legislation is promulgated at the national level, issuance of implementing regulations is typically left to local administrative authorities.

According to Blackman (2001), the result is that local regulations and interpretations can be inconsistent with laws promulgated by the central government. The absence of an independent judiciary with power to examine the legality of government authorities at any level means that there is no institution capable of insuring consistency or nationwide application of laws.

This legal Balkanization enables local protectionism to flourish. As we have seen, local protectionism promotes the economic Balkanization of China.

The absence of an independent judiciary

As complicated as the law-making process is, the process of obtaining adjudication of disputes through the courts is even more difficult. Yang (1999) notes that problems with Chinese laws are minor compared to problems with the way Chinese courts function in interpreting those laws. Part of the problem is the continuing prevalence of unqualified judges; even the Chief Justice of the SPC has criticized "non-professional and incompetent judges" for contributing to the unfairness of the legal system (Bray, 2002). In addition, the functioning of the courts is obstructed by both political influence and outright corruption.

POLITICAL INFLUENCE

In order to better insulate judges at local court levels from local political influence, efforts are under way to put in place a system whereby local judges are paid by the central government. Currently, however, employment, promotion and compensation of local judges are all in the hands of local government officials. Local government officials thus have the ability to influence the actions of local judges, and this authority is routinely used to exert "local legal protectionism." Yang (1999) identifies two forms of local protectionism.

One form involves local officials requiring judges to show favoritism to local litigants in cases where the other party is from another locality. This favoritism is an important tool in implementing the local government objective of protecting local enterprises from "foreign" competition.

The second form involves an even more direct and serious threat to judicial authority: the refusal of judicial and political officers in one locality to assist authorities from another locality. This is especially prevalent in cases where judicial authorities from another locality are seeking assistance in executing judicial monetary judgments against local residents.

CORRUPTION

Despite continuing efforts initiated by the party-state at the national level to limit it, corruption in China is a pervasive problem (Tjoa, Jianyu and Pykstra, 2005). Bribery and other forms of corruption pervade the professional activities of lawyers, judges and judicial officials (Lubman, 2000) and corruption within the judicial system is perceived as the most serious corruption problem in China, with the Chinese mass media reporting many cases of judicial misconduct (Zou, 2000).

The judicial corruption problem is not confined to lower-level municipal courts. During 2002 investigations uncovered corrupt acts by the head judges of two provincial people's high courts (positions equivalent to chief justices of an American or Australian state supreme court or Canadian provincial supreme court). The former chief of the Liaoning Provincial High Court was removed from his post for accepting bribes exceeding RMB 3.5 million (around US$420,000). He was subsequently sentenced to life imprisonment. His counterpart on the Guangdong Provincial High Court was punished after an investigation revealed that he and his family had accepted RMB 11.9 million (over US$1.4 million) in bribes (China Law and Governance Review, 2004).

Given the nature of China's legal system, Chinese society had to develop social structures that could protect individuals from arbitrary state action without resort to law. For both Chinese corporations and MNC operating in China, *guanxi* is the most significant of these structures.

The role of guanxi as a substitute for the rule of law

Although *guanxi* is a concept of considerable antiquity, it is still important to the conduct of business in China. Having *guanxi* avoids reliance on uncertain institutional environments. Both anthropological and management literatures have observed that *guanxi*, in the context of the PRC, acts as a defensive mechanism to replace or substitute for the legal relationships that structure both Western business transactions and the interactions between Western businesses and government regulators (Yang, 1994; Xin and Pearce, 1996; Luo, 1997).

The importance of *guanxi* to the conduct of business in Chinese-speaking societies both within and outside the People's Republic of China is attested to by references to it in several hundred articles in both scholarly journals and general business media. Despite the intensity of analysis, accurately gauging the effects of *guanxi* on management of enterprises has been difficult. One reason for this difficulty is the lack of an accepted definition of *guanxi*; the word does not appear in standard Chinese language dictionaries (Yang, 1994, 49–50; Luo, 1997).

It is not my purpose to join in the debate about the proper definition of *guanxi*. In Chapter 11 we will see that the executives with whom I spoke in China understand *guanxi* to refer to "relationships," which is an adequate phrase to encompass how *guanxi* operates in business.

The antiquity and diversity of guanxi

Fairbank and Goldman (1998, 84) refer to *guanxi* in terms of "personal connections" as being the means by which government officials advanced in the eighth century, even though the examination system had been instituted in the previous century by the Sui-Tang dynasty.

Some management researchers who treat "Chinese culture" as a unitary phenomenon also treat *guanxi* in the same unitary manner (Ahmed and Li, 1996). Other research has shown, however, that like "Chinese culture," *guanxi* is subject to geographic differences in interpretation. These differences are present in comparisons of overseas Chinese and mainland Chinese perceptions (Yi and Ellis, 1999) as well as in comparisons of perceptions between rural and urban regions of China itself (Yang, 1994, 76–8). Daniel Wen, the National Executive for China of WORLDWIDE, illustrated how he perceived the differing influence of *guanxi* in the latter case:

> *DW*: [W]hen you go to one part of China sometimes folks from another part of China are regarded as "foreigners" and so it's very difficult to generalize about China. [But] I would think that in areas with a high degree of local protectionism *guanxi* is very important. In areas with very open economic thinking, it becomes less important.

Guanxi *and local protectionism*

In November 2004 the central government dispatched an interagency task force made up of officials from seven different ministerial departments, including the Legal Affairs Office of the State Council, on an inspection tour of 28 provinces. The stated goal of the inspection was to monitor local government progress in eliminating local market protectionism. According to the head of the State Council's Anti-Trust Office, "local barriers won't just disappear . . . not until an effective legal framework is established will they start to break up" (Ting, 2004). Since establishment of such a legal framework seems to be somewhere in the future, businesspeople who are most affected by local protectionism must rely instead on *guanxi*.

On the local level, *guanxi* denotes a symbiotic relationship between local business and government. The measure of success for local government is how economic development and favorable treatment of local entrepreneurs can assist in this (K. Yang, 2002). At the same time, local entrepreneurs rely on local officials to protect them from competitors, both near and far (who have their own *guanxi* assets), as well as from actions by higher levels of government.

The officially sanctioned opening of Party membership to businesspeople resulted in some 20 percent of private entrepreneurs becoming Party members by 2000. Some entrepreneur Party members have gone on to become members of their local Party committees, which are a major political force at the local level, thus further cementing their *guanxi* with local political leaders (Dickson, 2004).

Finally, there is another, less appealing view of *guanxi* that equates it with "trading money for power" (*qianquan jiaoyi*), that is, with straight bribery (Fan, 2002). The executives with whom I spoke made clear differentiation between the two, and were emphatic that the two were not the same. Yang's (1994) extensive ethnographic study of *guanxi* in the PRC during the 1980s and early 1990s tends to support their views. Her basis of differentiation between *guanxi* and bribery is relational. Doing something for someone because of *guanxi* occurs as a result of a pre-existing relationship, often long standing. No such long-standing relationship is needed for a bribe; the social connection is established so that the bribe may be given (Yang, 1994, 61–3).

With varying degrees of success, MNC have learned to cope with the uniqueness of China. China's accession to the WTO has been welcomed by the MNC as the first step in "normalizing" the conduct of business in China. The final section of this chapter reviews MNC expectations of changes in China as a result of WTO accession, and to what extent these expectations have been met.

China's Institutional Environments, Multinational Corporations and China's Accession to the World Trade Organization

The importance of China for the global economy has focused attention on China's accession to the WTO. This landmark event is widely perceived as signifying China's acceptance of and participation in global institutional trading rules. At the same time, China's acceptance of its obligations under the WTO will result in profound changes in China's *internal* laws and institutional structures. Some observers believe (cf. Chan, 2004) that these changes are being undertaken voluntarily by China, while others consider that China is being forced to change by virtue of pressure from other WTO signatories. Whether the changes are voluntary or involuntary, they are still profound. Multinational corporations operating in China have expected that changes in China's institutional environments due to WTO accession would be beneficial to those MNC. The specific expectations need to be identified, before examining to what extent they have been realized.

MNC expectations and priorities

In a March 2000 speech, a top Motorola executive summarized his company's priorities for changes in China resulting from that nation's joining the WTO:

- tariff reduction or outright elimination, especially with regard to information technology (IT) products;
- elimination of mandatory technology transfer and trade-related investment requirements[28] for approval of direct investments;
- opening the Chinese services sector to foreign direct investment;
- promotion of the rule of law, especially with regard to protection of intellectual property rights (IPR);
- expansion of the rights of FIE to engage in trading and distribution within China (Brecher, 2000).

Three years *after* China's WTO accession, MNC priorities for WTO-influenced changes in China remained consistent. This was illustrated by the results of a July 2004 survey of the members of the US–China Business Council (USCBC), a

Washington, DC based trade and advocacy organization whose members include most of the largest US companies operating in China.

USCBC members listed their top WTO implementation issues, in order of importance, as:

- distribution – the ability to distribute products to wholesalers, retailers and end–users within China;
- intellectual property rights (IPR) enforcement;
- trading rights – the ability to import and export;
- non–tariff issues, including quotas and licensing;
- IPR legal framework;
- transparency of governmental processes, laws and regulations;
- specific market access service requirements;
- standards, technical regulations, and government assessment of conformity to those standards and regulations (Walton, 2005).

WTO: meeting expectations

In the introduction to the jointly produced *2004 White Paper*, the Chairmen of the American Chambers of Commerce, China (Beijing) and the American Chamber of Commerce, Shanghai voice their belief that, *with the exception of intellectual property rights*, China is substantially in compliance with its WTO obligations and specific obligations (American Chambers of Commerce, 2004, 4, emphasis added).

Given the nature of the current Chinese legal system, it is not surprising that the legal framework of IPR, and the enforcement of IPR protection, remain areas where foreign businesses feel that China is not yet in full compliance with its WTO obligations. The main obstacles to achieving full compliance were identified as lack of PRC government resources, and a low level of understanding of IPR in China (Walton, 2005). There are other issues, however, even in areas where China has literally met the letter of its obligations.

The opening of China's distribution system to full trading by WFOE may be accurately described as unprecedented. On December 11, 2004, in accordance with the accession agreement, China permitted WFOE to operate both wholesale and retail businesses, as well as to import and export products directly, without resort to one of the SOE trading companies. In accord with the equality of treatment requirements of the WTO, WFOE import-export and distribution companies will be subject to the same registered capital requirements as local companies, currently around US$62,500 for wholesalers and US$38,000 for retailers, to commence operations.

Having permission to conduct nationwide wholesale and retail operations is quite different, however, from being able to do so profitably. As mentioned earlier, the problems in China's internal distribution infrastructure translate into high internal logistics costs.

In addition, there are still restrictions on FIE wholesale and distribution operations at the national level. Retailers operating more than 30 stores will still be required to operate only through joint ventures, and prohibitions against wholesaling or retailing of certain classes of products remain in effect. Further, while the new regulations are intended to have national applicability, they will not override local or provincial land use and zoning regulations with regard to obtaining permission from local authorities to locate retail or wholesale facilities.

Zoning requirements for retail or wholesale establishments lead back to a point made earlier. MNC regard the single greatest obstacle to China's ability to fulfill its WTO obligations as the power of local and provincial governments to thwart national regulations on WTO implementation.

The issue of government transparency involves all governments in China, not just at the local or provincial levels. The concept of "transparency" can best be understood with reference to Western legal systems, whether based on common law or civil law. A basic principle of both systems is "certainty through openness." The legal process is intended to provide certainty through detailed laws and regulations enacted after public debate and publicly available to everyone. In China, the process is quite different. As explained in the *2004 White Paper*, "regulations are often promulgated without warning or consultation, and implementing rules are normally not issued until months later" (American Chambers of Commerce, 2004, 172). This lack of transparency can be understood through consideration of the *neibu* system.

Neibu or "internal" regulations, as the name implies, are not accessible to foreigners, or, for that matter, to Chinese who are not affiliated with the relevant government agencies involved.[29] The regulations act to prescribe standards of general and future applicability to the conduct of businesses, yet are not accessible to the businesses that must comply. Carver (1996) provides the most detailed examination of how the system works in practice, and provides an analysis of the case of regulations relating to foreign investment in telecommunications operations. Her work describes in detail the many difficulties encountered by foreign investors in trying to deal with *neibu* regulations.

Carver's critical views of the *neibu* system contrast with those of Duffy (1996), who argues that internal regulations, rather than a sign of an absence of law, or an excuse for graft and corruption, are instead "an important artifice permitting the regulatory process to remain flexible and pragmatic in a fast evolving and highly political environment." That may be correct, but Duffy's observation that Western investors are frustrated by the lack of transparency and predictability in the Chinese legal process more accurately sums up how foreign investors and managers view the transparency issue, and the operation of the Chinese legal system.

The WTO sought to deal with transparency problems by including Article I, 2(c), in China's WTO accession protocol:

> China undertakes that only those laws, regulations, and other measures pertaining to or affecting trade in goods, services, TRIPS,[30] or the control of foreign exchange

that are published and readily available to other WTO Members, individuals and
enterprises, shall be enforced. In addition, China shall make available to WTO
Members, upon request, all laws, regulations and other measures pertaining to or
affecting trade in goods, services, TRIPS or the control of foreign exchange before
such measures are implemented or enforced.

(quoted in D. Yang, 2002)

In his commentary on China's WTO accession agreement, D. Yang (2002) describes government transparency as one of the "basic principles" of China's WTO
deal, and describes this development as "unthinkable" for the party-state a decade
earlier. According to Lai's (2003) study, municipal and provincial governments in
China have begun making internal regulations available to the public through
various means including posting on websites, furnishing them to parties willing to
subscribe to official journals in which the regulations are published, and distributing
them on request.

Nonetheless, the very nature of delegated responsibilities among the national,
provincial and municipal governments within China can frustrate the opening of
markets, even when the intention is quite the opposite. The State Administration
for Foreign Exchange (SAFE) is the central government body charged with regulating foreign exchange transactions within China. In an effort to curb offshore
money laundering and tax evasion by Chinese citizens, SAFE issued regulations
requiring disclosure and approval of certain types of foreign transfers of business
assets by Chinese citizens. The effect of the regulations, however, is to interfere
with efforts by foreign investors to provide "startup" financing for Chinese entrepreneurs. The problems go beyond the wording of the regulations however.
Although the regulations are promulgated by a central government agency, local
government agencies are charged with actually granting or denying requests for
approval of transfers. In the view of foreign investors, the local offices do not have
sufficient staff to deal with requests, nor have they been furnished guidelines or
standards for processing the applications (Buckman, 2005). Problems of an inten-
tional nature also exist, and at the very highest levels of the central government.

China's WTO accession protocol contains specific provisions requiring, among
other things, that China apply and administer in a uniform, impartial and reason-
able manner all laws, regulations and other measures of both the central and
subnational governments. A short time after execution of the accession protocol,
a senior official in the Ministry of Agriculture was quoted in a published interview
as saying that after WTO accession, China should turn to "technical measures" to
protect its domestic markets (Wonacott, 2002c). This suggestion has been fully
implemented in the case of agricultural and food imports.

Both the USCBC surveys and the American Chambers of Commerce *2004
White Paper* describe continuing difficulties with China's enforcement of technical
standards and regulations. The *White Paper* devotes some of its harshest criticisms
to Chinese central government actions with respect to imports of food and agriculture products (2004, 100–7). The report lists examples of trade restrictions in

the form of arbitrary manipulation of quarantine regulations, implementation of protectionist sanitary and technical requirements on imports in order to protect domestic producers, and "unscientific, cumbersome and expensive testing and inspection procedures" that discriminate against foreign goods. Negotiations to resolve these issues are continuing.

The Way Ahead

The foregoing has introduced, in summary fashion, some of the major elements of China's unique institutional environments. We will return to this subject in Chapter 11, with a consideration of the processes through which the MNC that were studied coped with these institutional environment. The next four chapters are case studies of the four MNC.

PART II
The Cases

CHAPTER THREE

"According to Plan": Control and Coordination through the Discipline of Planning in an American Multinational Corporation in China

Introduction

Prior studies of control and coordination of global affiliates by multinational corporations (MNC) have focused on the organizational design or organizational behavior processes used to achieve these objectives. Little attention has been directed to the concept that corporate planning could be used by an MNC to control and coordinate its affiliates. MOTORS[31] is a highly successful US MNC operating globally through many divisions. MOTORS uses the mental discipline required by its rigorous planning system to inculcate a common "thought process" that serves as an integrative process for affiliates operating in diverse geographic and product markets. By operating "according to plan" division managers enjoy considerable autonomy to achieve goals that are established through a process that resembles the "management by objectives" advocated by Peter Drucker (1954).

Planning as a Control Process: General Comments

In the abundant literature on control and coordination within MNC, planning has been considered in two ways. First, planning is viewed as a structural element, that is, that the organizational site(s) responsible for the planning function and the monitoring of plan implementation represent a locus of control. Second, adherence to a plan is considered to be a control mechanism in its own right. In contrast, it is seldom recognized that the planning process itself can be an important means through which a parent MNC can control and coordinate its affiliates.

The idea is discussed in the following passage from Brooke and Remmers: "Planning also serves as an initial control over operations; for, in its final form, it makes a choice among alternative courses of action and uses of resources. In a similar way it is a device of commitment; for, in agreeing to the plan, subordinate managers are held responsible for its realization, or for explaining what went wrong" (1978, 90).

"Agreeing to the plan" is a central concept in the now out-of-fashion theory of management popularized by Peter Drucker and known as "management by objectives." In the Drucker formulation, management by objectives involves exec-utives and their subordinates agreeing to objective goals and measures by which their performance will be judged, and leaving to the subordinates the means by which those goals will be achieved. Corporate planning in general and corporate strategic planning in particular have come under increasing criticism as overly bureaucratic, too cumbersome for rapidly changing, technology-driven markets and destructive of morale in division and subsidiary management. In an era when much of the discussion, if not the practice, of organizational design is dominated by teams, management by objectives has been censured for discouraging teamwork. Drucker himself recognized problems with implementing management by objectives, but identified these as resulting from emphasis on procedures rather than on the concept itself.

Classifications of MNC by means of control structure or control style are useful as an organizing framework, but cannot provide explanations of the operations of a particular MNC. Further, many firms do not easily fit within the classifications, but have structures that incorporate elements from several classifications, and employ integrating processes that have not been explored in prior research. MOTORS is such a firm. It operates a very successful global, multidivision, multiproduct firm in which its diversified divisions are closely integrated by means of a discipline inculcated through MOTORS' planning process. This integration is achieved and maintained even for subsidiaries and affiliates operating in the challenging business environment of contemporary China.

MOTORS in China: Coordination "According to Plan"

MOTORS: a brief profile

FINANCIAL SUCCESS IN MATURE MARKETS

MOTORS is a New York Stock Exchange listed American MNC with head-quarters in industrial mid America. MOTORS operates through 40 divisions that manufacture a wide variety of industrial products in 380 factories throughout the world. MOTORS earned almost US$14 billion in the 2003 fiscal year. Asia accounted for 12 percent of total sales; international sales altogether accounted for 45 percent of total sales.

LEADERSHIP AND STRATEGIC FOCUS

MOTORS' CEO, Christopher Day, has led the company for more than 25 years. In an article in a leading US business periodical Day summarized the MOTORS philosophy:

> "[W]hat makes us tick at MOTORS is an effective management process. We believe that we can shape our future through careful planning and strong follow-up. Our managers plan for improved results and execute to get them. Driving this process is a set of shared values, including involvement, intensity, discipline and persistence. We adhere to few policies or techniques that could be called unique or even unusual. But we do act on our policies and that may indeed make us unusual."
>
> *(Knight, 1992)*

The manner in which that philosophy is implemented throughout the organization was related by Dan Truman, General Manager of a Shanghai joint venture in which MOTORS' wholly owned subsidiary, BRONWYN, holds an 88 percent interest:

> *STR*: Okay. MOTORS has a worldwide reputation for a very disciplined, very focused management style. Could you tell me a little bit about how that works at the level where you are managing?
>
> *DT*: First let me say, yes, you are correct. They do watch the money. It's a "very exciting and yet disciplined at the same time" approach to accounting. It forces you to not only understand where you are today but to very concisely plot your future. We know where we're going to be next quarter. We know where we're going to be next year. It's not "where we want to be," it is where we're going to be. And it's a very easy system . . .
>
> You've got to hit the target. And you as a general manager or a division manager or president or whatever you are, you have that number. And fortunately you have a tremendous amount of freedom on how you're going to make that number. But we all have this understanding that you are going to make that number. How, that's up to you. You can either cut heads, you know, headcount reduction, or you can cut discretionary spending. You can sell half the building. No one really tells you how you're going to get it. You just have to get it.

The culture and process of planning: setting the targets

PLANNING AND MOTORS' DIVISIONAL STRUCTURE

The MOTORS organizational structure is an "M-form" divisional structure. The presidents of each of the 40 divisions are responsible both for planning and for controlling the profits of their divisions' product lines. There is no intermediate organizational level, in which financial results are aggregated, between a division and MOTORS headquarters.

Both because MOTORS corporate staff is small for an MNC of its size and operating scope, and because of the absence of intermediate management layers between the divisions and MOTORS, in Day's words, "the people [divisional managers] who plan are the people who execute . . . it's their plan, not a corporate plan" (Knight, 1992).

THE DIVISION PLANNING CONFERENCE
WITH MOTORS OFFICERS

By his own calculation Day spends over one-half of his time each year on planning. Each year, from November through June, Day and other MOTORS corporate officers meet with the management of each division for that division's planning conference. For the conference the division is expected to produce certain standard exhibits. The first is a single page document called a "value measurement chart." This depicts long-term sales and profit growth, capital invest-ment and expected return on investment. Like other planning conference charts it covers "five back by five forward": that is, results of the previous five years and a five year forecast. The next two are "sales gap" and "sales gap line" charts. These display current and projected sales, based on market analysis, market growth, divisional market penetration, pricing and price changes and product introduc-tions and product line extensions. International growth is also reported. MOTORS assigns each division a growth target, which may be different for each division. The "gap" refers to situations where divisional projected growth does not meet the target, in which case divisional management must explain what it will do to close the gap.

The final chart is a profit and loss (P&L) chart describing 11 years of results; the current year is displayed along with the most recent five years as well as the five year forward projection.

While the charts themselves may be straightforward, the supporting documenta-tion can run to several hundred pages. Preparation for the planning conference by division management typically consumes several months. Preparation requires that division management adhere to the shared values that Day enunciated, especially involvement and discipline. In Day's words, "[t]o prepare properly requires that division presidents really understand their business. Every piece of data we ask for is something division management needs to know itself" and "[a] division president who comes to a planning conference poorly prepared has made a serious mistake" (Knight, 1992).

AFTER THE PLANNING CONFERENCE

Monitoring of plan implementation begins immediately after the group dinner that typically concludes the conference. Day writes a memorandum to the division president summarizing what was agreed at the conference (Campbell, 1999). More monitoring occurs on a monthly basis. Division presidents submit a monthly president's operating report (POR) to Day's office, called the Office of the Chief Executive, or OCE, at MOTORS. The POR reports the division's results for that month. Each division has its own board of directors, whose chair is an executive from OCE, and includes the division president and the president's senior executives. Division boards also meet monthly.

The MOTORS corporate planning conference takes place once a year, shortly before October 1, the start of MOTORS' fiscal year. The conference is attended by Day and OCE members, other senior corporate officers and the presidents and other senior officers of each division. Corporate officers discuss MOTORS' results for the fiscal year just ending, and announce the financial plan for the new fiscal year, and the strategic plan for the next five years. These are developed from information gathered at the divisional planning conferences and financial reviews, and aggregated and analyzed by MOTORS senior managers at the "corporate preplanning conference," held roughly one month prior to the annual planning conference. The significance of "hitting the target" is of immediate, practical importance to division executives. Their compensation depends on it. Each division executive is paid an annual base salary, and may receive a year-end "extra salary." The extra salary depends on division performance. If the division hits its financial target, members of the management team receive an extra salary. Extra salary is increased based on how much the target is exceeded but it is decreased based on how far division results miss the target.

Changing Strategic Focus to International Growth

In the 1980s, MOTORS was able to continue its enviable record of profit increases, principally due to cost cutting and asset rationalization. In the early 1990s, however, the company began to see slowing revenue growth. Day was characteristically blunt about the cause of the problem.

> "It's just been amazing to be sitting in these [planning] conferences, looking at these growth programs, and thinking 'Why the – haven't we done some of this stuff before?' Well, we didn't do it because we didn't have the resources to do it. And we didn't have the resources to do it because we were pounding the – out of profit margins."
>
> *(Henkoff, 1996)*

In consequence, MOTORS refocused on growth, and international growth in particular. By 1998 international sales constituted 40 percent of the company's total revenues. Despite what Day referred to as "a challenging environment in Asia," China played an important part in MOTORS' corporate growth plans. These plans, however, were implemented by different divisions using individualized strategies, only loosely coordinated by MOTORS' Asia-Pacific corporate office in Hong Kong. Before considering this, however, it will be necessary to briefly consider MOTORS' process of global growth through acquisition, in terms of both strategic conception and implementation.

Strategies of global growth: integration and coordination

THE EVOLUTION OF MOTORS' GLOBAL BUSINESSES

A review of past annual reports to shareholders discloses that MOTORS' internationalization process in some respects followed the "stages" model proposed by Johansen and Vahlne (1977): that is, manufacture for export, followed by licensing of products and technology in foreign markets, culminating in direct investment in foreign operations, whether through wholly or jointly owned affiliates. The history of MOTORS' globalization introduces an important variable to that model, however. MOTORS has been able to accelerate its global growth by acquiring both American and foreign companies that already operated significant worldwide businesses, and successfully integrating the acquisitions into MOTORS' global operations. The successful integration of these companies is an example of MOTORS' coordination through the discipline of planning, a discipline that is applied to both wholly and jointly owned affiliates.

PLANNING FOR ACQUISITIONS AND JOINT VENTURES

In a speech to a US conference on international management, Christopher Day explained that MOTORS treated domestic and international acquisitions and joint ventures in the same manner. All acquisitions involved extensive "due diligence." The objective was to buy profitable companies that were well managed, and whose business involved MOTORS' core manufacturing competence (Bonsignore, Houghton and Knight, 1994).

INTEGRATING THE ACQUISITION

Sterling Luo, the Co-Chief Executive of MOTORS, Asia-Pacific, explained the process of integrating an acquisition through the example of MOTORS' 100 percent subsidiary, CAPWELL, a leading manufacturer of compressors for HVAC applications, acquired by MOTORS in the late 1980s. CAPWELL exemplified the kind of company that was an attractive acquisition for MOTORS. It was a company with solid technology and products but without the internal financial resources needed to exploit growth opportunities.

Following acquisition, CAPWELL's CEO was replaced, but remained with the company, at first on a full-time and then on a part-time consulting basis, for three years. Everyone else in CAPWELL management was retained. Sterling Luo remarked that at a Hong Kong farewell party for a transferred CAPWELL executive, most of the 30 CAPWELL employees in attendance had been with CAPWELL for quite some time.

After acquisition MOTORS revised CAPWELL's financial reporting system, and then, over a three year period, CAPWELL became fully involved in the MOTORS planning process. As Sterling Luo explained, the integration process was facilitated because MOTORS acquired companies like itself; financially successful, well-managed manufacturers of products requiring substantial technologic expertise and discipline. CAPWELL was such a company and MOTORS followed its established policy of letting the newly acquired company manage itself. Because the companies were similar, they "talked the same language," as Sterling Luo put it.

JOINT VENTURES

MOTORS has been involved with both domestic and international joint ventures for many years, with extensive joint venture activities in Europe, and worldwide joint ventures with companies from European Union countries. A 50/50 joint venture was undertaken with a European company which was a major global manufacturer of hand-held power tools. MOTORS joined with a major global manufacturer of earthmoving equipment in another 50/50 joint venture, this one in power generation equipment. MOTORS sold its share of the power tools JV to its partner in 1996, and sold its share of the power equipment joint venture to that partner in 1999. Day described joint venture termination as follows:

> "Although joint ventures provided a quarter of MOTORS' total sales [in the period 1989–94] not all of our ventures last. About half of the joint ventures we have closed down were intended to be closed down. Short-term transfer of technology is one example of the hundreds of reasons why joint ventures end. 'Ending' is not necessarily 'failure.'"
>
> *(Bonsignore, Houghton and Knight, 1994)*

The MOTORS executives with whom I spoke held common views regarding the desirability of entering into joint ventures in China, and the management of joint ventures, if that ownership form was chosen. There was a clear preference for wholly owned affiliates, and the reason was cogently articulated by Sterling Luo: in a wholly owned situation you can concentrate on managing your business instead of spending time managing your partner. Both Raj Kumar, Co-Chief Executive of MOTORS Asia-Pacific, and John Kelly, MOTORS Asia-Pacific Chief Legal Counsel, mentioned that one reason to have a partner would be if the partner brought some type of value added in the form of market knowledge or market position in a market that MOTORS or its divisions are not presently participating in.

MOTORS' views of the issue of control in a joint venture are trenchantly summarized in the following remarks by John Kelly, who summarizes MOTORS' philosophy towards managing affiliates:

STR: Again, if I can offer up a general question with respect to joint ventures in China, let me just ask you about a couple of the traditional control mechanisms that US multinationals have used and have your view on the relative effectiveness. One would be insistence on, of course, majority ownership. Is that . . .

JK: I will try to summarize where I think you're heading with this. I don't think it's necessarily ownership. It's the responsibilities associated with having majority ownership. The success or failure, I believe, of any joint venture is in the management of the joint venture. What you get by having majority is the opportunity to control the entity. But that means that you have to be engaged in the control. That means you have responsibilities for planning; you have responsibilities for controls, financial as well as legal, as well as personnel. You have to implement them and that means you have to really be engaged with the joint venture. Majority control in China doesn't get you anything unless you exercise it; unless you actually implement what has been successful for your entities worldwide . . .

STR: So basically the management structure in a MOTORS joint venture would mirror the same structure that a wholly owned subsidiary would use.

JK: Yes.

STR: And the same management discipline would . . .

JK: Yes, we don't treat our joint ventures any differently. One of the reasons I think we have always gone for majority is to avoid the tendency of minority interest companies to not engage. If you have 30 percent of an entity, well I've seen other companies say that "well, it's not really important that we make decisions." So to avoid that, we have always stressed with our entities that they have control and they do engage and we've done that since day one in China. I think the commitment by our divisions and their managements has been remarkable as far as putting people who are quality people in place, minimizing the number of expatriates used, localizing the business, training the people, actually bringing the management structure of MOTORS and its divisions to these entities and bringing the disciplines that come along with it.

The accuracy of the summary can best be judged by now examining the actual operations of MOTORS and its wholly and jointly owned affiliates in China.

MOTORS' China Strategy: Concept and Implementation

Strategic motivation

MOTORS' motivation for direct investment in China has been twofold, as explained by Raj Kumar:

JK: I think MOTORS' whole objective in the last five or 10 years is to get higher growth. Our base markets grow at 3–4 percent in the US and Europe, maybe slightly less. So we have had to change the mix of our core product markets so that we have moved into things like telecom and electronics applications. The second thing is to invest in higher growth markets, geographic markets, and that's where Asia comes in. Any growth we get in Asia, the market is growing faster, is less saturated, and the infrastructure spending is growing at a rapid rate. The more business we get in Asia the higher our own growth, and as a percent of the business that keeps growing we have a fast growing chunk of our business here. And that's really our strategy with Asia. Now how do you do this? And the main thing is you've got to have a customer base that you serve as a local manufacturer.

The phrase "a customer base that you serve as a local manufacturer" is a reference to what Sterling Luo referred to as an "unwritten rule" within MOTORS. That is, MOTORS serves its customers globally. "If Whirlpool [an important MOTORS customer] started an assembly plant [in China] MOTORS would have a plant next door."

Implementation

While MOTORS' interest in investing in China dates from the early 1980s, several divisions preceded MOTORS itself as actual participants in Chinese markets. CAPWELL exported compressors to China beginning in the 1970s, considerably before its 1986 acquisition by MOTORS. STORMONT, a wholly owned subsidiary that manufactures process flow measurement and control equipment, first licensed its technology to a Chinese state-owned enterprise (SOE) in 1979. STORMONT's founder, who remained as company president following its acquisition, spent time in China and forged relationships with Chinese officials, including Zhu Rongji. During the 1980s STORMONT established a sales office in Hong Kong to sell its US manufactured products in China, and "representative offices" were established soon thereafter in Beijing and Shanghai. In 1992 STORMONT entered into a joint venture with an SOE to establish a manufacturing plant in the Pudong industrial area of Shanghai. STORMONT holds 60 percent of the equity in the venture.

In 1993 BRONWYN, another wholly owned subsidiary, engaged in manufacture of advanced industrial welding equipment, entered into a joint venture with an SOE to establish manufacturing operations in Shanghai. BRONWYN's initial equity share was 58 percent, since increased to 88 percent. MAYAN, initially a 49 percent owned UK company engaged in manufacture of power supply products for computers and telecommunications devices, established a manufacturing facility near Shenzhen in 1989. MOTORS acquired full control of MAYAN in 1997. While the above description might give the impression of unplanned activity, the divisions' various initiatives had been vetted through the MOTORS rigorous review processes described earlier. At the same time, the organizational structures for the divisions' China operations remain quite complex. In addition to those structures, MOTORS established MOTORS Asia-Pacific (MOTORS A/P) in Hong Kong. MOTORS A/P, however, while identified as MOTORS' regional headquarters, is not an intermediate authority interposed between the divisions and MOTORS. MOTORS A/P does have a number of important functions, described immediately below.

MOTORS A/P Hong Kong

Raj Kumar clarified the function of MOTORS A/P:

> *STR:* Do you think that MOTORS' influence over what you do in your responsibilities, because of the location as Asia, differs in some way from the way they relate to Europe, or Latin America for that matter?
> *PK:* Yes. Certainly, between Europe and Asia. In Europe businesses are grown by buying European businesses, fully running companies. So there's not much of a need for a corporate office. So our corporate office in Europe is smaller, does less development work and then does more of the treasury, currency, financial functions rather than the kind of things we do here. I think we do more strategy at the grass roots, building the business up, which in Europe they don't do because of the nature of the business that we have there, they are independent divisions who have developed their own management and their own strategies. So that's the difference here. I am more engaged in MOTORS business than would be the case in Europe.

MOTORS A/P serves two purposes in assisting divisions operating within Asia-Pacific. Within MOTORS A/P there are country managers, for example in China, who have business development responsibilities. In a situation where a division is thinking of undertaking an investment, whether by purchase or greenfield investment in a country in which it does not operate, the country manager has a corporate structure (in China, MOTORS China Holdings, Ltd) available within that country that provides "housing" for divisions going into new countries. This includes providing legal assistance and financial consultation and allowing them to view the country environment within an existing organization. If the division chooses to go forward in that country they can and do set up their own structures.

At the same time, as described by Raj Kumar, MOTORS A/P Hong Kong office is involved in helping the divisions recognize growth opportunities and providing financial, mergers and acquisitions and legal compliance assistance with regard to these and other business functions. There is also a centralized procurement function within MOTORS A/P employing 25 people and providing procurement services for all divisions within Asia-Pacific on an as-needed basis. However it is not mandatory to use the corporate headquarters' procurement function as long as the division can show that it can get a better deal doing things on its own.

In addition to Raj Kumar and Sterling Luo the Hong Kong office has two other senior MOTORS executives: John Kelly, Asia-Pacific Legal Counsel, and Corinne Lu, Human Resources Director. While the two officers have the same geographic responsibilities, their respective relationships with the divisions are necessarily different. John Kelly gave his view of the differences:

JK: MOTORS in many functions believes in autonomy. We don't want MOTORS corporate to ever get to the point where we are interfering with the operations of a division. However in my function that's a little different. The legal function is very involved in the divisions. We do not leave them to fend for themselves. For instance there is a standing rule that no one can engage counsel for Asia unless it goes through my office. No one is to seek guidance from counsel unless we have approved that counsel. As a result of this strictly enforced rule, we now work with a quality set of lawyers that we use throughout the region who give good advice.

The legal function is also closely involved in insuring compliance with the very high ethical standards promulgated at MOTORS headquarters in the US. John Kelly explained that these standards emanated directly from MOTORS' Chairman, Christopher Day, and are disseminated by means of a business ethics handbook printed in a number of languages and distributed to every employee in the company. All employees are required to sign an attestation that they have read the handbook; signature pages are filed in the employee's personnel file. John Kelly also conducts seminars throughout Asia-Pacific on business ethics, including review of MOTORS' business ethics standards, and the responsibilities of US companies under the US Foreign Corrupt Practices Act.

In contrast to the necessarily centralized direction of MOTORS' legal compliance function, MOTORS' human resources management policies reflect a more decentralized approach.

Corinne Lu is the Human Resources Director for MOTORS A/P. Her responsibilities are to support human resources services for all Asia-Pacific divisions, which total over 25,000 employees. Corinne characterized the divisions, in terms of HR, in two fashions. Some divisions relocate directly from the US in a startup mode, and for those divisions, at least initially, Corinne's organization provides detailed support in training, employee development, hiring, firing and legal compliance. However, other divisions have had a long-time presence in Asia, such as STORMONT and CAPWELL. These companies developed their own HR staffs and HR structures outside MOTORS. Her responsibilities for these companies are somewhat different. She keeps them informed of legal and compliance issues relative to HR, as well as the management philosophy of MOTORS.

Corinne reports on a dotted-line basis to the Vice President, Human Resources International, at the MOTORS world headquarters in the US. Eight people in Asia-Pacific directly report to her. She reports directly to Raj Kumar.

Corinne emphasized that MOTORS grows through its divisions and the divisions grow through acquisition, primarily by taking over existing workforces and management structures. MOTORS, therefore, is not interested in trying to integrate its various organizations into one uniform system worldwide. As illustration, Corinne emphasized that MOTORS' worldwide HR policies are remarkable for their scarcity. Business ethics are taken very seriously. There are very clear and detailed company policies on conducting business throughout the world under the highest possible, meaning US, ethical standards.

As a final illustration of the decentralized nature of the MOTORS HR function, Corinne referred to the agenda of the Asia-Pacific HR planning conference. This is neither dictated by nor the same as HR planning conferences within the US. For example, the topic of "localization" (replacing expatriate with local managers) is currently an important topic for Asia-Pacific in terms of management, management development and management recruitment. For MOTORS in the US, however, important issues are "lean" manufacturing and diversity in employment.

To understand how MOTORS actually relates to its China affiliates, this chapter concludes by examining CAPWELL, a wholly owned subsidiary, and two joint ventures: STORMONT Shanghai, and BRONWYN Shanghai.

MOTORS in China: Three China Affiliates

CAPWELL

CAPWELL operates worldwide as a manufacturer of compressors for both commercial and residential air conditioning uses, and for commercial refrigeration applications. CAPWELL is an original equipment manufacturer (OEM) for companies such as Carrier Corporation, and sells its products under the CAPWELL name as well. MOTORS purchased 100 percent of CAPWELL in 1986. CAPWELL maintains its own world headquarters in an American city several hundred miles from MOTORS headquarters. CAPWELL Asia-Pacific has its headquarters in Kowloon, Hong Kong, and is headed by a Chief Executive who reports directly to the CEO of CAPWELL in the US. CAPWELL Asia-Pacific has its own Chief Financial Officer, Director of Human Resources, and sales and marketing executives, all of whom report to the Kowloon-based Chief Executive. None report to anyone at MOTORS, either in Hong Kong or in the US. Within China, CAPWELL operates both a wholly owned subsidiary and a majority-owned joint venture. CAPWELL Asia-Pacific executives have considerable discretion over the performance of their duties within their own functional areas.

STORMONT Shanghai

STORMONT Shanghai was founded in 1993. STORMONT has three other China joint ventures and has a China holding company of its own, that is not a part of MOTORS China Holdings, Ltd. Wally Moon, the General Manager of STORMONT Shanghai, is also in charge of China sales for STORMONT. STORMONT maintains its own world headquarters in the US Southwest. Wally reports directly to the President of STORMONT Asia-Pacific, located in Singapore, and has no reporting responsibilities to anyone within MOTORS. STORMONT China Holdings has its own finance, sales and human resources staffs, although it does receive HR consulting services from MOTORS A/P as well as legal services.

With respect to operating the joint venture, Wally Moon directs day-to-day operations in accordance with STORMONT goals. The Chinese (40 percent) partner provides some assistance with the local government, and receives dividends. STORMONT Shanghai prepares budgets and operating reports in accordance with MOTORS guidelines, as part of the MOTORS planning process. Wally explained that "[w]e have some very rigorous financial and reporting guidelines but outside of that, we're fairly flexible to adapt rapidly to changing business conditions and we're fairly light on our feet."

BRONWYN Shanghai

BRONWYN is a wholly owned subsidiary of MOTORS and, like CAPWELL and STORMONT, operates a "stand alone" organization. BRONWYN owns 88 percent of the equity in the BRONWYN Shanghai joint venture; a Chinese entity affiliated with the Shanghai municipal government still retains a 12 percent interest. The General Manager for the past four years is Dan Truman, who is the only BRONWYN executive in the joint venture. The remainder of management are employees of the joint venture; however all were hired by Dan. BRONWYN Shanghai maintains its accounts under the BRONWYN system and submits its portion of the president's operating report to a BRONWYN financial executive in Hong Kong for consolidation. The human resources policies of BRONWYN Shanghai are "mirror images" of those of BRONWYN in North America with required adjustments for Chinese laws. A copy of MOTORS' human relations credo, the "Ten Principles," in Chinese, hangs in the BRONWYN Shanghai factory's elevator. As Dan put it, "[w]e try to instill the same quality and work ethic here as we would have anywhere in North America, and I use the word 'try' but we do not always succeed."

Other than submitting financial reports Dan has little contact with either BRONWYN in Hong Kong or MOTORS A/P, and no contact with anyone in BRONWYN in the US.

CHAPTER SUMMARY

MOTORS opened its first wholly owned manufacturing facility in China in July 1992, and in 1993 established a holding company, MOTORS China Holdings, Ltd, signifying that it had invested at least US$10,000,000 in China and operated at least three joint ventures. By 2005, 30 different MOTORS' wholly or jointly owned affiliates were operating in China, representing 25 of MOTORS' 40 divisions. MOTORS' growth in what is regarded as a difficult environment to do business reflects the company's ability to maintain its core business disciplines and transmit these, through the planning process, even to affiliates operating in China. Dan Truman's concluding remarks in my interview with him echo the MOTORS approach:

> *DT*: When you first come here you hear a lot of, this is China, this is different, that won't work. And if you believe that, then you're going to be a loser, like a vast majority of people that have come to China. Yes it's China, yes it's different, but it's the same. Money is still something everybody wants. And if you can show people a way to make it, a way to make as much of it as possible, wring every dime of profit out of your operation by using traditional business management tactics that worked for centuries in the United States . . . the common sense of business, instilled with discipline, you're unwavering in its enforcement, you'll be real successful. But don't buy the excuse that this is China; this is different; this is not going to work; because people that subscribe to that are the ones that are shutting it down, downsizing, losing money wholesale.

CHAPTER FOUR

"Control and Coordination through Goals": the Role of a Paramount Corporate Goal in Managing an American Multinational Corporation in China

Introduction

Prior studies of control and coordination of global affiliates by multinational corporations (MNC) have focused on the organizational design or organizational behavior processes used to achieve coordination. In the "strategy–structure fit" conceptualization, the organization's strategy determines the organizational structure needed to implement that strategy. Choice of control processes is, in turn, dictated by the management structure chosen. IMIGIS[32] is a US MNC operating globally through six primary business groups. IMIGIS' corporate goal of establishing a significant market presence for its businesses in China has involved creating a strongly focused country organization that operates with significant autonomy from the business groups, a situation unique within the company's global operations.

Classifications of MNC by means of control structure or control style are useful as an organizing framework, but cannot provide explanations of the operations of a particular MNC. Further, many firms do not easily fit within the classifications, but have structures that incorporate elements from several classifications, and employ integrating processes that have not been explored in prior research. Both statements are true of IMIGIS. As a pioneering MNC its organization structure grew, over time, to incorporate elements of several structural models and control types. This research was carried out at a time when IMIGIS operated globally by means of a unique "tri-matrix" organization, in which geographic management, product management and business function management coexisted.[33] The company's paramount goal of establishing a significant business presence for its subsidiaries and affiliates operating in the challenging business environment of contemporary China has served well to control and coordinate activities among the elements in this unique organizational structure.

IMIGIS in China: "Control and Coordination by Goal"

IMIGIS: renewal of an American icon

A BRIEF DESCRIPTION OF IMIGIS

IMIGIS is a New York Stock Exchange listed American MNC with headquarters in the American industrial Northeast.

IMIGIS' founder revolutionized the manufacture of a consumer entertainment product that is still associated with the company's name throughout the world – a name which itself is one of the most recognized global brands. In addition to its core consumer business the company also manufactures and distributes products in the medical, multimedia, document processing and graphic arts sectors. Total sales for 2003 totaled over US$13 billion; 56 percent of all sales were generated internationally. The company employs over 63,000 people, 38,000 of whom work outside the US. IMIGIS' products are manufactured in more than a dozen countries throughout the world.

FOUNDING PRINCIPLES

The company's founder set out four basic business principles for IMIGIS. They are still proudly listed in the "history" section of the company's website. These are: (1) mass production at low cost to enable competitive pricing; (2) marketing of products internationally; (3) extensive advertising; and (4) focus on the customer. These principles have not been forgotten.

IMIGIS was one of the first American companies to expand internationally. It opened its first foreign factory in 1891, in the United Kingdom. By contrast, Ford opened its first factory outside North America, also in England, in 1914. General Motors did not begin manufacturing outside North America until 1925, when it purchased Vauxhall, an English company. Furthermore, IMIGIS' foreign expansion was not confined to markets in the developed world. The company assigned an export sales manager to China in 1909, and opened its first facility in China in 1927, in Shanghai.

At the same time its founder established a tradition of paternalism towards IMIGIS employees. Pension and accident insurance funds were set up for employees long before institution of comparable US government programs, such as Social Security and Workers' Compensation. All employees were eligible for what was called a "wage dividend," an annual cash bonus plan. IMIGIS and its founder were benefactors to charities and educational institutions in the company's head-quarters city, as well as to institutions throughout the US, and the world.

THE PRICE OF SUCCESS

After a hiatus caused by World War II IMIGIS continued to expand vigorously throughout the world, applying the principles that had worked so successfully for so long. The company's success gave rise to serious problems, however. These problems were both internal and external. The internal problems were succinctly spelled out in a speech given by a senior IMIGIS executive several years ago.

> In the past the highly successful [IMIGIS] was a citadel of stability. It enjoyed market dominance, worldwide brand recognition and enviable margins and profits. Customers were extraordinarily loyal and employees looked forward to a lifetime of employment and security. Understandably, few people wanted to do anything to upset the status quo.
>
> *(Stopper, 1998)*

During the 1970s and 1980s however, the status quo was upset by events outside the company. While dominance in IMIGIS' core consumer business had always depended on its technological superiority, that dominance was successfully challenged by a new domestic competitor, employing innovative technology. IMIGIS had declined to purchase that technology when offered the opportunity some years before its introduction. At the same time, foreign competitors began to take market share away from the company in global markets, and followed up these successes by expanding into North American markets.

Organizationally, the company was not suited to respond to these challenges. Management was understandably attached to the status quo, an attachment reinforced by the tradition of generous paternalism. The discipline of planning was adhered to in principle, but sometimes not in practice. Product and sales forecasts often featured so-called "hockey stick" graphs depicting growth of sales, profits or market share as sharply accelerating. According to the author of a book recounting the company's decline and subsequent renewal, one senior executive was so angered by the persistent use of these graphs that she appeared at a staff meeting dressed in an ice hockey goalie's mask and carrying a goalie stick, and announced that she was not there to make such forecasts. There is no report of what other attendees thought of this (Swasy, 1997, 45–6).

Internationally, IMIGIS was originally organized on a "country manager" basis, with the country manager having profit and loss responsibility for all of IMIGIS' businesses in his or her country. While this had been satisfactory when only one or two IMIGIS products were sold internationally, it did not work well when the company entered several different lines of business. In the 1980s the company established product managers at headquarters for 17 separate product lines, giving them worldwide responsibility. At the same time, however, country marketing directors, who were part of an individual country manager's organization, were given marketing responsibility for certain product lines on a regional basis, while at the same time retaining responsibility for marketing all of IMIGIS' products within their assigned country. Despite the worldwide product line management structure at headquarters, country managers retained profit and loss responsibility for businesses in their own countries (Quelch and Hoff, 1986).

In the 1980s, senior management became involved in several ultimately unsuccessful attempts at diversification. Some new ventures, such as office copiers, were related to the company's core imaging businesses, while acquisition of a major pharmaceutical company brought IMIGIS into a part of the healthcare sector in which it had only a very small existing presence. One of the company's former CEOs admitted that IMIGIS missed several growth opportunities to expand its core consumer business with new products such as camcorders due to concentration on trying to make diversification work (Chakravarty and Feldman, 1993).

The effects of declining revenue from the once-dominant, pivotal consumer business were exacerbated by financial losses from the diversification efforts. Expense reduction programs featured massive layoffs that shocked IMIGIS' employees, who were used to lifetime employment, and endangered the paternalistic human resources management (HRM) tradition. Finally, in 1993 the company's board of directors reached outside IMIGIS, and hired as Chief Executive Officer, Jack Hunter, who was then head of an American MNC that was one of the leading global information technology companies. Hunter began implementing changes almost immediately.

Changing IMIGIS

Changing goals as well as the organization to implement them

Gradually, companies unrelated to IMIGIS' core imaging business were sold. In place of 17 product line organizations, the company was organized into six global lines of business: consumer, medical, entertainment, document processing, professional/graphics and digital products. Supporting these were global functional units representing both operational functions comprising manufacturing (of which HRM was a part), research and development, and supply chain management, as well as staff functions such as legal and finance. Country managers remained, but with lessened responsibility, with China being the important exception, as explained below. Some operating and staff functions were housed within regional organizations. In the case of China, headquarters of the Greater Asia Region is situated in Shanghai, and the President of Greater Asia, Henry Peterson, also serves as President of the Greater China "country" organization, encompassing China, Hong Kong and Taiwan. Therefore, some operating and staff functions whose headquarters were in Shanghai serve both Greater China and the larger region.

The importance of the Greater Asia Region to IMIGIS can be understood from the following statistics. The region encompasses 21 countries and areas, including India, Greater China, Japan, the Philippines, Malaysia, Singapore, Thailand, Indonesia and Australia, with a total population of over 3 billion people. IMIGIS has 11,000 employees within the region in 60 offices. Fourteen of the company's 28 global manufacturing facilities are located in the region, and there are over 13,000 retail outlets handling the company's products (Swift, 2000). Of these totals, IMIGIS has five factories and 5,000 employees in China itself; its products are sold through over 8,000 retail outlets throughout China.

The actual process by which the country and product (business group) management work together was explained by John Victors, IMIGIS' HRM Director for Greater Asia, and Kirk Tang, Senior Legal Counsel for Greater Asia:

> *STR*: With respect as far as certain functional areas, as far as the division of responsibilities between who does what within IMIGIS China, versus either IMIGIS regional or back at headquarters, does the China country manager prepare a capital budget for the various China units?
>
> *KT*: No, I think that he manages it.
>
> *JV*: He is involved within the bigger picture, trying to fit it inside the big picture, both Asia and worldwide . . . For example, the decision to manufacture digital products in China was jointly made at a global level. However the capital requirement needed to implement that is going to be generated at the local level and then go back up so the local unit would say "okay, this is what you wanted us to do, this is what it's going to take to do it." So how you're defining that, it's sort of a little of each.

This process was further explained, with specific reference to capital asset acquisition and operating budget development, by William Lobashevski, head of equipment manufacturing for Greater China:

> *WL*: IMIGIS' basic business structure is primarily a "business unit" type of structure. As such the company is divided into six basic business units and the business units control the investment that goes into R&D, capital assets and so forth. So, whoever controls the cash really controls the decision making process.

He replied in the affirmative to my question whether his organization's ROI was set on a company-wide basis, under a standard that all IMIGIS business units are expected to meet: "we follow the same global requirements; the investments that we make have to meet the corporate 'hurdle rate.' Each of those is done in conjunction with the business unit that sponsors the project or activity that would come into our operation." Mr Lobashevski explained that the budget process was a mixture of "top down" and "bottom up":

> *WL*: I would say that it is a mixture. There is a large degree of bottom up at the start. The top down element comes with respect to broader goal achievement, what the corporation needs to do and the requirement to adjust the bottom up plan as necessary, and, if possible, certainly, and if practical, to adapt [the bottom up plan] to those goals if top down goals are different from what the bottom up process produces.

He also explained the manner in which the functional organization fits into this structure:

> *WL:* Because of IMIGIS' structure I actually report to two people. One is in Shanghai, who is Regional President [Greater Asia Region] who is responsible for all of our business activities throughout Greater Asia. Now, as I said, we have six different business units. Consumer . . . and so forth. Then we have functions within regions that support the activities of the business units. Functions are R&D, manufacturing and so on. So, I also report to the worldwide Manufacturing Director, who is located back at our headquarters.

When asked if this was something that academics would call a "matrix" structure, William replied that "Yes, you could apply that nomenclature. Russell Ackoff would call it a 'network' organization."

Creation of a global strategy emphasizing China and emerging markets

In his previous CEO position Hunter had been directly and extensively involved in his company's large investment in China (Swasy, 1997, 127). He agreed with the assessment of General Electric's CEO that, "[I]f you want to be a world leader in your industry, you must be the leader in China." For Hunter, market growth statistics provided compelling support for the move into emerging markets. In the 1997 Annual Report to Shareholders Hunter pointed out that volume growth in the consumer business in the US and Japan over the previous two years had averaged 5 or 6 percent per year. In China, volume for the core consumer product grew 17 percent from 1996 to 1997, and in India [starting from a much lower base] volume for the same product during the same period grew 125 percent. According to Hunter, the new organizational structure, with some operating functions lodged in regional headquarters, was intended to aid IMIGIS in implement the following operating principles for emerging markets (Swift, 2000):

- manage emerging markets as a portfolio;
- accept volatility within individual country markets;
- make products where you intend to sell them;
- make products to a world–class standard.

Changing IMIGIS' management

Part of the changes in the company following Jack Hunter's appointment as CEO involved the process of opening the company to new ways of doing things, and to new people. IMIGIS manufacturing staff visited and studied Motorola manufacturing facilities in order to prepare for implementation of "Six Sigma," a statistical process quality control methodology whose goal is to virtually eliminate product defects from manufacturing operations, and which Motorola is credited with developing.

Just as IMIGIS was opening itself to ideas from outside, it was opening itself to hiring from the outside. John Victors, the HRM Director for the Greater Asia Region,[34] is an experienced international executive hired from General Electric. Kirk Tang, Senior Legal Counsel in Greater Asia, was hired from the China office of a major US Wall Street law firm. At the same time, veteran IMIGIS executives such as William Lobashevski, who had considerable experience in managing in China and elsewhere, were given increased responsibility; in Lobashevski's case, responsibility for manufacturing operations in Greater China.

IMIGIS in China: the Plan

Personal involvement by the CEO

As discussed above, Jack Hunter had considerable personal experience with China, the country, as well as in negotiating with Chinese government officials. The experience was gained during his prior work as CEO of a major US information technology company that had made investments totaling over US$2 billion to manufacture high-technology products in China. That experience helped shape what IMIGIS executives described as the company's key operating strategies in China (Swift, 2000):

- develop a partnership with the Chinese government;
- deploy "world-class" technology in China;
- develop "best in class" management practices;
- recruit the best local people;
- emphasize training;
- create a performance-based corporate culture;
- recognize the benefits of diversity;
- adhere to core values, with local characteristics;
- emphasize communication.

At the same time, IMIGIS had very clear ideas as to "must have" provisions in any agreement with the Chinese government that would lead IMIGIS to a commitment to make major investments in China. These were:

- sufficient operating and legal flexibility to enable IMIGIS to earn an attractive return on its investment;
- no investment that would involve the assumption of either non-productive assets or liabilities;

- compensation for technology introduced;
- IMIGIS' control of its affiliates in China;
- IMIGIS' ability to manage its manufacturing facilities as an integrated whole;
- temporary prohibition on other foreign investment in the sector in which IMIGIS would initially invest;
- "dramatic" reductions in import duties on certain components and raw materials.

These were formidable negotiating goals, but quite logical in view of IMIGIS' objective of gaining significant market share in China as soon as possible. IMIGIS did have significant experience in China in the period since 1979, however. A representative office was opened in 1981, and in 1984 IMIGIS entered into a contractual agreement to assist a state-owned enterprise (SOE) to build a factory in China.

IMIGIS' involvement in building the factory created a favorable impression of the company in China. Also, the company's investment initiative came at an opportune time from the Chinese point of view. The central government was faced with the need to rationalize capacity within the state-owned enterprises operating in the sector in which IMIGIS wished to invest. The government was also eager for IMIGIS to introduce advanced technology into that sector, in terms of both manufacturing methods and products produced.

An agreement was ultimately reached in 1998 that largely satisfied both parties' objectives. IMIGIS committed to an investment of over US$1 billion. A commitment of US$340,000,000 was made by IMIGIS as investment in two new companies. IMIGIS gained 70 percent share ownership in one company, with an SOE as 30 percent owner. In the other, IMIGIS held an 80 percent interest, with two SOE holding 10 percent each. These investments were essentially a purchase of the assets of the minority shareholders. However IMIGIS assumed none of the liabilities of any of the SOE in the transactions (Swift, 2000).

Furthermore, the new companies were *not* joint ventures. Rather, they were formed as "companies limited by shares" under the Chinese Company Law. Under the Company Law IMIGIS was able to more effectively exert management control over each company as majority shareholder than it would have been with equal or greater ownership share in a joint venture operating under terms of the Joint Venture Law. Under the Company Law IMIGIS would not be subject to the restrictions imposed on foreign joint venture partners by the mandatory provisions required in any joint venture agreement.

In addition to the asset purchases, IMIGIS also committed more than US$700,000,000 for subsequent capital investment in China. The Chinese government agreed to impose a four year moratorium on additional foreign investment in the sector in which IMIGIS had invested. The government also closed two obsolete plants in the sector.

With the conclusion of the agreement IMIGIS had achieved most of its negotiation goals. Now it was time to initiate the structure and deploy the assets to achieve its strategic business goals.

IMIGIS in China: Implementing the Plan

The continuing focus on China by IMIGIS' leadership

Personal focus on China by IMIGIS' top management was intense during the negotiation of the agreement, and remained at that level following conclusion of the agreement. In 1995 IMIGIS established the Greater China Region (GCR) to serve as regional headquarters for the company's operations in China, Hong Kong and Taiwan. To emphasize the importance of China, in 1997 Hunter established a "branch office" of the Office of the Chief Executive Officer, located at the GCR's headquarters in Hong Kong. This office was permanently staffed by one of Hunter's two Deputy Chief Executive Officers.

Hunter also continued to be a regular visitor to China, a practice that was continued by David Bass, his successor as Chairman and CEO. John Victors explained the role that these visits played in IMIGIS' China strategy and operations:

> *JV*: I figure that this has to be the most visited country in the world [for IMIGIS executives] because China is such an important market . . . I think that, to the businesses it's important that they spend time, try to understand China, and also the importance to IMIGIS, from a government relations point of view, to have people like David Bass come in and interface with senior officials. This is very important to us and very important to doing business in China, very important to our strategy. So I think because it is important to China, and also because it is important to [our] businesses to understand China, that we get a lot of visitors to China.

The unique position and role of the Greater China country manager

In 1999 the Greater Asia Region (GAR) was established, with headquarters in Shanghai. In 2000 IMIGIS revised certain reporting relationships so that the President and Chairman of GAR, Henry Peterson, now reports directly to David Bass. Henry Peterson is also General Manager of IMIGIS (China), the country organization covering Greater China.[35] Henry Peterson's unique role was explained by John Victors:

> *STR*: What is the role of Henry Peterson?
> *JV*: Henry is the General Manager. He is the head of China, the country, and he is the person who clearly represents IMIGIS when it comes to external affairs. The government relations area is a big part of his role and media relations, that's very clear. *And then, in terms of his role in the businesses, that's probably less well defined, yet it tends to be the case that in China he plays a more direct role in the businesses than would country heads in most other countries because of the need to*

coordinate what goes on in China. Quarterly, each of the business unit heads would report to his or her global product head. But, and this is true for every country's General Manager, they would also report to the country's General Manager in a matrix reporting relationship, as you called it. *I would say, though, that in the case of China the dotted line to the General Manager is stronger than in any other country in the world.*

STR: That was going to be my next question, which is, based on both of your experiences, taking it from a different direction, whether the type of influence that IMIGIS headquarters has over what goes on in China, if that's different than the kind of influence they would exert say in Singapore or in Europe?

JV: I would say that to the degree that there are overriding considerations with development in China as an overall market for IMIGIS and the importance that China has strategically across all business units, that the person in Henry Peterson's role probably has a greater ability to influence what goes on than would be the case elsewhere. In other countries the businesses would operate more independently. There would be less need for the country manager in Singapore, for example, to do so, less sensitivity and less need for him to interfere with his local business unit managers. (emphasis added)

Managing IMIGIS in China: control of the affiliates

In its global operations IMIGIS utilizes several different types of ownership structures. IMIGIS participates in a number of joint ventures, most importantly with leading information technology companies, as part of IMIGIS' drive to rapidly develop its digital products business. Joint ventures, however, have not been limited to IMIGIS' digital business. As example, IMIGIS is a partner with a large multinational chemical company in a 50/50 joint venture to supply specialty chemicals to the global graphic arts industry. Less than wholly owned enterprises are also utilized, such as IMIGIS' 51 percent ownership interest in a Japanese company that manufactures digital products.

IMIGIS' operations in China also reflect a mixture of ownership structures. Yet whatever the structure, majority ownership of the enterprise by IMIGIS predominates. As described earlier, the "company limited by shares" ownership structure was chosen for the two companies that would utilize the majority of IMIGIS' US$1 billion initial investment precisely so that IMIGIS would be able to exert maximum managerial control over the two entities.

In addition to the "companies limited by shares" and two wholly foreign-owned enterprises (WFOE) organized under the Foreign Investment Law, IMIGIS also participates in several joint ventures in China. The ownership strategy with respect to these entities was explained by John Victors and Kirk Tang:

> **STR:** With respect to the joint ventures, is it accurate to say that IMIGIS is a majority owner in each joint venture that it is engaged in?

JV: Yes.

STR: And by that I mean at least 50.01 percent.

JV: Yes, at least. Usually it is a little more than that.

STR: Is that a function of a deliberate strategy or the way that the capital contributions came in?

KT: Well, there is always the control issue or aspect for us. And part of this is that we are protecting, husbanding a brand and a brand name, and we don't feel like any company that is not IMIGIS should manufacture products or provide services and not be managed by us.

William Lobashevsky added a perspective regarding his own operations:

STR: Is it accurate to say, with respect to the joint ventures, that you, meaning your business unit, has control both in the sense of majority equity and in the ability to appoint the people who you want to appoint to management positions?

WL: Yes, at least in the ones that I am familiar with and am directly responsible for, we have that discretion.

STR: Is it fair to say that you would regard that as essential in a joint venture arrangement?

WL: I think that for a successful JV, if it is not essential, then it is certainly the preferred way to proceed.

IMIGIS in China: managing people

The coexistence of global and local management systems within the IMIGIS China organization is illustrated by the relation between John Victors' Greater Asia HRM organization, and the HRM organization contained within William Lobashevski's manufacturing operation. William Lobashevski described his HRM organization:

STR: With respect to hiring executives for the business units that you are responsible for, is this a process that you initiate as far as announcing a need, and then John Victors or someone else is going to go out and find you candidates?

WL: The way it works is that we have a fairly strong HRM organization internally. My relationship with John and his organization is more a strategic relationship, if you will, from a policy-making standpoint, broader policy changes. What you described I would put in the tactical category, and from a tactical standpoint, recruitment would be handled by the infrastructure that I have within my own manufacturing organization, which is linked to John's organization.

STR: So the recruitment would be on a local basis, first?

WL: Yes. The default choice would be that, wherever possible you would want to recruit locally. First of all it makes economic sense. More importantly, it creates an environment that helps us with job retention. It is a very dynamic market, particularly in the Shanghai area, and the more examples there are of advancement opportunities that are filled by local candidates the better it is both for the individuals and from a perceptual standpoint, where it shows that IMIGIS provides superior advancement opportunities for an individual . . . In each of our operations we have no more than one expatriate manager. All of the rest are local managers . . . We are talking about PRC nationals, not Hong Kong or Taiwan.

John Victors explained the interaction of local and global HRM practices:

> *STR:* John, with respect to HRM practices, are these conducted on the basis of global policies and standards?
>
> *JV:* Many things are. We certainly try to have principles around human resources and things like executive development and executive compensation are very much done on a worldwide basis. In fact, our executive compensation system operates globally and ignores both market practice, and, to some degree, market competitiveness on a country-by-country basis. We just have one variable pay program and the percentages of variable opportunity don't vary based on what is normal practice within a particular country. Then when we get lower down in the organization we tend to try to follow local patterns and practice both in terms of the quantity and use compensation both in terms of quantity and pattern, or you know I'd say, not only how much you get paid, but how it's delivered, we try to align more with local practice and we try to establish a country-by-country framework particularly for compensation and then try to say to the businesses, you operate within the framework and then justify yourself away from that based on business necessity and market practice . . .
>
> *STR:* And with respect to non–executive people, let's say, take for example, within China, and let's take both the case of a joint venture and the case of a wholly owned entity, is there some policy that says at a certain level below which they will be employees of the affiliate and above they will be employees of IMIGIS the global corporation?
>
> *JV:* Well, technically and legally speaking, they are also employees of whatever entity employs them. From a practical operational experience we tend to let everybody think of themselves as "IMIGIS." They don't think of themselves as being IMIGIS Shanghai Limited, or being part of IMIGIS Digital, Shanghai. They think of themselves as "IMIGIS" first, and we try to move people across those entities so we try to have systems that allow us to do that.

The success of IMIGIS' HRM policies can be appreciated by considering the performance of its China manufacturing facilities, as delineated by William Lobashevski:

> *STR:* With respect to the actual manufacturing operation, "Six Sigma" is a frequently used, probably excessively used buzzword. Other people talk about

"Copy Exactly." Are your manufacturing operations performed to an internal IMIGIS standard, or to meet an ISO standard?

WL: Each of our operations has been certified as ISO certified, either 9001 or 9002. They have been ISO 14000 certified for environmental compliance. From a quality standpoint, in order to differentiate ourselves in this business environment, we have really embraced Six Sigma methodology. In fact, more than three years ago, we produced our first Six Sigma quality product from our Shanghai operation. It was actually IMIGIS' first equipment product to achieve that quality level. We did it here in Shanghai. Since then, we have really embraced that process and that methodology and every product has achieved Six Sigma quality level. Now, there are other companies that are still thinking about whether it is possible to implement Six Sigma. In contrast, at IMIGIS we have a whole group of people who take it for granted . . . "Of course it can be Six Sigma."

CHAPTER SUMMARY

IMIGIS' concentrated pursuit of a significant market presence in China has been rewarded relatively quickly. Within three years of investing over US$1 billion in the People's Republic of China, IMIGIS is credited by media reports as having a 63 percent market share in its core consumer product market (Gilley, 2001). Total sales in a recent year were estimated at US$500 million, which would represent more than 10 percent of the company's worldwide consumer product sales. Innovative digital products for the consumer market that are developed and manufactured by IMIGIS in China are now introduced in China prior to introduction in North America. All of this has been accomplished while operating with a unique management system that balances geographic, product and functional business groups. John Victors summed up the IMIGIS system:

JV: I guess the only thing that I would say is that it is complex and it is sometimes difficult, at least for me to always know who's doing what to who and for what reason. Our organization is complex: we do try to simplify it but there are a lot of entities working here and you have the operational level and you have the legal [entity] level of organizations. Those two don't always line up. They cross. But it is fun, and that is quite the challenge of it all.

CHAPTER FIVE

"Global Replication": Control and Coordination through the Discipline of Replication of Organizational Processes in an American Multinational Corporation in China

Introduction

Prior studies of coordination of global affiliates by multinational corporations (MNC) have focused on organizational design or organizational behavior processes as means of achieving needed coordination. Research has emphasized the importance of coordination mechanisms in the context of the relative utility of these mechanisms in addressing the perceived challenge facing all MNC. That challenge is how best to organize and coordinate activities throughout the world in order to integrate operations across many markets while at the same time remaining responsive to local conditions in different individual markets. This is often referred to as the "global–local" challenge.

The conceptualization of this challenge focuses on coordination by means of different organizational structures as well as coordination by means of different processes or styles of coordination. It subsumes the concept that an MNC's business strategies and management practices must be aligned to allow operational integration as well as local variation. Research has characterized such alignment as essential if an MNC is to expand successfully in global markets (Rondinelli, Rosen and Drori, 2001).

At the same time other researchers including Hickson, Hinings, McMillan and Schweitzer (1974) and Child (1981) have pointed out that some MNC have adopted what Rondinelli and his colleagues categorize as a "universalist" approach, that is, that effective management does not depend on the geographic/cultural context within which it is practiced. Further, the important although generally unrecognized research of the Hong Kong scholar, Yao-Su Hu (1992), has called into question the existence of "global" corporations, as distinct from national corporations that operate internationally. ELECTRONS is an example of the "universalist" approach.

ELECTRONS[36] is a leading US MNC. Although founded in the 1960s, the company's relatively brief history reflects both consistent high profitability and technological leadership in the information technology industry. The company's operations throughout the world are governed by a process that I call "global replication," in which the company literally replicates its operating and management system at all of its worldwide facilities. This replication is exemplified by the company's manufacturing process known as "Copy Exactly," described below.

At the same time, the processes that comprise what ELECTRONS executives refer to as its unique "culture" facilitate the interchange and use of knowledge (called "best known methods" or "BKM" in company jargon) throughout the global organization, regardless of geographic origin. ELECTRONS' operations in China reflect the successful transplantation of the "global replication" process, including "Copy Exactly" and "BKM," to the unique Chinese business environment.

ELECTRONS and Prior Research on MNC Control Processes

Classifications of MNC by means of control structure or control style are useful as an organizing framework, but cannot provide explanations of the operations of a particular MNC. Further, many firms do not easily fit within the classifications, but have structures that incorporate elements from several classifications, and integrate operations through combining different integrating processes. Both of these statements are true of ELECTRONS, as we have now seen them to be true for the other cases.

ELECTRONS and the Bartlett and Ghoshal typology

In terms of Bartlett and Ghoshal's typology of MNC corporate structures discussed in Chapter 2, it is true that ELECTRONS has some elements of a *global* firm. It is also true that ELECTRONS embodies important characteristics found in *transnational* firms, especially in regard to the integrative linkages among dispersed units. These are discussed below, with reference both to the company's operating systems, and to how those systems are implemented within ELECTRONS Technology (China) Ltd (ETCL), the subsidiary that was the subject of the field research reported here.

ELECTRONS and styles of control

As discussed in Chapter 2, prior research had identified three principal models of organizational behavior control processes, that is, *personal* (also called "direct" or "centralized"), *bureaucratic* (also called "formalized") and *normative* (also called "cultural" control or "control by socialization"). ELECTRONS shares characteristics of all three processes yet does not fit neatly within any of the three.

ELECTRONS' primary control process is the discipline imposed by global replication. Global replication will be described first in terms of its role in the management of ELECTRONS, and then in terms of its role in controlling and coordinating ELECTRONS' Shanghai manufacturing operations. The essence of global replication is the setting of global standards, implemented through rigorous quantification of every business process. While these standards are driven, in the first instance, by the need for global product uniformity (the "Copy Exactly" process), they are implemented throughout the ELECTRONS organization and affect every business unit, including human resources management (HRM).

At the same time, decision making is pushed down through the organization through heavy use of cross-functional teams and the famous "two in a box" dual leadership structure. Yet throughout its many reorganizations, the company has continued to grant centralized authority over manufacturing to only one business unit, the Technology Manufacturing Group (TMG), located at company headquarters in the Silicon Valley, California.

Before beginning examination of ELECTRONS and global replication, it is important to note that ELECTRONS' successful use of global replication is quite different from strategies of global uniformity pursued by other US multinationals, particularly IBM and McDonald's.

IBM has maintained a highly centralized management structure, centered on its US headquarters since its founding, as has ELECTRONS. IBM, however, has also consistently maintained a "single leader" hierarchical chain of command structure throughout its existence, quite unlike the collaborative "two in a box" ELECTRONS approach. Further, while ELECTRONS has made proprietary manufacturing under central control the cornerstone of its business since its founding, IBM, during the 1970s and 1980s, evolved into an organization that would rather buy than make things (Mercer, 1988, 85).

The global uniformity of McDonald's "golden arches" also offers an example of successful global replication of an American operating and management system. As with ELECTRONS, McDonald's has a very strong corporate culture. This culture is transmitted by having all franchisees train at "Hamburger University" in the US, a facility equipped with simultaneous translation equipment to permit non-English-speaking franchisees to attend classes (Love, 1995, 149). Yet the means by which the necessary global uniformity is maintained is different for McDonald's. While ELECTRONS relies on internal control, McDonald's relies on external control, specifically the legal compulsion available to enforce its agreements with franchisees and joint venture partners, as the ultimate control process for insuring global replication (1995, 401–8).

The success of ELECTRONS' global replication system flows from its leadership and principles. These will be considered next, followed by the implementation of global replication within ETCL in Shanghai.

ELECTRONS in China: Success through Global Replication

Profile: from startup to global dominance

ELECTRONS was founded in 1968 by Richard Nye, one of two scientists who independently invented the integrated circuit, the device that makes all modern information technology possible, and Gerald Mohr, a brilliant research scientist in his own right, and the leader in the effort to bring the integrated circuit from the laboratory to commercial application. Their first employee was Arthur Graves, a European-born refugee who attended university in New York and then earned a PhD from the University of California at Berkeley and subsequently succeeded Mohr as Chairman and CEO.

The company's products are at the heart of 70 percent of the personal computers sold in the world each year. Its core businesses remain design and manufacture of microprocessors, chipsets and flash memory. At the same time, however, the company has vigorously pursued expansion into manufacture of chips used in routers, the devices that transmit and direct traffic over the Internet and corporate intranets.

Year 2003 revenues exceeded 30 billion US dollars. International revenues accounted for 75 percent of this figure. Manufacturing facilities are located in the USA, China, Costa Rica, Ireland, Israel, Malaysia and the Philippines.

Founding principles: open leadership

In the words of Nye's biographer, "There were always two people running [ELECTRONS]" (Tedlow, 2001, 411). A dual leadership structure is not unknown in business, nor was it unusual for ELECTRONS, considering the long-time relationship between Nye and Mohr. The same type of relationship characterized the joint management of another successful Silicon Valley startup, Hewlett-Packard, by David Packard and William Hewlett until William Hewlett's death (Packard, 1996, passim). Binational companies such as Royal Dutch/Shell Transport & Trading and Unilever PLC/Unilever NV also have dual chief executives. The structure has recently been advocated as a potential means of smoothing the integration process in newly merged companies (Troiano, 1999).

At ELECTRONS, however, there are two important differences. First, dual leadership at the top survived Richard Nye's departure from the company and subsequent death. Arthur Graves joined Mohr in running the company, and when Mohr retired another senior executive became Chief Operating Officer (COO) while Graves succeeded Mohr as Chairman and CEO.

More important, unlike the other businesses cited above, shared leadership, that is, "two in a box" in ELECTRONS jargon, is implemented throughout the organization. For example, the Assembly Test Manufacturing (ATM) Group is the second largest business unit within the TMG, itself the largest group within ELECTRONS in terms of employment. ATM is co-managed by an executive in Malaysia and his co-manager in Silicon Valley.

Open management is reflected through the heavy reliance on cross-functional teams that are assembled outside the structure described in the organization charts, in order to deal with specific tasks. Bian Chen, an ELECTRONS executive at ETCL, described one such team:

> BC: ELECTRONS runs "virtual factory meetings." Many of the sites run the same products . . . We have virtual teams with meetings across platforms and the BKM[37] are being shared through these meetings. Let's say Manila is running a little slower than Shanghai; the teams will assess both operations; in this case they found that Shanghai is doing a better job at implementing certain processes. They will look to see whether the implementation process itself is something that can become a BKM, and be shared with Manila.

In the case of organizational structure, ELECTRONS is organized as a matrix with both product and functional groups. During the 1990s the company was reorganized on an almost biennial basis. It has been the product groups, however, that have been reorganized. In part this reflects the company's strategy of moving forcefully into Internet-related products and services, as well as the growing importance of mobile computing, in which ELECTRONS' flash memory line of products is the global leader.

While product groups are reorganized periodically, the two key functional groups have remained unchanged for quite some time. The Technology Manufacturing Group (TMG) remains responsible for all ELECTRONS manufacturing worldwide, and will be discussed in detail throughout this chapter.

Equally important is the Finance Group, which not only has responsibilities for finance but also has the company's human resources management (HRM) function reporting to it. The Finance Group, referred to in company jargon as the "finance network," maintains matrix relationships with client groups. While not quite a "two in a box" relationship, most ELECTRONS general managers and business division heads have a dedicated controller as their counterpart (Burgelman, Carter and Bamford, 1999, 3).

An example is Dick Cahn, Financial Controller of ETCL. He reports directly to the ATM Group Controller, located at ATM "co-headquarters" in Malaysia. At the same time he reports on a dotted-line basis to Jim Liu, General Manager of ETCL at the Shanghai facility where Dick works:

DC: My fundamental role is to help Jim Liu with his business planning. Making sure that we look at this operation [ETCL] both from a business and also from a financial point of view. I have an analyst under me whose job it is to support the ETCL management review committee.

Another part of the open management system is the egalitarianism that is a characteristic of what ELECTRONS likes to refer to as "our culture." The absence of reserved parking spaces at company headquarters in Silicon Valley has been remarked on by almost every business journalist who has visited there, and it is true that parking spaces are available only on a "first come, first served" basis. Because of the employment expansion, anyone arriving in mid-morning must park quite a distance from the headquarters complex, regardless of rank.

A more significant indication of the egalitarian mindset is that every ELEC-TRONS employee not working on the factory floor has roughly the same size cubicle. This is true for the General Manager of ETCL as well as for Mohr and Graves. Although there are conference rooms, there are no "offices" at ELEC-TRONS in the conventional sense, nor are there "private dining rooms" segregated by rank. The administration building at ETCL boasts an excellent cafeteria, and everyone who works at the facility, regardless of rank or job, eats there.

The egalitarianism is best summarized by a Chinese immigrant chip designer who now works at ELECTRONS in California: "America is like [ELECTRONS] because success is merit-based; it is not about where you come from" (Miller, 1998).

Founding principles: the discipline of setting precise goals

In an interview in *Harvard Business Review* Nye described ELECTRONS as a highly disciplined organization, and put the company's emphasis on measurable results this way: "The people we want to attract are . . . high achievers. High achievers love to be measured . . . because otherwise they can't prove to themselves that they are achieving" (quoted in Tedlow, 2001, 399).

Part of the discipline involves observance of certain rituals, but in ELEC-TRONS' case, all rituals have congruent business purposes. For many years the company maintained "late sheets" on which were recorded the names of any employees, of whatever rank, who arrived for work after the 8:00 a.m. starting time without good business reason. The uniform starting time was enforced at every company facility. While the policy was clearly intended to inculcate disciplined behavior,[38] it had other, more specific business purposes. The uniform start time insured that telephone conference calls, the standard pre-Internet means of communication between geographically dispersed offices, could be reliably scheduled and held. It also insured the scheduling integrity of meetings within ELEC-TRONS facilities and with nearby customers and suppliers.

ELECTRONS still maintains a policy that is referred to in company jargon as "Mr Clean." Once a month a senior executive at every ELECTRONS facility conducts an inspection of that facility, concentrating on safety and cleanliness issues. Any defects found must be remedied as soon as possible, usually within 24 hours. In a business that requires immaculate factories, it makes sense to inculcate the discipline of cleanliness throughout the organization.

Founding principles: the discipline of measurable performance

An ELECTRONS executive with knowledge of the facts has identified the genesis of what was first known as "ELECTRONS management by objectives" (EMBO) and is now known as "management by plan" (MBP), as a series of 1973 meetings attended by top ELECTRONS managers and outside consultants (Yu, 1998, 180–1).

Under MBP *every* business group, department and individual within ELEC-TRONS has a quarterly set of goals broken down into clear measurable items ("deliverables," in company jargon) that must be accomplished during the forth-coming quarter. All goals are linked to the company's corporate strategic objectives (CSO) discussed below. Goal accomplishment is evaluated at the end of each quarter, and goal setting for the next quarter is related to what was and was not accomplished in the prior quarter.

Everyone at ELECTRONS is a part of this process. Shao, the Deputy Site Manager for Public Affairs at ETCL, described the process for his department:

> S: Yes, every department has performance plans; and we have to work out a performance plan; six objectives maximum, and we regularly update on the progress of making these objectives. We have one clear objective, to build good relations with local authorities, so that the company can do business easily in Shanghai. Then we have to define what activities are going to contribute to achieving this objective. Also, every month I prepare a report, "the monthly business environment scan." That goes to the Management Review Committee [of ETCL], headed by Jim [Liu, General Manager of ETCL].

MBP also involves communication with employees. At the end of each quarter "business update meetings" are held with all employees, at which time the com-petitive environment, company status and key accomplishments of the past quarter are all reviewed. These meetings are reinforced by posters and bulletin boards displaying progress towards goals.

Individual business units produce a plan of record (POR) that reviews unit P&L, budgetary allocations and plans. For example, Jim Liu and his staff produce an annual POR for ETCL.[39] This is adjusted quarterly to explain variances in key cost categories such as head count. According to ETCL's controller, Dick Cahn, the POR is simply ELECTRONS' expression for a unit's budget. A unit's budget is produced "bottom up," with financial analysts within departments at the indi-vidual sites each producing a segment. These are consolidated at the level of ATM management. The lowest level of approval of POR is, in the case of manufacturing, at the level of the executive heading TMG.

The setting of corporate strategic objectives (known in ELECTRONS jargon as "CSO") is, by contrast, a "top down" process that has been driven by Arthur Graves since he became Chief Executive Officer. CSO for a three year period are established at an annual three day meeting held in April attended by 20 top managers; there is another three day meeting in November to review progress towards achieving the goals established in the CSO and determine whether revisions are needed. The planning process itself is called strategic long range planning (SLRP). The April SLRP meeting traditionally begins with Graves reviewing the current business environment, the progress towards meeting current CSO and proposed changes. Following the "decision meeting" format, there is open debate about what to do and then agreement. Task-based teams are then established to develop plans and action strategies. After these are agreed, the CSO are published and displayed on posters and bulletin boards throughout the company.

Each business group (product and functional) has a monthly meeting with the CEO and COO where strategy relevant to the particular group is reviewed; a separate monthly meeting among the same parties is held to discuss operational issues (Yu, 1998, 110–11).

Founding principles: developing people to meet precise goals

Employee development at ELECTRONS is in two parts; training in working within ELECTRONS' culture, and training for a particular job. Kyle Urban, the head of design engineering within the flash memory factory at ETCL, explained the globally uniform nature of the process:

> *KU*: Every ELECTRONS division has a development plan template for each job. Every ELECTRONS employee has a development plan; there are a set of internal classes as far as ELECTRONS culture, how we do work here, how you are expected to behave, legal aspects such as safety. *All of that is standard anywhere that you go.* Then, for the job itself, that is where my training comes in. I prepared an introduction to flash memory that has been codified within the division. Basically, it says "You need to understand these things." (emphasis added)

This six month standardized orientation for every new ELECTRONS employee has been likened by one American management writer to "boot camp," an American colloquial expression that originally referred to the arduous basic training course that recruits to the United States Marine Corps must undergo (Mieszkowski, 1998).

Employees are introduced to the discipline of meeting precise goals immediately. On their first day on the job they view a video featuring Arthur Graves and attend a briefing by a senior executive on company business strategy, mission and objectives. They then go into a meeting with their direct manager where they are introduced to "deliverables," the tangible results that are to be accomplished within their first quarterly performance review period.

After about 30 days on the job employees attend an all-day class specifically devoted to the ELECTRONS culture. In addition to the quarterly performance reviews, new employees are interviewed by an HRM staff member after six months with the company. The final question of the interview asks the employee to state what he or she thinks it will take for them to succeed at the company. The new employee's co-workers have a vested interest in making sure that he or she completes the orientation to ELECTRONS and its culture; their bonuses are reduced if the new employee does not complete the course (Mieszkowski, 1998).

Founding principles: the discipline of the marketplace

The essential product development philosophy of ELECTRONS was succinctly spelled out in these words:

> One thing that has always been true of this industry is that recovery from a down cycle never occurs with old products. Technology evolves so rapidly that the market moves to the next generation and beyond. Thus, to be successful it is necessary to continue investing in new products even during the down periods.
>
> *(Moore, 1996)*

ELECTRONS' strategy for developing those new products has represented a sharp contrast with historic technology leaders such as IBM and AT&T.[40] ELECTRONS waited until 28 years after its founding to establish a central laboratory for conducting basic research. While ELECTRONS' research and development expenditures lead those of competitors, as well as those of most other information technology companies, most of the company's "R&D" expenditures during its first two and one-half decades was on "D."[41]

Rather than a central laboratory complex located at headquarters, ELECTRONS maintains three major and 80 smaller laboratories around the world (Chesbrough, 2001). Almost all of these are located immediately adjacent to or near an ELECTRONS manufacturing facility.[42] Each of the three main laboratories focuses on a product group, and the head of the laboratory reports directly to the head of that product group. The emphasis is clearly on rapid product development and introduction in the marketplace, or, in company jargon, "ramping up quickly."

Ramping up quickly is expedited by the global replication process. The equipment in the labs is closely related to, if not the same as, equipment actually employed in ELECTRONS' manufacturing facilities.

The focus on the marketplace is exemplified by Graves' choice of cubicle location. He sits on the same floor at headquarters that is occupied by ELECTRONS' sales and marketing staff.

As with every other process that can be observed at ELECTRONS, entry into foreign markets follows a precise plan (Dellacave, 1997). The plan involves three steps. In the first, ELECTRONS establishes a sales and marketing presence in a new market, referred to in company jargon as a "beachhead." The objective is to create demand for ELECTRONS' products in the local computer hardware and software industries. As these industries grow, the market is then classified as "emerging." As ELECTRONS' position within the market as the leading supplier to these industries is established, the market is classified as "developed." As discussed below, this has been the path followed in China.[43]

Linking the Disciplines: Global Replication through "Copy Exactly"

The linkage between the processes of discipline described above is the global replication process. Global replication can be understood through an examination of "Copy Exactly." Before describing "Copy Exactly" it is necessary to understand the importance of the Technology Manufacturing Group (TMG) to ELECTRONS, and how TMG represents an operationalization of the economics of the semiconductor business.

> TMG is the heart and soul of [ELECTRONS]. It is the most "ELECTRONS-like" organization, and it is the biggest organization by far; it's where we are going to spend the bulk of the $7 billion [in capital expenditures] that we are going to spend this year. *[ELECTRONS] cannot be understood without understanding TMG.*
> *(Arthur Graves, company press release, emphasis added)*[44]

ELECTRONS is justly proud of its reputation as a company characterized by manufacturing excellence. It is important to note at the outset that the emphasis on manufacturing excellence has had important consequences both for the company's internal organization and for its relations with its customers.

As noted above, while ELECTRONS' product groups have been reorganized on an almost biannual basis over the past dozen years, TMG has been constituted in its present form for at least 15 years, as far as I can determine from reviewing organization charts.

Further, TMG has, with few exceptions, historically been responsible for *all* ELECTRONS manufacturing of silicon wafers, microprocessors and memories. While the company engages in joint ventures and alliances worldwide to enable entry into new product markets, especially with regard to Internet technology, the company's manufacturing operations are conducted in its own factories.[45]

The internal organization of TMG reflects the steps in the process of manufacturing wafers, microprocessors, chipsets and flash memory components. The silicon wafers that go into these products are manufactured at facilities called "fabs." After creation they are sent to other factories, called "assembly and test" facilities, run by the Assembly and Test Manufacturing (ATM) Division within TMG. At ATM facilities, such as the ELECTRONS Technology (China) Limited (ETCL) factories in Shanghai, each wafer is cut into individual silicon dies, packaged, and tested for functionality, before shipment to customers.

ELECTRONS' success in manufacturing has been accomplished through recognition of the basic economics of semiconductor manufacturing, and the successful molding of its manufacturing organization to benefit from the basic economics.

Silicon chip complexity (that is, the number of active elements on a single semiconductor chip) is expected to double about every 18 months, and this law has held true for three decades. For the law to remain valid, however, chip size (the area of the silicon wafer) must increase in order to accommodate an increasing number of elements on the chip. This has become even more important as microprocessors (which in company jargon are referred to as "computers on a chip") have replaced memory chips due to the growth of the personal computer market. As long as these two trends are maintained the semiconductor industry will continue to grow. This is due to what has been described as the favorable "real estate" equation: the industry has been selling an area equal to an acre of semiconductor space for roughly one billion US dollars for the last 30 years. The amount of computing elements that can be put on that acre, however, has increased by several orders of magnitude, so that the cost per device element has correspondingly decreased by several orders of magnitude (Moore, 1996).

The necessity of increasing wafer size reflects the favorable "real estate" equation. According to the company, a 12 inch (330 mm) diameter wafer offers twice as much surface area, and 240 percent more individual microprocessors per wafer, compared to the 200 mm wafers that were the current industry standard. ELECTRONS expects that the manufacturing cost of the 300 mm wafer will be at least 30 percent less than that of 200 mm wafers.

High volume alone, however, is not sufficient to realize the magnitude of profitability that ELECTRONS has been able to achieve. To realize the benefits of increasing wafer size there must be an increase in the "yield per wafer," that is, the number of functioning microprocessors produced on each wafer. Microprocessors, however, are much more complex than DRAM memory chips because they are multifunctional and even take over some functions (such as floating point decimal calculation) previously performed by PC software. The quality of the manufacturing process is thus as important as the ability to manufacture in large volumes (Meieran, 1998).

The current cost of constructing an ELECTRONS "fab" amounts to more than one billion US dollars and ELECTRONS' ATM facilities cost between five and six hundred million US dollars.[46] In order to deal with the need for high-volume, high-quality manufacturing while meeting the need for rapid "ramping up" in order to get new products to market quickly, ELECTRONS developed "Copy Exactly."[47]

Put simply, "Copy Exactly" involves one manufacturing facility being chosen as the "development plant" to devise processes for production of chips for certain types of products. As the development plant creates the new process technology, managers from other ELECTRONS plants around the world will participate on site in the development process.

Thus when the process is complete, it will have been tested not only for manufacturing performance and reliability, but also for its feasibility for the high-volume manufacturing required by ELECTRONS. The process is then implemented at other ELECTRONS' factories.

At first only the equipment used and the output parameters were copied exactly. During the last decade however, *everything* at the development plant, including process flow, equipment, suppliers, plumbing, clean rooms, and training methodologies, has been chosen to meet the needs of high-volume manufacturing, recorded and then "copied exactly" to ELECTRONS' factories around the world. During and after implementation, joint teams made up of engineers from R&D and factory engineers conduct audits to uncover and correct any variations from "Copy Exactly."

"Copy Exactly" has its own change methodology. Having R&D facilities at or near factories allows R&D to be constantly conducted to improve processes. Similarly, manufacturing engineers are encouraged to submit suggestions to R&D for improvement.

Cross-functional teams known as "change review boards" are responsible for operation of "Copy Exactly," and once a change has been accepted it must be implemented at all manufacturing sites. The boards are also responsible for overseeing introduction of new equipment, while the R&D laboratories are charged with testing new equipment and materials and working with suppliers to educate them on "Copy Exactly" requirements. In terms of internal training on equipment, processes and procedures, since these are "copied exactly" each facility uses the same training documents, whether paper or electronic.

"Copy Exactly" extends beyond the manufacturing process to the design of electronic components, as Kyle Urban explained in response to my question as to how "Copy Exactly" influences the design of flash memories:

> *KU*: This originated on the fab side, and it has proved to be a very powerful concept, and we use it to set up all our satellite sites. We will try to use the exact same workstations, the exact same programs with the exact same revisions. For example, we have just finished a project to allow the worldwide flash memory design organization to synchronize on the small "glue" programs that we make or have made for us to enable us to do design engineering work, building models faster, keeping databases up to date; those sorts of things. We have synchronized to have one source, and to propagate from that source out to the rest of the world, to all the sites that produce flash memories. We are trying to use the same programs, same hardware.

The global replication that is exemplified by "Copy Exactly" has enabled ELEC-TRONS to achieve notable financial and marketing success. It is now appropriate to consider how the company implements global replication in the unique Chinese business environment.

ELECTRONS in China: Implementing Global Replication

The development of ELECTRONS' China business and organization

The development of ELECTRONS' China business has followed the pattern for entering new geographic markets discussed above. Although the company established a representative office in China during the 1980s, sales and marketing efforts did not begin until 1993 when a wholly owned subsidiary, ELECTRONS Architecture Development Ltd (EADL), was established, with principal offices in Shanghai and Beijing (Everatt, 1999).

EADL was the "beachhead" for the company's expansion. The phrase "architecture development" is company jargon for having ELECTRONS engineers work with non-company software developers to develop applications software that will run on personal computers that use ELECTRONS microprocessors. Besides direct support EADL has also fulfilled educational functions that include conducting technical seminars throughout China, and donation of the latest ELECTRONS microprocessors to Chinese academic and private software developers.

In 1994, in order to further influence the emerging Chinese computer industry, the company departed from its strategy of conducting the entire microprocessor manufacturing process within its own facilities. It licensed a subsidiary of a large state-owned enterprise (SOE) to test and package ELECTRONS microprocessors that were imported into China already assembled. For both the Chinese computer industry and the Chinese government, this represented significant foreign recognition of the capabilities of the Chinese computer industry (Paterson, 1994).

At the same time ELECTRONS was able to achieve substantial political and marketing recognition within China at relatively little cost. The microprocessors that the Chinese SOE would be testing were "last generation" microprocessors that were already being superseded by faster and much more complex models. Further, a few weeks after reaching agreement with the SOE, the company announced that it was entering into negotiations with the Chinese government to build an ELECTRONS ATM factory in the Shanghai area.

ELECTRONS' China organization has expanded rapidly in line with its increasing business. Although reporting relationships in China, as in the rest of ELECTRONS, are "complicated," to use Jim Liu's phrase, they replicate the characteristic matrix arrangement.

The representative office became ELECTRONS China, Ltd (ECL), a wholly owned subsidiary located in Beijing and responsible for relations with the central government. Finance personnel who share offices with the ECL staff prepare the financial and tax reports required by Chinese laws and regulations, but report directly to the head of Finance at Silicon Valley headquarters. I found no indication that the head of ECL has either direct or dotted-line reporting relationships with the heads of the other China business units, although for legal purposes the various operating companies are structured as subsidiaries of ECL.

EADL now has 13 offices throughout China, although Shanghai and Beijing remain the two largest. The head of EADL reports to the head of Marketing at ELECTRONS' US headquarters.

There are now six R&D facilities in China. In addition to three facilities in Shanghai that focus on software development, three laboratories in Beijing work on speech and handwriting recognition, wireless technology and Internet architecture, respectively. The labs report to the heads of their respective product groups as well as to ELECTRONS' Chief Technology Officer, all of whom are located in the US (Liu, 2000).

ETCL[48] represents ELECTRONS' manufacturing presence in China, producing both flash memories and chipsets. Shortly after I completed my interviews at ETCL, ELECTRONS announced that it was investing another US$300,000,000 to expand ETCL's Pudong facility. The expansion brought ELECTRONS' total investment in the Pudong facility to one-half billion US dollars and quadrupled manufacturing area floor space (Xinhua News Agency, 2001).

ETCL: implementing global replication

The dialogue with Gene Ma, Engineering Manager of ETCL, summarizes my visual impressions of ETCL. With the exception of the Chinese characters used interchangeably with English on posters and messages, there are few other differences between ETCL and ELECTRONS headquarters in California:

> *STR*: It seems to me that you can walk through the door here [in Pudong] and, other than the Chinese characters, you could be in Silicon Valley?
> *GM*: Yes, ELECTRONS heavily emphasizes its culture and it wants all employees to behave in a very similar manner. That way, we can have meetings by telephone with people thousands of miles away and we are speaking in a common language, using the same terms. The culture is quite similar from location to location.

ETCL has a very small employee parking lot because most employees still commute by bicycle or by company-provided bus service that serves 30 locations throughout Shanghai. Uniformed guards and fences are part of the landscape in Pudong and absent (in the case of uniformed guards, at least absent from direct view) in Silicon Valley. The excellent employee cafeteria in Pudong serves Shanghai Chinese cooking; California cuisine appears to be totally absent, as do other Chinese regional cuisines.

The physical similarities are more significant than the differences. The similarities reflect an intent that things be done the same throughout the world, as the General Manager of ETCL, Jim Liu, explained:

STR: If you can make this comparison, please do, and if you cannot, that is okay, too. As far as the way your operation relates to Malaysia or the US, are you in a unique relationship with Mr Wan [co-head of ATM] or with the people in California, or is this pretty typical of the way that ELECTRONS would manage its subsidiaries wherever they are located?

JL: First of all, to get back to your last statement first, you mentioned that we are a subsidiary because I told you we are a subsidiary, but that is only because we are set up that way as a legal entity. But in every feel and look, we are just an ELECTRONS factory. You cannot even tell that we are a subsidiary. Our employees are ELECTRONS employees. We are a subsidiary only for purposes of a legal entity.

That leads to your next question, "Do we deal with ourselves differently from other ELECTRONS sites?," for example, in dealing with customers, or management structure. And the answer is "no" with the exception of complying with local laws and local cultures.[49] When we deal with the divisions, we don't want the divisions to be overly concerned with where things are manufactured. We want to have the manufacturing flexibility to manufacture products anywhere. That is why, in ELECTRONS, manufacturing is centralized, so that we can deal with ups and downs of each division.

Our concept is very much that all the factories look the same. You have heard the term "Copy Exactly" so everything is the same and we certainly don't want customers to start worrying about which factory is making their parts. Also, we want to take the worry out of the division as much as possible. (emphasis added)

Management processes: open leadership

The management of ETCL replicates the process of open leadership. As General Manager of ETCL, Jim Liu is responsible for everything that happens at the "site." At the same time, only four business functions report directly to him: external affairs, human resources, engineering[50] and strategic planning.

As described earlier, Dick Cahn, the site's Financial Controller, reports directly to the Finance Director at ATM, and dotted line to Jim. The Information Technology Manager reports directly to ELECTRONS' Chief Information Officer in California, and dotted line to Jim. The two factory managers report directly to the co-heads of ATM, and dotted line to Jim. As Jim explained, "As far as day-to-day factory operations, that is the responsibility of the factory managers, and I tend to stay out of these."

The Management Review Committee (MRC) at ETCL is another example of open leadership. It is *not* a "board of directors" as that term is used in Anglo-American company law; it has neither legal existence nor legal authority. It is, however, a cross-functional team that assists Jim by consulting on and exchanging information about business issues that cut across functions or departments, and that can or may affect the site as a whole. Thus it reviews reports, such as those by external affairs called the "environmental scans," as well as financial, manufacturing and IT reports, that have impact on the entire operation of ETCL.

Management processes: replication

As discussed earlier, global replication has a significant impact on functions and activities beyond manufacturing. The Deputy Site Manager for Public Affairs clarified whether he had any responsibility for formulating policies for dealing with the Shanghai government, or whether policies came from ELECTRONS, either in Beijing or in California:

> *S*: Everything we do with any part of the Chinese government, we follow ELECTRONS' "business principles" which are established and sent down from ELECTRONS headquarters in the US. The business principles tell us what we can and cannot do. We don't have our own guidelines . . . Basically we follow US law, local law and ELECTRONS' business principles.
>
> ELECTRONS is a more mature company, in the area of external affairs, than the [Sino–US] joint venture I worked for before I came here. For example, if I want to offer you a meal, or I want to give you a gift, what is the amount that I cannot exceed? ELECTRONS has very clear guidelines about what can and cannot be done. In the JV, if the Chinese chairman says 'okay' then it can be done.

The process of replication does not depend solely on written guidelines, nor is it established only by directive from California headquarters. Bian Chen, ETCL's IT Manager, provided a detailed explanation of the process, in response to my question on setting standards:

> *STR*: Within ELECTRONS, who sets the standards by which your unit is judged?
> *BC*: Management standards?
> *STR*: Yes.
> *BC*: Okay. We say we always want to have a very strong ELECTRONS culture which managers can take advantage of as a baseline, to exercise global standards, what we call "BKM" or "best known methods." A lot of sensitive management processes are set by corporate-level teams; processes such as C&B [compensation and benefits]; these are set by global corporate management [at headquarters].
>
> The second area I would call well-defined management practices; this is the wisdom collected through years of global operations. This is not set by senior management; it is the collective wisdom from all parts of ELECTRONS. This is what we call BKM. How to conduct a staff meeting, how do we plan? Planning processes, for example. These are almost always globally similar. I am not saying exactly the same but very similar. Same with performance management.

In terms of manufacturing operations management, we have a term called "Copy Exactly." In this term we are not just talking about manufacturing operations, we are also talking about management processes. The second portion is the major portion, that is 80–90 percent of management practices. If you go around to ELECTRONS sites, all over the world, and I do, you see these processes flowing throughout ELECTRONS. You go to another ELECTRONS site in a different part of the world, you do not feel like you are a stranger because you talk the same language. When you talk about "POR" people know what you mean. When you say "capacity planning" or "performance management" people know what you are talking about.

Management processes: individual initiative

As befits a company with manufacturing facilities in the US, Asia, Latin America, Europe and the Middle East, and whose products are sold in almost every country in the world, ELECTRONS' global replication process is still flexible enough to allow for individual initiative exercised on a local level. Jim Liu gave an illustration of this flexibility when he responded to my surprise at the fact that he had a strategic planning function at ETCL:

STR: You mentioned earlier a function at this site called strategic planning. To have subsidiaries do their own strategic planning is highly unusual within most multinationals, so could you explain a little more about what the strategic planning function is involved in at this site.

JL: Sure, but let's change this question to "Why do you, as a factory, do strategic planning?," because we view ourselves as a factory rather than as a subsidiary. But even as a factory, you can say that you go with what your central planning group tells you, except, we are charged with maximizing the benefit of this site to ELECTRONS. And, if you look at ELECTRONS, the reason that we're here [in Pudong] is the China market, and then you ask, "How do you know that you're maximizing your presence here?" And another reason that we're here, that I didn't mention before but that I want to mention now, is that we are facing a worldwide shortage of very competent high-tech people, and we can get our share in China. China certainly has very good universities that can produce such people, so . . . we are expected to help ELECTRONS deal with the crunch in high-tech resources.

So, if you look at everything together, what we do in strategic planning, we look at our mission which is specific to China, and look at what we want to do, and then integrate that with the overall Assembly Test Manufacturing (ATM) plan. For example, ELECTRONS does a lot of acquisitions, so we may say, that kind of acquisition or that kind of product is going to be a major factor for ELECTRONS' revenue in the future. ATM may say that we have to try to have what we call "early involvement" to understand that product and be engaged with that division, so that when that becomes a major force within

ELECTRONS we won't be caught not knowing what to do with it. Now, we as a site will look at that product and ask "How does it fit into China?" For example, we said that China will probably be the biggest wireless market in the world. It may already be, with 94–100 million subscribers it may exceed the USA already. So if its wireless, we say, we should bid for it, that is, develop the capabilities, then we look at what it takes to do it, do we have the space here, how many buildings are we building, is this space here best allocated for this product or that product. Then we formulate a plan, but it is not final, because we still have to integrate it in the overall ATM plan, but ATM is counting on us to say what is right with this site.

As explained in the above quotation, encouraging individual initiative also permits free interchange of important information between the global sites and headquarters. "Best known methods" (BKM) are a product of this information interchange. As the engineer responsible for expanding the chipset factory at ETCL told me, one of ELECTRONS' important advantages in implementing "Copy Exactly" in new factories is that the company has built many factories globally and the accumulated body of experience has been distilled into BKM for factory construction.

Bian Chen explained that BKM also plays a role in localization:

BC: The third aspect of BKM is what I call "localization practices." For instance, in Shanghai, I am "local people" and we are managing ELECTRONS' operations here, and we have lots of local practices because you have to obey local laws and regulations. And, you have to try to integrate local people into the ELECTRONS culture. Sometimes you have conflict, but maybe you add more value into the ELECTRONS culture. Like good things in Chinese culture bring good things into the ELECTRONS culture. So we have a little bit of localized management practices, and, if these prove to make sense to ELECTRONS as a whole, we can share them with other ELECTRONS sites around the world.

For instance, [ELECTRONS' plant in] Israel is the global leader in performance management, so that practice [developed there] is being shared throughout ELECTRONS.

ELECTRONS' management processes are configured to allow coexistence between global standards and local practices, as exemplified by compensation and benefits (C&B) practices. Although C&B policies are centrally set by a group within Human Resources Management at California headquarters, the policies are implemented at each site, individually. Jim Liu elaborated on C&B philosophy:

STR: In terms of compensation structure, is this set centrally someplace within ELECTRONS, say at headquarters, for overseas operations, or is this something that you have authority to vary, or is there some intermediate person?
JL: That's a good question. We have a central group at ELECTRONS called C&B [compensation and benefits], and we have a C&B philosophy, which is

too complicated to get into, but our C&B policy is basically to be competitive with the market. If you asked, "How do you determine your C&B policy?," the simplest answer is "the market." Every geographic location has a different market, so every site has a different C&B. The central C&B group has the expertise, and works with consultants who are doing surveys to establish C&B. Every year, the C&B group proposes to us changes, increases, etc., which I, as site manager, have to approve. At the same time, I have to be "in sync" with it, and to champion it.

This is not intended to leave an impression that individual initiative in any way diminishes the company's disciplined approach. Kyle Urban's answer to my question regarding responsibility for quality control (QC) is illuminating:

STR: The perception by non-engineers is that QC standards are set at a high organizational level, that is, at corporate headquarters, and then spread down through the organization. Is that how it works at ELECTRONS?
KU: No. Corporate wide, when we send products to customers we have an overall, ELECTRONS global quality requirement. But doing the work to produce each product, each division provides its own quality requirements and its own system to track that. Recently, that is, within the last few years, there has been a real drive to push the concept of quality down the chain of command to the individuals who are working on the product. In my group [flash memory design] you, as a design engineer, are expected to take great care to insure that electrical design rules, interactions that you cannot simulate, are all taken care of before the product leaves your control. There is no "quality control" expert who has the final say. It is expected to be done at the working level.

CHAPTER SUMMARY

ELECTRONS established its first sales offices in China in 1993, and first began producing flash memories in China in 1998. It presently produces both flash memories and chipsets at its Pudong factory, which represents an investment of over 500 million US dollars.

Although the company declined to give exact market share figures, company executives did state that ELECTRONS is the leader in flash memory sales in China. China is the largest and fastest growing wireless telephony market in the world, and the principal use of flash memory is in wireless telephony. Observers have credited ELECTRONS with having over 80 percent of the Chinese microprocessor market and a similar share of the Chinese flash memory market.

ELECTRONS' rapid growth in the challenging Chinese business environment reflects the success of its management processes that I have called "global replication." ELECTRONS' dynamic expansion in China mirrors the success that it has enjoyed since its founding, success that seems to have been "copied exactly" in China.

"The Genetics of an Operating System": Control and Coordination through the Transmission of Shared Management Processes in an American Multinational Corporation in China

Introduction

Prior studies of coordination of global affiliates by multinational corporations (MNC) have focused on organizational design or organization behavior processes as means of achieving needed coordination. Within the study of organization behavior processes much attention has been devoted to the concept of "normative" control (also called "culture control" or "control by socialization") in which coordination is achieved by imbuing managers with common beliefs and expectations. Research efforts have sought to identify analytic models that explain how an organization can coordinate global affiliates through transmission and inculcation of the organization's "culture."[51] There has been no work, however, on the concept that the coordination process may follow a model based on evolutionary genetics.[52] WORLDWIDE[53] is a US MNC that is one of the world's largest industrial companies. Its history, which spans more than 100 years of successful operation in diverse product markets throughout the world, has made it one of the businesses most studied by practitioners and academic scholars.

WORLDWIDE's history provides a record of the development of the process by which the company has succeeded in controlling and coordinating its affiliates in many different geographic and product markets. This process is described by the company as its "operating system," defined in the company's 2000 Annual Report as the WORLDWIDE "learning culture in action." The WORLDWIDE operations in China reflect the transferal of the operating system to the unique

Chinese business environment, and its successful implementation in that environment. In my view, an evolutionary model is useful for understanding WORLD-
WIDE'S ability to accomplish this transference and implementation.

Normative Control and Coordination Processes and the Evolutionary Model

Normative control and coordination processes

WORLDWIDE'S conceptualization of its operating system as its "learning
culture in action" incorporates both the concept of "culture" as a pattern of
beliefs and expectations shared by the organization's members (Schwartz and
Davis, 1981, 32) and the concept of "learning" as the process by which organizations encode inferences from history into routines that guide behavior (Levitt
and Marsh, 1988). The "action" element is the subject of this chapter: "action"
being the dissemination of the "learning culture," dissemination which serves as
the mechanism through which the WORLDWIDE organization is coordinated
globally.

An evolutionary perspective on coordination

At the conclusion of their article on organizational learning, Levitt and Marsh
note that "there is adequate evidence that the lessons of history, as encoded in
routines, are an important basis for the intelligence of organizations" (1988, 336).
They also acknowledge (1988, 320) that their use of "routines" builds on the
work of Nelson and Winter (1982).

Biological evolutionary theory seeks to explain how changes in the genetic
composition (gene pool) of a species from generation to generation produce
changes in that gene pool and may produce new species (Bothamley, 2002).

What does all this have to do with control and coordination processes in
MNC? Nelson and Winter's biological analogy characterizes "routines" as playing
the same role within an organization that genes play in biological evolutionary
theory. By this, they refer to genes as the place where genetic characteristics
are stored. However genes also contain deoxyribonucleic acid (DNA) which
serves as the medium by which the genetic characteristics[54] of every living cre-
ature are *transmitted*. In the words of a popular work on evolutionary genetics,
genes pass "discrete bits of information from one generation to the next" (Wills,
1989, 19–23).

In WORLDWIDE it is this transmission process that puts the "learning culture"
in action, and provides the control processes for the WORLDWIDE organization.
To better comprehend this it is first necessary to examine the historical foundation
of WORLDWIDE'S routines.

WORLDWIDE: Control and Coordination through Transmission of Shared Organizational Processes

WORLDWIDE: a brief profile

A MODEL OF BUSINESS LONGEVITY

WORLDWIDE is a US MNC that is one of the world's largest industrial corporations. It operates globally through 12 major business groups, ranging from aircraft components through multimedia, and includes industrial systems, electric products for industry and consumers, power generation systems, medical equipment, industrial materials and transportation equipment. WORLDWIDE has operated seven of the 12 businesses for at least 70 years, and during its 100 year history has had only eight chief executives. It employs several hundred thousand people in facilities throughout the world. In its most recent fiscal year it enjoyed sales of over US$150 billion, 40 percent of which were earned outside the US.

DEVELOPMENT OF WORLDWIDE'S SHARED MANAGEMENT PRACTICES

The company's 1989 Annual Report summed up the unifying principles of its businesses in these terms: "[In] our seemingly diverse businesses there is a unique common thread – *shared management practices* – that binds them together and creates what we call integrated diversity" (emphasis in original). These shared management practices, the "genes" in the evolutionary model, can be grouped under three broad categories: entrepreneurial decentralization/market focus (the "genetic content"), knowledge development (the means by which genetic content is transmitted), and global concentration (the process by which the genes are encoded in a specific environment). Each plays a role in WORLDWIDE operations within China. Each will be described in sequence, before considering WORLDWIDE'S China operations.

ENTREPRENEURIAL DECENTRALIZATION AND MARKET FOCUS: THE "GENES" OF ORGANIZATIONAL ROUTINE

WORLDWIDE began its existence in the 1890s as a decentralized organization by virtue of a business strategy common in late nineteenth century America; the organization of a new business through horizontal integration of several smaller existing businesses.[55] In WORLDWIDE'S case the common factor in these businesses was their genesis in patents covering various products that had been obtained and commercialized by one of the company's founders. The company built on its heritage of invention through a formidable research and development organization and an emphasis on excellence in engineering and manufacturing.

Through its participation in defense production during World War II, WORLD-WIDE became involved in new technologies whose commercialization was to have a major impact on postwar industry; among these were radar, jet propulsion and atomic energy.

After the war the company recognized that it needed to move aggressively to exploit new technologies while maintaining strength in core business groups. The answer was to create an organization that was decentralized into as many as 150 different business groups, called "profit centers." This was coupled with a rigorous system of monitoring through enhanced financial controls, and the redevelopment of product-specific factories, closely related to the profit centers.

These changes were authored by WORLDWIDE'S postwar CEO, Robert Cormier. He explained the rationale for the reorganization in these terms:

> The underlying rationale for reorganizing [WORLDWIDE] that no organization chart can show is the drive we are trying to instill, that will cultivate entrepreneurial decision makers throughout the length and breadth of this mammoth organization. We want to put all of our managers constantly at risk; we want them all to be real entrepreneurs.
>
> *(Vaghefi and Huellmantel, 1998)*

Some 40 years later these goals were echoed in the company's 1992 Annual Report by James Walls, the then CEO, who said that "What we are relentlessly trying to do is to get that small company *soul* – and that small company *speed* – inside our big company body" (emphasis in original).

The changes at WORLDWIDE instituted during the recently concluded tenure of James Walls as CEO are customarily described by adjectives such as "revolutionary." Yet the principle used as cornerstone for his initial restructuring efforts was a contemporary restatement of the approach of one of his predecessors 20 years earlier: WORLDWIDE would operate only in those lines of business where it could be either number one or number two in the world. Businesses that could not meet this market target would be closed or sold. In the 1980s this resulted in the divestiture of several dozen businesses, the reorganization of the company into 14 principal business groups[56] and a 150,000 person reduction in global employment.

Several books and several hundred articles have been written about the changes wrought by James Walls at WORLDWIDE and no attempt will be made to recapitulate their content. It should be noted, however, that all of Walls' initiatives followed WORLDWIDE'S traditional shared management practices. Vigorous demolition of many layers of management has been intended to install and maintain entrepreneurial skills. As noted above, the market focus has been translated into concentration on lines of business in which WORLDWIDE is number one or two in the world in terms of market share. This is congruent with Walls' renewed global concentration, one that emphasizes China, India and Mexico as markets with the highest growth potential. Finally, Walls followed WORLDWIDE'S tradition of knowledge development by strengthening the company's commitment to acquiring and disseminating knowledge to all levels throughout the organization. That area is reviewed next.

Knowledge development: the "search routines"

As described above, WORLDWIDE began through the consolidation of companies that held patents granted to a famous inventor who was one of its founders. Commercialization of knowledge was thus the foundation for the company's initial rapid growth. Its knowledge development activities began with scientific research, and then expanded into management education. Its search routines include internal learning, both through management development programs and through the company's own planning processes, formal "initiatives" to transmit knowledge throughout the company rapidly, and learning from others, whether competitors or partners.

Following World War II a formal management training center was established by Cormier as part of his decentralization initiative. The management training center was the first of its kind in a major US company.[57] The faculty included professors from leading US and European management faculties as well as prominent private business consultants, including Peter Drucker (Noel and Charan, 1992).[58]

The arrival of James Walls as CEO brought major changes. The management training center was renamed the Management Development Institute (MDI) and given a new mission statement. One of its missions was "to serve as an instrument for culture change." As another human resources scholar observed, Walls used the MDI as an instrument for molding the new culture of the company (Evans, 1995, 652).

The new mission was accompanied by a complete revision of the way in which MDI transmitted knowledge. The traditional program was replaced by what WORLDWIDE called "action learning." The typical format involves five to seven person teams, made up of MDI students drawn from different parts of the WORLDWIDE organization. The teams work on actual business projects presented by a senior executive from the business under study. The only restriction on participation is that a team member cannot be from the business being studied. While working on the project the teams also receive classroom instruction from MDI faculty that include both WORLDWIDE executives and business school professors, and also conduct offsite interviews and research in the course of preparing their recommendations to senior management of the business being studied.

In addition to the pedagogical implications of action learning, implementation serves another important purpose. Having students who are experienced managers work on problems of other, different businesses serves as a very effective means for diffusing knowledge throughout a diversified global company. Thus MDI serves not only as an agent for cultural change but also as a "search routine," to transfer management practices throughout the organization.

Knowledge diffusion is also built into the company's corporate planning organization. Among the many changes instituted by Walls was the replacement of a large strategic planning bureaucracy by the Corporate Executive Council (CEC). In a much-quoted interview in *Harvard Business Review* Walls described CEC this way:

> We also run a Corporate Executive Council, the CEC. For two days every quarter we meet with the leaders of the 14 businesses and our top staff people. These aren't stuffy, formal strategic reviews. We share ideas and information candidly and openly, including programs that have failed. *The important thing is that at the end of the two days, everyone in the CEC has seen and discussed the same information.*
>
> *(Tichy and Charan, 1989, emphasis added)*

The same knowledge diffusion is built into the other elements of the company's annual planning process. These include the Operating Managers Meeting in January, attended by 600 top executives, and the Corporate Officers Meeting in October, attended by 150 top executives. The Operating Managers Meeting also serves as the forum in which the company CEO unveils new "initiatives," which are another important element of the knowledge development process.

The initiative process

"Initiative" is the term used by James Walls to refer to the institutional process by which WORLDWIDE engages in company-wide change. Cormier's decentralization and the marketing focus of his successor, Bosch, were both initiatives, although not labeled as such. Initiatives are generated by the CEO, but their source need not be within the WORLDWIDE organization. Walls' first initiative, an empowerment and feedback process designed to break down bureaucratization within the company, resulted from an open meeting attended by Walls, the director of the MDI and several hundred WORLDWIDE employees, held at the MDI. To design a program to implement the initiative WORLDWIDE called on an organizational development scholar at a leading US business school.

Joint venture partners, especially Japanese companies, were particularly fruitful sources of ideas that became initiatives. "Bullet train thinking" was borrowed from the Japanese partner in a medical equipment joint venture. The concept involved redesign of manufacturing processes to meet cost reduction goals previously thought unobtainable, in the same way that Japan's "bullet" trains involved complete redesign of railroad systems to achieve speeds previously thought unobtainable. It was adopted throughout WORLDWIDE manufacturing operations and achieved significant cost savings (McClenahan, 1997).

The most significant initiative involved WORLDWIDE adoption of Six Sigma. It is discussed in detail, both in this section and in the section dealing with WORLDWIDE in China, because the successful transferal of Six Sigma to China illustrates WORLDWIDE'S capacity to transmit its shared management practices to a much different environment, and successfully implant those practices in such an environment.

Six Sigma refers to a statistical quality control measurement in which manufacturing processes are carried out correctly 99.99966 percent of the time; this would mean 3.4 defects in one million production operations. It became the manufacturing quality control standard of Motorola during the 1980s, in response to Japanese competition in key Motorola product markets. Six Sigma, at WORLDWIDE as well as at other companies, has expanded to become the quality standard for all business processes.

Walls was introduced to Six Sigma by a former WORLDWIDE vice chairman who had left to become CEO of another US manufacturer, and whose company had studied Motorola's use of Six Sigma. Also through his former vice chairman, Walls was introduced to a consultant specializing in Six Sigma implementation and who had helped develop Motorola's Six Sigma manual. The consultant was retained by WORLDWIDE and helped develop the company's Six Sigma course content, and to identify key individuals within each business to receive initial Six Sigma training (Henderson and Evans, 2000).

To implement Six Sigma, Walls laid down three requirements: (1) every "exempt" employee (that is, every employee who was not a member of a trade union) would receive training, (2) every employee being trained would receive a minimum of 13 days' training, and (3) consideration for promotion would depend on successful completion of basic Six Sigma training (referred to as becoming a Six Sigma "green belt": Six Sigma skill levels are denoted by terminology borrowed from Japanese martial arts). Walls decreed that Six Sigma would be fully implemented throughout WORLDWIDE by the end of 2000. It was.

These goals were accomplished through a process in which employees who had been assigned to receive initial training (people with education/background in quality control) were trained to the master black belt (highest) skill level and then returned to their business units to train others. Feedback structures were put in place to monitor successful implementation.

Six Sigma implementation with reference to its implementation in China is discussed in the section of this chapter dealing specifically with WORLDWIDE China operations. It is appropriate, however, to conclude the present discussion of Six Sigma by quoting Terence Deng, the general manager of WORLD-WIDE'S Beijing-based medical equipment joint venture. When I asked him about implementation of Six Sigma in his organization he responded this way: "*Well, Six Sigma is for me, well, my brand new term is, I call it my DNA*" (emphasis added).

Knowledge development also interacts with the third shared business practice, global concentration.

Global concentration: implanting the encoded genetic material

WORLDWIDE has had a long tradition of involvement in international business, including China, where it established a factory in Shanghai in 1919.

Due to destruction of foreign physical assets during World War II and the need to repatriate capital to finance postwar expansion and new product development in the USA, WORLDWIDE drastically reduced its activities outside the Western hemisphere in the postwar years (Wilkins, 1974, 295). It was to be one of the newest of WORLDWIDE'S many businesses that was responsible for its return to prominence in global business in later years.

The rise of WORLDWIDE Aircraft Components

WORLDWIDE began manufacture of aircraft components as part of its role as a major producer of US military equipment during World War II.[59] After the war several factors combined to enable the Aircraft Components division (AC) to expand internationally using a model that proved successful first in Europe and later in China. AC's international expansion also exemplifies the decentralized nature of WORLDWIDE, as the expansion took place at a time when the rest of the company turned away from international business.

International expansion through licensing

When the Korean War began, procurement of modern jet aircraft by the US military was greatly accelerated and AC, which made many of the components for these aircraft, thrived. At the same time, the creation of the North Atlantic Treaty Organization (NATO) was followed by institution of American financial aid to NATO members to enable them to expand their armed forces. Some of that aid was "tied" to purchase of US military equipment, and US aircraft became standard equipment for most NATO air forces.

As a result AC began licensing manufacture of its components to companies in Italy, Germany and Belgium, and later to Japanese companies (Garvin, 1998, 8, 56–7). As part of the process AC engineers began to travel frequently to European and later Japanese factories, and, over time, built up close relationships with their foreign counterparts. As Garvin noted, the licensing programs created personal relationships of trust through technical collaboration between AC and European manufacturers.

The European joint venture

While AC prospered in the decades following World War II, its business was concentrated on supplying components for military aircraft. It had been largely unsuccessful in penetrating commercial markets. An opportunity to enter these markets was created by the procurement program for the family of European wide-body passenger aircraft being designed and produced by Airbus Industrie (Airbus).

AC entered into a co-production agreement with the leading French and German components manufacturers to manufacture components for the new Airbus aircraft. As part of the new agreement key AC technology was licensed to the Europeans, and the revenue-sharing provisions were favorable to the European partners. The co-production agreement resulted in the US-French-German consortium obtaining the contract to supply major components of the first jetliner manufactured by Airbus, and in AC entering into the passenger aircraft components market. This co-production agreement then led to a joint venture with the French member of its Airbus consortium.

This collaboration was structured as a joint venture with each company owning 50 percent. All revenues would be shared, along with equal sharing of research and development, marketing and sales expenses (Sparaco, 1999). The joint venture, in Garvin's (1998) words, would have only a "skeleton" staff. Manufacturing, engineering, marketing and product support would be performed for the venture by its partners, with work shared on a 50/50 basis (1998, 131). Both partners would manufacture for the joint venture at their own factories. As Garvin explained, integrating the marketing responsibilities was more difficult, in the venture's early days, than was integrating the technical work, where the partners got along smoothly from the beginning (1998, 130). The initial difficulties were soon overcome however; the joint venture is still in full operation after more than three decades.

Patterns of international expansion

AC's international expansion followed the pattern that it developed in Europe in the 1950s and 1960s. This is illustrated by the Chinese example, discussed below. AC entered China through a modified form of technology licensing, and most marketing activity has been carried out through the AC-French joint venture.

The Medical Equipment business group (ME) pursued diverse strategies. As seen in the case of China, also discussed below, ME entered through joint ventures that assembled components manufactured elsewhere into completed systems. In less than 10 years the joint ventures have almost all been replaced by wholly owned subsidiaries, and complete systems are being manufactured in China under Six Sigma standards, for global customers.

By contrast, ME's European expansion was undertaken by purchasing 100 percent ownership in European competitors when favorable purchase prices could be obtained. Otherwise, joint ventures were used until equity interests could be obtained. In Japan a third course was followed. ME entered into a joint venture with a major Japanese competitor which provided important management skills (the "bullet train thinking" concept of restructuring manufacturing processes) as well as access to new markets. ME then acquired a minority interest in its Japanese partner, and eventually achieved majority ownership.

Having examined the basic "genetic material" or "routines" that comprise WORLDWIDE'S business processes, and reviewed the "search routines" by which information is acquired for transmittal, this chapter concludes by examining how the transmitted genetic material is implanted, grows and mutates in a new environment. In this case the environment is China.

WORLDWIDE in China: Implanting the Routines

WORLDWIDE involvement in China dates from establishment of an electrical equipment manufacturing joint venture in Shanghai in 1919. Following the founding of the People's Republic of China (PRC) in 1949 the joint venture was nationalized, and WORLDWIDE had no further involvement on the Chinese mainland until 1979. Substantial investments began in the 1990s and involved all eight of WORLDWIDE's industrial business groups. According to the company website, its China operations employ 12,000 people working in 36 separate affiliates. According to media estimates, WORLDWIDE's China operations produced sales of US$4 billion in 2004.

WORLDWIDE in China: Strategy and Structure

The National Executive

In countries where WORLDWIDE already has a strong presence, the National Executive is usually a senior executive from one of the business groups' local affiliates who handles the job on a part-time basis (Humes, 1993, 189–90). In China, India, Japan and Mexico, countries in which WORLDWIDE is concentrating its international expansion efforts, the National Executive is an officer of WORLDWIDE International (WWI) assigned full-time to this responsibility. Daniel Wen, WORLDWIDE'S China National Executive, explained his role in China:

> *DW*: You know each [separate] business [group] has its own China operations leadership and the function for the National Executive is to have one face to the government from the company perspective and to have local support for all business development initiatives for WORLDWIDE regardless of which business.

While representation is centralized, strategy making is decentralized. As Walls put it, "We don't have a 'China strategy' for WORLDWIDE. Medical [the medical equipment business, ME] has a China strategy, plastics [the industrial materials business] has a China strategy, AC has a China strategy. In many ways we're the sum of the business strategies" (Rohwer, 2000). Daniel Wen stated that, within the common objective of growing the business, tactics varied depending on the line of business and the market environment.

China strategy: common elements

Before examining the way that the different business groups pursue their own strategies, it is necessary to identify the common elements of WORLDWIDE'S expansion process in China. One, the decentralization of strategy making, has already been identified. Another element relates to the question of management control over individual affiliates.

WORLDWIDE in China focuses on exercising control over affiliates, whether wholly or partly owned. Daniel Wen's comments are illustrative. They are in response to my question whether, in his experience, wholly owned affiliates in China are managed differently than Sino-foreign joint ventures.

DW: I would think that the difference is not between wholly foreign-owned enterprises and joint ventures. The difference is between controlled entities and not controlled entities. So joint ventures with majority control and wholly foreign-owned enterprises rightfully should be operated similarly. However in China that doesn't sometimes happen because again China is very different and it has a lot of history that is very different from how the Western public and corporate communities view things.

With regard to WORLDWIDE policy, in cases where it acquired a part of a formerly state-owned enterprise (SOE), Daniel Wen was quite specific as to control policies:

STR: In terms of carving out [part of an SOE], am I right to assume that these would involve buying let's say, in US terms, a division and then running that as a wholly foreign-owned enterprise? So WORLDWIDE would have total management control.
DW: Either as a joint venture or as a wholly owned.
STR: And the managers in the joint venture would basically be WORLDWIDE managers.
DW: Absolutely.

WORLDWIDE pursued this policy in one of its first joint ventures in China.[60] It acquired a 65 percent interest in a Shanghai-based joint venture that manufactures electrical equipment; the 35 percent owner was a Chinese private company that had begun as a Township Enterprise and grown large enough to have shares listed on the local stock exchange. The joint venture ended several years later when WORLDWIDE bought out its Chinese partner. From establishment until termination through buyout the partners were in conflict – a conflict that the Chinese partner publicized in the Asian business media.

The Chinese partner's objections centered on WORLDWIDE'S spending. WORLDWIDE brought in production line equipment, and, when it found local components inferior to its standards, began importing foreign product components as well. It also imported foreign managers, not only Americans but also nationals of its East European subsidiary, perhaps in the belief that the Europeans, having been trained in a state-run economy, would better be able to relate to Chinese managers trained in the same environment. Increasing personnel costs began to hurt the venture's profitability. An executive of the Chinese partner observed that:

> "[F]or them [WORLDWIDE] they are just maintaining the same standard as they would for managers in America. But for a Chinese company, whose products sell for a much lower price, which have a much lower profit, such standards are a luxury. These management costs put pressure on the joint venture."
>
> *(Yatsko, 2001, 238–9)*

Daniel Wen had a very different view of the joint venture. In his words:

> "[W]e did a joint venture with an existing operation. We did not build the joint venture from scratch, so that we had to fix old processes and bring in new technology. We needed to change the mindset of a lot of people. For instance, it was a lot just to convince the factory manager to put more lights in the factory and keep them turned on. This required a change of mindset. 'Don't scrimp on every penny. Spend money where it matters.' This was effort-intensive . . .
> Communication was not good. We did not want to argue points *ad infinitum*. We had a burning sense of urgency. You can argue that they did not feel that their views were listened to. Sure, there were a lot of those kinds of feelings. *Given what we were facing, it was better to do it the way we did it. Life is short.*"
>
> *(2001, 229–41, emphasis added)*

Daniel Wen's words were echoed by those of James Walls:

> "One of the things people don't really understand is that having a company you work for acquired is probably the worst thing that can happen to somebody, other than the loss of a family member . . . when we've been the acquirer, I don't think we've been as sensitive as we could have been over the years. But in most cases we went too slow in trying to get the new company to adapt to our ways. You know. 'Let's not give our culture to these people; let's let them be themselves.' [But] [t]hat's the lesson. You've got to take the actions, get it done, and get on with the game."
>
> *(Loeb, 1995)*

Strategy implementation: aircraft components

As was the case with WORLDWIDE'S reentry into international business, AC was the business group that led the company's return to China.[61] That return began with AC engineering executives being invited to Beijing in April 1979 to give a technical seminar for Chinese engineers. Detailed preparations included bringing an anthropologist and a historian to AC's US headquarters to brief the AC delegation on China. Although the seminar produced no immediate business, it served to introduce the Chinese to AC's product line and the products produced by the AC-French joint venture. It also served to inform WORLDWIDE as to how it was regarded by the Chinese.

The company had been pursuing legal claims against the PRC government to obtain compensation for the 1949 nationalization of the company's Shanghai factory. Notwithstanding this history, the Chinese at the Beijing meeting were not only not interested in "political memories," but held WORLDWIDE "in awe," as Garvin recalled to me in an interview.

Sales opportunities soon materialized when the ministry that operates Chinese civil aviation, known in English as the Civil Aviation Administration of China (CAAC), needed to buy parts for US passenger jet aircraft that it was purchasing. After successful participation in the Airbus program AC and its joint venture were important factors in the passenger jet market, and obtained a contract for the parts. A potential obstacle arose when the Chinese made it clear that they expected the parts to be manufactured or assembled in China. AC's own extensive international experience, and learning from another US company, overcame the obstacle.

As it had two decades earlier in Europe, AC decided to enter the Chinese market through licensing local factories to make its parts. Robert Garvin explained the problem with this strategy, and how it was solved, in an email to me:

RG: To allow such parts made in China under subcontract to be installed and used in our [products] required that they complied with the QC (quality control) rules of the [US] Federal Aviation Administration (FAA) . . . and that the manufacturing process was precisely the same as used for the certification test parts [parts tested as part of the product's certification by the FAA] and controlled to remain that way. Some manufacturers in the US and Europe can now get a "facility certification" from the FAA, the aviation equivalent of the ISO 9000 process. In those days, none of that was on the cards.

Instead, the FAA simply made [AC] responsible for the quality of the parts we had made in China, just as if Liming [site of one of the Chinese factories] had been a WORLDWIDE factory. The concept had been pioneered by Douglas [then McDonnell Douglas Corporation, now a part of Boeing] when it began to make MD-82s [US passenger jet airliners] in Shanghai.

We stationed a quality control engineer in Beijing. He made the rounds constantly of Liming and Xian [site of the other factory], interpreted blueprints, helped with specifications, spot-checked the manufacturing process, and witnessed the inspection of parts . . . Stationing an expert in China wasn't cheap. Such a person probably cost as much as half a million [US dollars] a year with all the extras, plus occasional visits by other of our QC experts. But it was part of the process of establishing a common technical language with the Chinese industry.

Prior to the Chinese beginning manufacture of the AC parts, a Chinese delegation from the Liming factory made a three week visit to the US as guests of AC. They visited AC's factories and thoroughly reviewed production processes for manufacturing the parts that Liming was to make. Garvin noted that the Chinese delegation felt "quite at home" in the US factories. Conversation was facilitated because AC employed highly qualified scientists and engineers of Chinese ancestry, who volunteered to help as interpreters and explain manufacturing processes (Garvin, 1998, 202).

Strategy implementation: medical equipment

In contrast with its European strategy of buying an entire company to provide manufacturing facilities and market access, the ME group entered China via a joint venture.[62]

In 1991 it acquired a 65 percent interest in a joint venture to manufacture medical imaging equipment; the PRC Aerospace Ministry took 25 percent and the Health Ministry the remainder. Having the Health Ministry as a partner offered a strong marketing advantage; the ministry is responsible for licensing the import into China of foreign-manufactured medical equipment. As Terence Deng, ME's general manager at the Beijing joint venture, explained, ME's manufacturing plants were established to break down the barriers to importing medical equipment into China. By 1999 ME had acquired the Aerospace Ministry interest; the Health Ministry still retains 10 percent share. Only one employee from the Chinese partner remains, the Deputy General Manager, whose salary however is paid by ME.

The acquisition of the Aerospace Ministry share had an effect on manufacturing operations in the joint venture, as Terence Deng explained in answer to my question about the *danwei* work unit system:

> *STR*: What about the *danwei* work unit system that prevailed here in the old days?
> *TD*: No, not really. In this joint that is almost gone. I don't see that. I don't feel that; maybe I'm dumb, but I don't feel that. It used to be, but last year or the year before last, my predecessor went through a massive house cleaning before and after we bought off the 25 percent share from aerospace department. Because the people with more seniority, they came from that family. A lot of them are not there anymore.

According to Terence the joint venture became profitable soon after its inauguration, due to its ability to import and reassemble medical imaging equipment, especially CT scanners.[63] He described the venture's first eight years:

> *TD*: We started to make money and the reason for that was CT and digital imaging, mainly for CT. CT is a controlled item for importing into China. So

for these many years we mainly did what we call the SKD. SKD means "semi-knockdown." Semi-knockdown means you assemble machine 100 percent somewhere in Japan or US, most of them actually in Japan. Then we tear it apart, not in detail, but some big portion, bring it back to China, we screw them together, send them to test, put on a new label, sell it in China. That gives us mainly, not necessarily a tax advantage, that is not really the one we are looking for. It gives us the flexibility of being able to participate most particularly in a tendering system. After all, government in China they favor local factories, local people, local joint venture compared with 100 percent import and so there's a reason these places exist. Very limited engineering competency except try to do a small scale modification of the product to make it a little more localized. That's a small scale of localization in terms of material. That's what we've been doing for eight and a half years. Starting in 1999 we changed.

The change was generated by ME management, then headed by an executive who subsequently succeeded James Walls as CEO of WORLDWIDE. ME's new configuration was as a global product company (GPC). The new strategy involves producing medical equipment anywhere in the world that offers the right combination of local engineering talent, best overall cost base, and best marketing opportunities for the equipment being manufactured there. ME's China management considers its China operation to offer the most economical CT manufacturing facilities in the world (Rohwer, 2000). According to Terence Deng, "[as far as] moving to China, if we only consider labor, we're kidding ourselves. We are moving here because we want the people. We want the people who are engineers. We have the best engineers in the world and with a very competitive salary."

Terence Deng further explained the impact of GPC on his operation:

TD: [A]fter we put together the GPC, we started to grow our engineering capability. So right now we are designing, not only transferring. There are four stages, really. You transfer the product, you localize the product, you "value engineer" the product, and you design the product bottom up. Some of this, like my X-ray operation, we are able to do the bottom up design, we design everything here; sourcing will be a big part of it because design is such a tedious operation so you need sourcing to be a big part of this because you have to get whatever component that you have to have in order to put the product together, to test it, and then to go. So I have a whole team of sourcing people who do that part. And when the product becomes mature, that means starting mass production.

The implementation of the GPC in China could not have taken place without what Terence Deng called a "Cultural Revolution . . . like the Cultural Revolution in China 30 years ago; you had to be part of it." This "revolution" was the implementation of Six Sigma at ME in China. Terence Deng was one of the people responsible for starting and promoting the revolution, and his words are instructive in understanding why WORLDWIDE chose to impose Six Sigma, and how it is applied in the joint venture's operations:

> *STR*: But Six Sigma is . . . much more beneficial [than the Cultural Revolution]?
> *TD*: Well, yes it's beneficial because Six Sigma has to be part of our life, we knew it was coming, there was no way we could get away with it, and after this many years I turned to be an even firmer believer in Six Sigma . . . Six Sigma helps us stabilize the operation. *We use Six Sigma, it's not necessarily the mechanical part, the statistical application of Six Sigma that we're focusing on. I think we're looking at Six Sigma as a concept. It's a concept of listening to your customers, of hearing your customers' voice to take the CTQ (critical tool of quality), decide what is critical to the quality and how to do the measurement, how to collect the data, and how to make a process, how to design a process, what does it mean to have a process met. And thus we make sure that all these white collar people here or supporting people, they know what it means too. They can apply it.* (emphasis added)

Six Sigma was applied at ME in China in exactly the same manner as described, for WORLDWIDE as a company, in an earlier section of this chapter:

> *STR*: Please tell me when Six Sigma was introduced, what was the means of instruction? Was it in terms of bringing people in from outside China to train an initial group of people who then trained others?
> *TD*: That's how we did it. I was the one who was brought into China from Taiwan. So what I did was, I trained because sales was my specialty, so I trained a handful of people, about a dozen of them, and within six months I handpicked and trained about another 70 people. We call it "black belt." And among these black belts I picked about 10 percent of them and they became what we call "master black belt." And so we had champions, master black belts, black belt, and this was spread out all over the place within this 1,400 person organization, they were everywhere. So their job is to push and prompt and teach people and just push them to go through the first barrier. That had pretty much finished by the end of last year. By the end of last year we were 100 percent certified.

The successful transmission and implementation of Six Sigma has been discussed at length because it illustrates WORLDWIDE'S capability to transmit its management practices to China and implement them successfully. ME now has a 54 percent share of the Chinese medical equipment market; its nearest competitor has half that. The Chinese market is now number three in size in the world, behind only the US and Japan.

But the greatest continuing challenge for WORLDWIDE in China will be to find the "genetic material," that is, the people within which to inculcate WORLD-WIDE'S shared management practices and then apply them in China. Daniel Wen expressed the company's confidence in achieving this result at the conclusion of our interview:

DW: One of my visible responsibilities is to create a process for the company by which we can then develop a pipeline of local leaders. We believe that local leadership should be folks who understand China very deeply by nature of, this is where they come from. At the same time they should understand WORLD-WIDE very deeply by nature of who we are as a global company. And if what we run in China is disconnected from the rest of the corporation we will never be successful. So therefore the kind of people we're looking for are a kind of a duality type of people, and they are very hard to find. So I would certainly agree with you that, and those other executives, that this is one of our principal challenges. Our problem is the same.

CHAPTER SUMMARY

The detailed longitudinal analysis of WORLDWIDE's management processes presented in this chapter is the most effective means of understanding WORLD-WIDE's ability to transmit to and implement in China the genetics of what the company calls its "operating system." Management control is provided through the discipline of adherence to the operating system. The successes enjoyed by WORLDWIDE's Medical Equipment and Aircraft Components business groups are notable, yet perhaps not surprising considering that WORLDWIDE's current management processes have evolved within a company that has enjoyed more than a century of success.

PART III

Comparison and Analysis across the Cases

CHAPTER SEVEN

Cross-Case Comparison Summary

Introduction

In the words of one scholar, the vast literature dealing with MNC reflects a "preoccupation" with the relation between parent companies and their subsidiaries (Tahib, 2000, 114–15). The parent–subsidiary relation has traditionally been expressed in terms of an opposition between global integration (centralization) and local responsiveness (decentralization) (Malnight, 2001). Resolution of this opposition within an MNC is usually conceptualized in terms reminiscent of Hegel's dialectics. The literature reflects the view that there is some synthesis or "balance" that can be arrived at between the two opposing forces that will permit MNC to operate efficiently. The search for such balance has encompassed research on organizational structure, general business strategy, specific business function strategies and organizational behavior.[64] This last research area has traditionally emphasized study of management control systems for MNC; more recently attention has also been given to the hypothesized effect of national or ethnic cultures on MNC organization and management.

Implicit in the "global–local dilemma" is the concept that foreign operating affiliates are managed differently depending on the type of affiliate (that is, whether wholly owned or joint venture) and the host country context within which it operates.

The evidence from the Chinese affiliates of the US MNC studied here shows that, rather than being subject to global–local conflict, the affiliates are managed so that they are simultaneously integrated into the MNC global organization and also responsive to the needs of China's unique market. This can be understood by distinguishing between the "internal face" and the "external face" of the affiliate.

The affiliates studied are managed internally (their "internal face") using management processes developed by their respective parents through prior global experience, and transferred to and implemented within the China affiliate in ways that result in the processes not meaningfully varying from the processes used by the parent's other affiliates worldwide.

At the same time, the processes by which the affiliate deals with China as a market[65] (the affiliates' "external face") involve adapting organizational forms and strategies to meet the demands of that market, as well as increasing the use of local rather than expatriate managers to implement the global management processes transferred to the affiliate from the parent.

The affiliates studied are focused on "market centered" goals established by their parents. The goals, generally, are to seek opportunities in markets offering high absolute and relative growth in sales volume and profits. Both the strategies and the organizational structures that must be implemented to accomplish these goals are driven by market objectives. In the companies studied, strategies and structures are means to accomplish goals, not goals in themselves.

The MNC affiliates studied are externally focused on meeting the demands of Chinese markets and internally focused on implementing globally successful management processes. The message of many hours of conversation with MNC executives can be summarized this way: "*We manage in China the same as we do in other countries, but approach China's markets using strategies and organizational structures differently than we might in other countries.*"

The cross-case comparisons will now be presented in five short chapters. The first chapter deals with important concepts of definition and discusses how shared management routines and values ("corporate cultures") are transmitted from the parent MNC to their respective affiliates and the means by which these processes are implemented within the affiliate. The second chapter covers the "market-driven" goal setting process within the MNC and how that process is translated into strategy creation and organizational structure selection (wholly owned versus joint venture) within MNC China operation.

The third chapter deals with human resources management processes within the affiliates, and the fourth chapter with processes to control and coordinate manufacturing and internal financial operations. The final chapter discusses control and coordination of the affiliates' responses to China's institutions and cultures.

The accompanying table provides a cross-case comparison summary.

Management Processes, Routines and Cultures

The importance of shared processes within the MNC

Some research has stressed the need for "internal differentiation" within the MNC, whereby management processes are differentiated depending on host country, product or function (Doz and Prahalad, 1993, 27). Other research, however, has emphasized that MNC do have the ability to transfer management processes globally (Bartlett and Ghoshal, 1989; Nelson, 1991). Additional studies have provided examples of effective transfers (Wilms, Zell, Kimura and Cuneo, 1994; Nolan, 1995; Child, 2001).

Cross-Case Comparison Summary

	ELECTRONS	IMIGIS	MOTORS	WORLDWIDE
Global organization	Product groups with centralized independent manufacturing and finance organizations	Organized around worldwide product groups	"M-form" organization of 40 separate product divisions, with their own self-contained staff organizations; MOTORS has a small corporate staff within its US headquarters, the main function of which is to set detailed financial and operating goals for the divisions, and administer the detailed planning process that monitors the divisions' achievement of those goals	Twelve principal "businesses" (business groups) that are each product specific, with self-contained staff organizations. Headquarters has a small staff, which, like MOTORS, is primarily engaged in setting financial goals, acquiring and disbursing capital, and monitoring the business groups' performance
Organization for China	Beijing-based holding company handles relations with central government and preparation/filing of Chinese tax returns. Operating companies, all of which are WFOE, report to either the Technology Manufacturing Group (global manufacturing) or one of the global product groups	"Country Manager" for Greater China Region (GCR) who, reflecting the importance of China to the company, is also Head of Greater Asia Region (GAR). Heads of operating companies within China report to the Country Manager, as well as the heads of their respective product groups in the US. The company uses WFOE as well as partly owned affiliates in China: however the company owns a majority share in all partly owned Chinese affiliates	The Asia-Pacific regional organization in Hong Kong (A/P) reports to MOTORS headquarters. At the same time the divisions operate their own organizations within China, using WFOE as well as JV. All JV are majority owned, however	The business groups that operate in China each have their own organization. There is also a WORLDWIDE China "country organization," which is responsible for providing staff assistance, primarily in the legal and HRM areas, to the business groups, as well as assisting new operating companies to establish China operations, and handling merger and acquisition activities. China affiliates are both WFOE and JV, but JV are all majority-owned by the company
Management control processes	"Copy Exactly" and "best known methods"	The company has a paramount goal of establishing a strong market presence in China and this focus is the predominant control process over the China organization. Financial objectives are set at US headquarters and monitored through detailed reporting requirements; however the company does not currently have a global corporate culture	The corporate culture is characterized by discipline and planning. These shared values are implemented through the routine of the planning process, which is based on management by objectives (MBO)	The company's "operating system," which it describes as its "learning culture in action." This is a combination of a modified form of MBO, coupled with very disciplined financial and operating planning processes, and the global implementation of business processes such as Six Sigma

Cont'd

Cross-Case Comparison Summary cont'd

	ELECTRONS	IMIGIS	MOTORS	WORLDWIDE
Processes within functional areas				
Human resources management:				
Administration	Local (Shanghai) managers administer HRM with respect to local non-executive workforce; administration of HRM with respect to executives is based on globally standardized processes	Administered through the country organization but at the same time individual operating companies, especially the manufacturing organization, have their own HRM staff	Although there is a small HRM staff within the A/P organization, almost all HRM functions are handled through the divisional organizations	Within China, the China country organization plays a major role in HRM, and not merely with respect to insuring that the company's global HRM practices are implemented. The HRM staff plays a major role in providing training, recruitment and management advancement opportunities across business group lines. HRM administration for non-executives is, as with the other companies studied, handled at the operating company level, as is compensation
Selection	Selection methodology is globally centralized, with the goal of localizing management as soon as possible	The goal, as with the other companies studied, is to staff executive and non executive positions with Chinese citizens. At the same time, expatriates predominate within the country organization	As with the other companies studied, the emphasis on management recruitment and advancement is to hire and develop Chinese citizens to manage affiliates within China	The emphasis in recruitment and advancement of executives within China is to develop Chinese citizens as managers as soon as possible
Training	Methodology and content are globally standardized: differentiation is task specific	Training goals within China are the same as training goals elsewhere, for example, implementation of Six Sigma business processes, and the company's Chinese factories were the first to achieve Six Sigma standards, as well as the first to receive ISO 14000 certification. Training is conducted by the operating companies, assisted by the HRM staff within the country organization	Training is handled by the divisions except that training in and compliance with MOTORS' global ethical standards is done through the A/P organization	Training processes are implemented pursuant to global standards with additional localized instruction, e.g. English language skills
Compensation	Differentiated only with respect to non-executive local workforce	Executive compensation is on a global standard; non-executive compensation is based on local labor markets within China	Each division sets compensation standards	For executives, compensation policy is globalized; for non-executives it is localized

Cont'd

Cross-Case Comparison Summary cont'd

	ELECTRONS	IMIGIS	MOTORS	WORLDWIDE
Advancement	Globally standardized for executives	Senior executive promotion is done through global processes; junior executives formerly were promoted within the China operating companies of the product groups, but recently IMIGIS has established procedures whereby junior executive positions throughout GCR/GAR are available to candidates within the regions regardless of the operating company or product group in which they are employed	Controlled through the divisions, but the A/P HRM organization is also attempting to open job recruitment for open executive positions within the 21-nation A/P region to candidates throughout the region, regardless of which division employs them	As noted above, the China HRM organization is involved in providing advancement opportunities across business group lines
Finance	Acquisition and disbursement of capital are centrally controlled through US headquarters. Global financial controls and reports: differentiation only to the extent necessary to prepare Chinese tax returns	Acquisition and disbursement of capital are centrally controlled through US headquarters. Financial goals are prescribed by headquarters, which also establishes financial controls and financial reporting requirements	Acquisition and disbursement of capital are controlled through MOTORS US headquarters, which also sets financial goals for the divisions and monitors compliance with those goals. Financial reporting requirements are established and monitored by US headquarters	As with the other companies studied, acquisition and disbursement of capital is handled by US headquarters, which establishes the financial goals as well as the reporting requirements needed to monitor achievement of those goals
Manufacturing	Global manufacturing standard ("Copy Exactly")	Global manufacturing standards (Six Sigma, ISO 9000 and 14000) are implemented in China and products, whether for Chinese or foreign markets, are manufactured to these standards. Products are not differentiated for internal, Chinese consumption	Each division is product-specific so that, while global manufacturing standards are used, the extent to which products are differentiated for specific Chinese markets depends on the product. At the same time, some of the Chinese affiliates are the single source for certain products for their respective divisions	Like the divisions that comprise MOTORS, WORLDWIDE's business groups are product-specific. Manufacturing is done pursuant to global standards, principally *Six Sigma*, but the extent to which a particular product is differentiated to meet the requirements of specific Chinese markets depends on the product. Some operating companies are the global single source for certain products manufactured by their respective business groups
Relations with China's institutions	Global standards of conduct established through US laws and ELECTRONS' codes of conduct; all government relations are handled by ELECTRONS employees who are Chinese citizens	Global standards for legal compliance and ethical standards are implemented. Due to the importance to the company of success in China, top management from US headquarters is more heavily involved in relations with China's national, regional and local governments than is the case with the other companies studied	Global standards of conduct are established by US headquarters and compliance is monitored by the A/P legal and HRM staffs	Governmental relations are among the principal responsibilities of the head of the China country organization, and he has a staff of Chinese citizens with day-to-day responsibility for this function. Legal and ethical compliance standards are globally uniform and compliance within China is monitored by the country organization

Practitioners view the global sharing of standard management practices within the MNC as achievable and desirable. The then head of Unilever has written approvingly of the process of "Unileverization." This is a process through which company executives from many different ethnic and geographic origins are inculcated with Unilever's shared management philosophies (Maljers, 1992, 4–5).

The importance of using management processes that have been historically successful within the global MNC for the success of MNC affiliates in China is illustrated by two quotations. The first is from my interview with Dan Truman, head of BRONWYN, one of MOTORS' Shanghai joint ventures. Dan's remarks, quoted in full earlier, reflect MOTORS' strong management process:

> *DT*: When you first come here you hear a lot of, this is China, this is different, that won't work. And if you believe that, then you're going to be a loser, like a vast majority of people that have come to China. Yes it's China, yes it's different, but it's the same. Money is still something everybody wants. And if you can show people a way to make it, a way to make as much of it as possible, wring every dime of profit out of your operation by using traditional business management tactics that worked for centuries in the United States . . . the common sense of business, instilled with discipline, you're unwavering in its enforcement, you'll be real successful.

The second quotation is from my interview with an executive of a US-owned WFOE, and describes the situation at his previous employer, a US MNC that did not have strong management processes:

> *MM*: Now, this is very, very typical of any foreign investment or foreign company coming into China. When they establish a business in China they just build the plant, they don't build the system. And also, they know when they start the plant, they pick the people with the language skill. They don't pick the people with the business skill and the technical skill.
> For example, I was the project manager, and I had been telling the plant manager who was assigned by headquarters, at the beginning of the project, "you should be setting up your planning system, and setting up your financial systems and setting up your everything." He said, "Oh no, no no." I saw that not only in that company but in a lot of other plants. And I think that they are paying for it [now].

In an insightful special survey of MNC, Adrian Wooldridge of *The Economist* observed that MNC need to make sure that what is transplanted into China is actually the way the MNC does things worldwide, rather than what he labeled as a "bastardized," localized version. Wooldridge then opined that this meant that MNC in China needed powerful control systems.

All of the parent MNC of the affiliates studied here have identifiable corporate management control processes. These processes differ in extent and intensity of application, but control processes are only part of managing affiliates in China. Control itself is only a part of a larger process. That process is described by Wooldridge in these terms: "The art of management in this region is very much the art of transferring knowledge, implanting western business methods in Chinese minds" (1995, 13).

What is transferred: processes, routines, cultures

A process refers to a course of action as to how something is done by an individual, group or organization (Nicholson, Schuler and Van de Ven, 1998, 445). A business process reflects business operations involving a number of sequential steps that combine physical and intellectual efforts, such as processing sales orders, or designing semiconductors. Management processes encompass the way managers do their jobs, that is, how they make, communicate, implement, monitor and revise decisions (*Harvard Business Review*, 1995). Business and management processes are both included within Nelson and Winter's (1982, 14, 97) conceptualization of a business's routines; that is, the regular and predictable behavior pattern of firms and individuals and groups within firms.

The inclusiveness of the concept of "routines" is appropriate because the processes that parent MNC transmit to the China affiliates that were studied cannot be neatly separated into business or management processes. For example, ELEC-TRONS' "Copy Exactly" manufacturing process clearly satisfies the definition of a business process, but depends for its success on a management process that itself is a reflection of what ELECTRONS executives refer to as ELECTRONS' unique "culture."

As discussed earlier in the WORLDWIDE case, a leading organizational culture scholar has observed that dissension among organizational culture researchers about fundamental questions such as what it is, how it should be studied and what effect it has on firm performance make "organizational culture" difficult to define (Martin, 1998, 376). This is certainly true, but the executives of the affiliates studied used the phrases "culture," "corporate culture" and "organizational culture" consistently in discussing their own organizations. Also, they did so in a consistently positive way that expressed the concept that their respective "cultures" were a source of strength.

One scholar recently observed that leaders are easy to identify but incredibly difficult to define (Mische, 2001, 196). The same can be said of an organization's culture.[66] Contemporary works on corporate culture recognize this difficulty (Kotter and Heskett, 1992; Kets de Vries, 1995b). Yet, the executives with whom I spoke all knew to what they referred when they spoke of their organization's culture. Based on what I learned from them, I have concluded that what they were referring to includes both routines, that is, shared management practices, and culture, that is, shared values. I will use the definition of "corporate culture" that I derived from my conversations with them. Corporate culture is a set of shared routines, practices and values within a particular enterprise. Further, when used in this book "corporate culture" refers to the shared routines, practices and values *specific to* the companies studied, and not to "organizational culture" or "corporate culture" as generalities.

Corporate culture as a combination of routines, practices and values is illustrated in the following quotation from an interview by Manfred Kets de Vries with Percy Barnevik. At the time of the interview Barnevik headed the Swiss-Swedish MNC, ASEA Brown-Boveri (ABB). Barnevik answered Kets de Vries' question about the "glue" that held ABB together in these terms:

> "Well, there are two sorts of 'glue,' the hard and the soft kind. The hard kind is the overall reporting system, 'Abacus,' that ties us together in a numbers sense. As for the soft kind, that glue is described in what we call our policy bible . . . [i]t describes our mission and values, where we want to be several years from now, and gives guidelines for our overall behavior."
>
> *(Kets de Vries, 1995a)*

Another example is specifically related to the affiliates studied. US federal laws, that is, those laws enacted by the US Congress, typically have extraterritorial effect. These laws govern the conduct of US citizens, whether individuals and corporations, throughout the world. One such law is the US Foreign Corrupt Practices Act (FCPA).[67] The FCPA prohibits Stock Exchange listed US companies operating in foreign countries from paying bribes to various classes of foreign officials, and establishes extensive accounting control requirements for corporations so that foreign transactions are accurately reported.

It is important to understand that the FCPA is not a "paper tiger." American companies take their obligations to obey US laws in their China operations quite seriously. Two examples from mid 2004 illustrate this.

In the first, Citigroup fired two high-ranking China executives for alleged breaches of the company's ethical codes of conduct; one of the discharged executives was the daughter-in-law of a former high official of the Chinese government. In the second, Lucent Corporation fired its four top-ranking China executives for perceived violations of the FCPA (Underwood, 2004).

We will now briefly consider the tools used by the affiliates to respond to FCPA requirements. The first set of tools involves deployment of routines. The routines include the establishment, maintenance and implementation of accounting information and control systems throughout the global organization. They also include the preparation and dissemination of legal guidelines from corporate headquarters and enforcement of those guidelines throughout the organization.

While routines are crucial to FCPA compliance, the routines are rendered much more effective because they are combined with a set of shared values as to the ethical conduct expected of all employees. The comments of MOTORS' Asia-Pacific Legal Counsel illustrate this point:

STR: Am I being accurate in saying that the standards both of ethical conduct in the marketplace and particularly with respect to relations with foreign governmental authorities are brought directly from MOTORS headquarters?

JK: Yes. The standards are brought directly from our chairman at MOTORS headquarters. In addition, without the involvement of senior management all the way to the top it would be impossible, I think, to convey the proper message. Luckily they are strong advocates of a highly ethical company; they have made repeated statements that under no circumstances are we to deviate from those standards. It comes from the top down and it's actually practiced. It makes my job a lot easier to be able to go out and to be able to show that all the way to our chairman level, he believes that philosophy.

At the same time, as discussed earlier, the means through which management processes, that is, both routines and culture, are transmitted to and implanted within affiliates by the parent company involve *both* control and coordination.

To coordinate the transmission and implementation of ethical standards requires shared values. The shared values, however, are created through both consent and control. People within an organization share values through consent (Barnard, 1938, 82–4). As a former head of Unilever explained, maintaining generally accepted standards of corporate behavior depends as much on everyone in the global organization understanding and accepting them as on formal instruction manuals (Maljers, 1992).

Yet those values that are shared in common by the multiethnic workforce of an MNC operating globally must have some central source and direction. In his brilliant essay "Is International Management Different from Management?", Simon (1994, 5) points out that if the modern MNC is to succeed, it must find an effective replacement for the powerful motivating forces provided by ethnic homogeneity. Shared values may serve as such replacement, but someone must initially set out the values of an organization that its members are expected to share. In other words, someone must "instruct the actions or behavior of others." This is the control element and it is coextensive with the coordination element.

Corporate Culture as a Control Process

In their often-cited survey of research on control in MNC, Martinez and Jarillo (1989) observed that during the decade prior to publication of their article, research attention had shifted from studies of what they described as formal control (or "coordination" to use their words) mechanisms to studies of control from the viewpoint of acculturation and informal communication networks. They posited that this shift reflected trends in actual management practice during the same period.

Barley and Kunda (1992) have disputed whether there has been a permanent, rather than an episodic, shift in what they call "management rhetoric" from investigation of formal control to investigation of informal control mechanisms within organizations. Whichever view is correct, however, the importance of corporate culture as a process or mechanism of control has been recognized by academics and executives for many years.

Concepts of corporate culture

I use "corporate culture" in this work to refer to the shared routines, practices and values that are *specific to* the companies studied, and not to "organizational culture" or "corporate culture" in general.

Corporate culture as an integrative mechanism in MNC

Kuin's (1972) description of the role of what he called "corporate acculturation" in the management of Unilever provided an early discussion of corporate culture as an integrative mechanism in an MNC whose international success was of long standing. Kuin had joined Unilever in 1948 and was an executive director of the company from 1961 until 1970.

Kuin's work provided a unique longitudinal perspective on the company's management practices during his years of service. He commented at length on Unilever's practice of international rotation of managers, regardless of their national origin, to positions throughout the Unilever organization.

His explanation for this practice was that young managers, even if their final assignment was in a high position within their own country of origin, had to acquire understanding of what he called "the basic nature and policies of the company." He quoted another Unilever senior executive to the effect that, in order for people from many different cultures to work together effectively, they must acquire not only a common language of communication, but a common culture as well. This encompassed a pattern of behavior that reflected an accepted way of doing things that would be readily understood everywhere in the Unilever organization.

The need for such an integrative mechanism has been recognized by Simon who, as noted earlier, observed that if the modern MNC is to succeed, it must find an effective replacement for the powerful motivating forces provided by ethnic homogeneity (1994, 5). More than 25 years after Kuin's article, Prahalad and Lieberthal (1998) noted that "The need for a single company culture will also be more critical as people from different cultures begin to work together. Providing the right glue to hold the companies together will be a big challenge."

Spreading the corporate culture: expatriate managers

In their pioneering case study of transfers of managers within four European MNC, Edstrom and Galbraith (1977) introduced the concept of "control by socialization." They made a distinction between, on the one hand, transfer of managers for socialization, and, on the other, both transfers to meet staff needs in countries without indigenous managerial resources and transfers for purposes of management development. They posited that transfers for purposes of socialization, a process observed in two of the four MNC studied, were designed to develop what they called "international, verbal information networks" of executives which permitted greater organizational decentralization than bureaucratic control processes.

It is important to note more precisely what Edstrom and Galbraith stated. They observed two objectives for "control by socialization": to make managers from different cultures comfortable with and able to work among people from other cultures, and to create commitment to the organization as a whole. This echoed Kuin's observations and, in fact, they quoted the same statements by a senior Unilever executive that Kuin had quoted in his article.

They went on to make other, equally important observations. One was that what they called "control strategies" were cumulative, rather than "either–or," and one strategy was only able to partly substitute for the other. Another observation was that transfer of executives *per se* was not solely a function of a socialization control strategy. Use of expatriate general managers in national affiliates, in their view, was done more to implement a "personal control" strategy than as part of a "socialization control" strategy. It was a control process similar to the practice of having executives from headquarters who travel almost constantly among foreign affiliates.

The research presented in this book, among other things, clears up the considerable misunderstanding of the use of expatriate executives by US MNC that is present in earlier studies.

The study by Hulbert and Brandt (1980) attributes US MNC employment of local rather than expatriate executives as a reflection of American companies' exclusive use of bureaucratic control mechanisms. In their depiction of the views of US MNC management, local executives, if they master "the book" (of approved management practices), may safely be entrusted with management of local affiliates (1980, 145–8). Their study contrasts this with the more normative control mechanisms employed by European and Japanese MNC, both of which, in their view, require employment of expatriate European and Japanese executives.

Jaeger (1983) conducted a case study of foreign affiliates of two US MNC located in Brazil. Jaeger was interested in contrasting what he categorized as a "traditional type A" US MNC with a "type Z" US MNC; these categories were developed in an earlier work by Ouchi and Jaeger. Type A represented a "bureaucratic control" firm and type Z represented what Jaeger called a "culture control" firm.

Leaving aside certain limitations of the study's methodology, Jaeger made important observations about the US MNC that he labeled "Company Z" (because it represented the type Z organization). One observation was that Company Z simply ignored the question whether it was possible to transfer the company's management practices to its Brazilian affiliate; it simply proceeded to do so. The research results reported here confirm that this reflects US MNC practice.

Jaeger also observed that the process by which the transfer was accomplished was through heavy use of expatriates, at least in the initial stages of the venture, as well as by intensive training of local staff, both in Brazil and in the US. English language instruction was an important part of the curriculum, and courses in both managerial and technical subjects were taught in English. Jaeger also noted that Company Z received a large number of visitors from US headquarters.

In their insightful work, Lebas and Weigenstein (1986) point out the inaccuracy of the view that US MNC have relatively weak cultures, and cite what they call many famous American examples of strong organizational culture. My research supports their view.

My findings also support another, equally important observation that they made. According to Lebas and Weigenstein, culture removes the need for personal supervision, through establishment of a system of norms and informal rules which spell out how people are to behave most of the time, and allows them to extrapolate quickly in new situations. Thus, once a corporate culture is instilled in a foreign affiliate, there is no need to have numbers of expatriates present to personally supervise the details of the day-to-day functioning of the affiliate. The affiliates that I studied typically had only one US expatriate, the general manager.

This last point was not considered by Kobrin (1988) in his criticism of what he called the failure of US MNC to use sufficient numbers of US expatriate managers in foreign affiliates. Kobrin observes that "if most employees are local then there are precious few who either have an encompassing knowledge of the worldwide organization or identify with it or its objectives" and that "the virtual elimination of expatriates affects control adversely." My research findings show that US MNC use several different control processes. The process that Jaeger calls "culture control" successfully creates and maintains identification by and linkage of all employees with the routines, practices and values of the parent companies. Formal processes, such as regular, detailed financial and operational reports, are complementary control measures. The relative absence of expatriates in the affiliates studied is not accompanied by any observed adverse effect on control.

The parent MNC of the affiliates studied both control and coordinate their China affiliates. To understand how they do so it is necessary to consider the similarities and differences in their respective corporate cultures. This consideration builds on the individual cases but, in so far as possible, the material from the cases is presented in summary form rather than repeated. Before doing so, it is also important to note that transmission and implementation of corporate culture do not depend on the ownership structure of the affiliate.

Although the IJV among the affiliates studied were all majority owned by their respective US parent, earlier research on US–Chinese joint ventures that had balanced, i.e. 50/50 ownership, has reported that even within balanced ownership IJV the US executives of the IJV instilled the parent's management culture and processes at the earliest opportunity (Newman, 1992; Yan and Gray, 1994).

Similarities and Differences in Corporate Cultures

The center and scope of corporate culture

Three of the MNC whose affiliates were studied, WORLDWIDE, MOTORS and ELECTRONS, have self-identified corporate cultures. As noted in the case analysis, IMIGIS (which is the oldest business among the parent MNC) had a strong corporate culture throughout most of its more than 100 years of existence. Yet it was IMIGIS' corporate culture that its own executives and outside analysts both identified as a prime source of IMIGIS' business and financial reverses. The case also describes the efforts of new management to create a new corporate culture for IMIGIS. This effort, however, is a "work in progress." IMIGIS' China operations are as much coordinated with those of its parent as the respective operations of WORLDWIDE, MOTORS and ELECTRONS, at least in terms of focus. In IMIGIS' case, however, coordination is achieved by virtue of top management focusing the entire organization on success in China, rather than through applying shared management practices and values.[68]

The remaining three companies all have corporate cultures that are global in scope. These cultures are similar in routine in that they all employ variations of management by objectives as the foundation of management practices. Yet ELECTRONS is unlike either WORLDWIDE or MOTORS in that ELECTRONS' corporate culture is both centrally directed through control, and representative of shared routines – the "BKM" that are developed in and diffused among affiliates globally by coordination. This is explained best by Bian Chen, a Chinese executive at ELECTRONS' Shanghai affiliate:

BC: Okay. We say we always want to have a very strong ELECTRONS culture which managers can take advantage of as a baseline, to exercise global standards, what we call "BKM" or "best known methods." A lot of sensitive management processes are set by corporate-level teams; processes such as C&B [compensation and benefits]; these are set by global corporate management [at headquarters].

The second area I would call well-defined management practices; this is the wisdom collected through years of global operations. This is not set by senior management; it is the collective wisdom from all parts of ELECTRONS. This is what we call BKM. How to conduct a staff meeting, how do we plan? Planning processes, for example. These are almost always globally similar. I am not saying exactly the same but very similar. Same with performance management. In terms of manufacturing operations management; we have a term called "Copy Exactly." In this term we are not just talking about manufacturing operations, we are also talking about management processes. The second portion is the major portion, that is 80–90 percent of management practices. If you go around to ELECTRONS sites, all over the world, and I do, you see these processes flowing throughout ELECTRONS. You go to another ELECTRONS site in a different part of the world, you do not feel like you are a stranger because you talk the same language. When you talk about "POR" people know what you mean. When you say "capacity planning" or "performance manage-ment" people know what you are talking about.

In WORLDWIDE's case the corporate culture[69] is centrally generated and trans-mitted globally through "initiatives" that for decades have originated from the Chief Executive Officer. This is true both of internally generated initiatives such as the reorganization into strategic business units in the 1960s, and of recent initiatives such as "bullet train thinking" (borrowed from a Japanese joint venture partner) and the more significant Six Sigma initiative, whose original source was Motorola.

After the decision is made to implement an initiative throughout the company, transmission of processes and values takes place through local, onsite "implementers." The method used in China was explained by Terence Deng when he discussed the process of implementing Six Sigma in his manufacturing joint venture located outside Beijing:

> *STR*: Please tell me when Six Sigma was introduced, what was the means of instruction? Was it in terms of bringing people in from outside China to train an initial group of people who then trained others?
> *TD*: That's how we did it. I was the one who was brought into China from Taiwan. So what I did was, I trained because sales was my specialty, so I trained a handful of people, about a dozen of them, and within six months I handpicked and trained about another 70 people. We call it "black belt." And among these black belts I picked about 10 percent of them and they became what we call "master black belt." And so we had champions, master black belts, black belt, and this was spread out all over the place within this 1,400 person organization, they were everywhere. So their job is to push and prompt and teach people and just push them to go through the first barrier. That had pretty much finished by the end of last year. By the end of last year we were 100 percent certified.

Cross-organizational transmission also takes place through the executive training programs at the company's Management Development Institute. Mid-level and senior executives from different business groups study and learn as teams through analysis of actual operating plans and decisions of different business groups, thereby dis-seminating "best practices" throughout WORLDWIDE when they return to their own organizations.

MOTORS represents a very different corporate culture, with a different trans-mission process. MOTORS differs from the other MNC parents whose affiliates were studied because of its structure. It is the only MNC that operates in a multi-divisional structure that resembles Chandler's "M-form." It comprises 40 separate, incorporated[70] divisions, each of which is a wholly owned subsidiary of the parent company.

MOTORS uses the mental discipline required by its rigorous planning system to inculcate a common "thought process" that serves as the coordinating mechanism for the many divisions and their affiliates operating in diverse geographic and product markets. By operating "according to plan" division managers enjoy considerable autonomy to achieve goals that are established through a process that resembles the "management by objectives" advocated by Peter Drucker in *The Practice of Management* (1954, 129, 138).

The lengthy description of the planning process contained in the MOTORS case will not be repeated here. What should be noted is that the frequent, detailed meetings across geographic regions, business functions and operating divisions that occur throughout the year serve as MOTORS' means of transmitting routines and values. At the same time, the planning process is not only a means of coordination, but also a means of exercising control.

The MOTORS culture includes both routines and values. As noted in Chapter 3, the philosophy underlying the culture can be summarized best by the following excerpt from an article in *Harvard Business Review* quoting Christopher Day, MOTORS' CEO for the past 29 years:

> "[W]hat makes us tick at [MOTORS] is an effective management process. We believe that we can shape our future through careful planning and strong follow-up. Our managers plan for improved results and execute to get them. Driving this process is a set of shared values, including involvement, intensity, discipline and persistence. We adhere to few policies or techniques that could be called unique or even unusual. But we do act on our policies and that may indeed make us unusual."
>
> *(Knight, 1992)*

Management routines within the respective cultures

As noted in the case analyses and earlier in this chapter, MOTORS, ELECTRONS and WORLDWIDE all employ management routines based on management by objectives (MBO). I follow the definition of MBO given by Packard (1996, 152), that is, a system in which overall objectives are clearly stated and agreed upon and which gives people the flexibility to work towards those goals.[71]

Interviews with IMIGIS executives disclosed that its China affiliates are managed in a similar manner as affiliates located elsewhere, that is, that the affiliates are "locally managed" with review by headquarters business group managements focused on accomplishment of financial objectives. This has several elements of MBO, but there was no indication that the setting of managerial objectives was determined through interaction between levels of management.

MOTORS affiliates' executives identify MOTORS' management process specifically with reference to MBO, as exemplified by the remarks of the Asia-Pacific Finance Director for MOTORS' CAPWELL subsidiary:

DK: I think that it would be helpful to explain a little about the impact of MOTORS' culture on the way things are done within CAPWELL . . . MOTORS is a culture of focus and of discipline.

STR: And by "discipline" . . .

DK: MOTORS is a classic management by objectives company. Through the CAPWELL planning meetings, agreed on performance objectives are set. I've got my objectives, yet how I go about achieving those objectives is my business. Now, some of those objectives may be stated as directions: "don't factor accounts receivable," "no bad debts," "keep a low DSO" [daily sales outstanding]; again, though, how I achieve those objectives is up to me.

At ELECTRONS the management process uses "management by plan" (MBP).[72] Under MBP every business group, department and individual has an agreed quarterly set of goals broken down into clear, measurable terms (called "deliverables" in the company jargon) that must be accomplished during the forthcoming quarter. All subordinate goals are linked to ELECTRONS' corporate strategic objectives and goal accomplishment is evaluated at the end of each quarter. The next quarter's goals are directly related to what was or was not accomplished in the prior quarter.

ELECTRONS' management process is characterized by a rigorous quantification of goals and processes, yet MBP applies to non-quantitative goals as well. The Deputy Site Manager for Public Affairs at ETCL explained that his department has its own performance plans and objectives. As he put it, "We have one clear [continuing] objective, to build good relations with the local authorities so that ELECTRONS can do business easily in Shanghai. Then [in MBP] we have to define what activities are going to contribute to achieving this objective." A maximum of six interim objectives that are correlated with these activities are identified quarterly, and progress on accomplishment is reported quarterly as well.

By contrast, WORLDWIDE's operating system, as explained in the company's Annual Report for 2000, and as discussed in the case analysis, comprises both "hard" and "soft" elements. WORLDWIDE still drives its business groups to achieve the objective of being number one or at least number two in global market share in their respective lines of business. In the MBO tradition, business unit managers have considerable discretion in choosing and implementing strategies to achieve this goal. Also in the tradition of MBO, and like MOTORS and ELECTRONS, there are continuous meetings, spread throughout the year and spread organizationally and geographically throughout the business groups to establish and agree to plans and goals, and review implementation and achievement.

Performance measurement is practiced on a company-wide basis through Six Sigma, the company's current global management initiative. The company rightly identifies Six Sigma as a management process that extends beyond the factory floor. By the same token, however, it also represents a rigorous quantitative goal for reduction of errors in every business transaction that the company undertakes.

Critics of the manner in which MBO was implemented at WORLDWIDE in the 1950s and 1960s emphasized that implementation relied too heavily on achievement of financial objectives, thus stifling promising business proposals that could not meet a centrally imposed "hurdle rate" (Pascale, 1990, 187–8). Whether or not the criticism is accurate, by the early 1990s some WORLDWIDE business groups changed to a "balanced scorecard" approach that emphasized non-financial criteria such as customer satisfaction and product quality (Davis, 1996). The Medical Equipment (ME) business group revised Terence Deng's performance objectives so that, although he heads ME's manufacturing operations in China, he no longer has profit and loss responsibility for the joint venture and the two WFOE that he manages. Instead, his performance goals are expressed in terms of 40 different performance measurements, related to product quality, production rates and "time to market." Despite the continuing quantification, the company also emphasizes what James Walls refers to as its "soft values" (Annual Report for 2000). These begin with what Walls identifies as "the first and foremost" value, integrity, and include obtaining the best people, providing the maximum training to develop leaders (the "global brains"), continuous learning from all sources, customer focus, orientation to change, and reduction of bureaucracy.

While these may seem like nothing more than warmed-over clichés of corporate "image consultants," the case analysis goes into some detail in showing that these values are part of the "genetic material" of WORLDWIDE and have been successfully implanted throughout the global organization, along with the "hard" concepts mentioned earlier.

Successful implementation of the corporate culture in China

This section discusses successful implementation of the corporate culture. For MOTORS, ELECTRONS and WORLDWIDE, it refers to implementing the totality of the respective corporate cultures of these three firms, all of which have truly global corporate cultures.[73]

The commitment to transplanting the entire corporate culture that is common to MOTORS, ELECTRONS and WORLDWIDE does not depend on the parent's internal organization, or on whether the affiliate is wholly owned or a joint venture. MOTORS' Asia-Pacific Legal Counsel put it this way:

> *JK*: I think the commitment by our divisions and their managements have been remarkable as far as putting people who are quality people in place, minimizing the number of expatriates used, localizing the business, training the people, *actually bringing the management structure of MOTORS and its divisions to these entities and bringing the disciplines that come along with it.* (emphasis added)

In my interview with Gene Ma at ELECTRONS in Shanghai I remarked that walking through the door of the Shanghai facility was, with the exception of the Chinese characters on the directional signs, like walking into ELECTRONS' Silicon Valley headquarters. He agreed, and added that "ELECTRONS heavily emphasizes its culture and it wants all employees to behave in a very similar manner. That way, we can have meetings by telephone with people thousands of miles away and we are speaking in a common language, using the same terms."

Daniel Wen, WORLDWIDE's China National Executive, made it clear that, in acquiring parts of Chinese SOE, whether ultimately structured as wholly owned subsidiaries or joint ventures, these affiliates would be managed by WORLD-WIDE managers, using WORLDWIDE management processes. WORLDWIDE's practice of incorporating the whole of its management practices in affiliates is discussed in the case analysis.

The importance of transplanting the totality of the parent's corporate culture has been recognized in prior research. Buckley, Clegg and Tan (2001), in their case study of the China operations of Motorola and Shanghai Bell, quote a Motorola executive thus:

> "Our [Motorola's] competence comes not only from every bit of the firm, such as advanced technology, but also the whole firm, [the] integrated organization. Motorola is very competitive in all aspects of a firm: technology, management, and more important, corporate culture. If you want to understand Motorola, you have to understand its culture first."

Other scholars who have studied Sino-foreign joint ventures have identified the benefits resulting from the foreign partner transferring its entire corporate culture into the joint venture (Peng, 1997).

American multinationals are not the only foreign firms in China that stress transplantation of the corporate culture. When the Fiat subsidiary Iveco estab-lished its Naveco manufacturing joint venture in Nanjing in the late 1980s it first hired several hundred Chinese employees who then received Italian language instruction from 32 teachers brought to Nanjing from Italy by Iveco. Following language instruction, the new employees were then moved as a group to Iveco Italian factories. There they learned Iveco's manufacturing processes and its corpor-ate culture, as well as being exposed to the Italian way of life. Naveco has been successful since its founding. At present it has only eight Italians among its 3,000 employees. The Managing Director and Finance Director are both Italian; the Managing Director has headed Naveco since it began. Italian is still spoken through-out the Naveco factory (Harding, 1999).

CHAPTER SUMMARY

This concludes consideration of the "internal face" of the affiliates studied. We have seen that management of the affiliates incorporates management processes and shared values common to the parent and its other affiliates. We have also seen that these processes and values are transmitted by the parent to the affiliate and implanted in the affiliate by means of the parents' respective corporate cultures.

This chapter has featured concepts of uniformity. The remaining chapters, depending on subject matter, reflect degrees of diversity. They deal with the affiliates' "external face." All of them discuss the affiliates' approaches to China's unique marketplace and institutions. These approaches require degrees of adaptation of both organizational strategies and structures – adaptation that takes place within affiliates that are simultaneously being guided by global corporate cultures.

CHAPTER EIGHT

Setting Goals, Selecting Strategies, and Adopting Organizational Forms

Introduction

The use of a common corporate culture shared between parents and affiliates permits the affiliates to concentrate their efforts on development of strategies and organizations that will enable them to achieve designated corporate objectives within China's unique business and institutional environments, without having to simultaneously revise basic management processes. This chapter and the three that follow will review these efforts. This chapter is concerned with the parents' "market-driven" corporate objectives and the processes by which the affiliates adapt strategies and structures to meet those objectives in China. It is necessary to begin the review by describing "market focused" objectives and how they drive the affiliates' strategy selection processes.

The Market Focus of MNC and MNC Objectives

The difference between objectives and strategies

As one of the earliest writers on strategic game theory noted, the core of business is the market (McDonald, 1950, 73). As explained in the previous chapter, I use "market," whether singular or plural, in the businessperson's sense, that is, to refer to a collection of selling opportunities.

Although rediscovered in the literature only recently, a fundamental business concept is that objectives drive selection of both strategies and organizational forms. "Strategies" are simply integrated concepts of how a business can achieve its objectives (Hambrick and Fredrickson, 2001). Formulation of objectives must take place before development of strategies to achieve those objectives (Anderson, 1982). An early scholar of organizational theory noted more than 40 years ago that the founders of great enterprises regarded the division of work or work assignments within an organization not as predetermined, but rather as dependent on objectives; an organization was like "a road to market" (Dale, 1960, 26). Maljers (1992) reflected this perspective when he described Unilever as evolving through a "Darwinian" process of retaining what was useful and rejecting what no longer worked. In his words, the evolution took place through actual practice as a business in responding to the marketplace.

In the parent–affiliate relations studied here, the parent MNC all have very specific market-driven objectives. These objectives drive the affiliates' selection of strategies and use of organizational forms. To paraphrase Bartlett and Ghoshal (1989), the parent thinks globally, setting objectives, and the affiliates act locally, to achieve them. Objectives and strategies are determined within different places in the same organization.

Parent company objectives

In American companies business objectives are customarily expressed quantitatively, in terms of financial or marketing performance. Often both are combined. New business proposals are currently evaluated under standards that typically require the proposed investment to contribute to a 20 percent return on equity for the firm as well as after-tax profits of at least 10 percent. Market growth potential should exceed 10 percent per year (Merrifield, 2000).

These objectives can be related specifically to investment in China. A Chinese lawyer who has advised American MNC on China business for over 20 years described his US clients' current objectives in investing in Sino-US joint ventures in these terms: profit growth of 15–20 percent per year, with between 70 and 80 percent of sales coming from local (Chinese) markets and no more than 20–30 percent representing exports. Also, the Chinese partner must be well managed. He explained that the last requirement meant that the Chinese partner(s) must show actual profits from existing businesses (Ma, 2002).

As discussed in the IMIGIS case, the company had very specific goals which were presented to Chinese negotiators during discussions that led to IMIGIS investing over one billion US dollars in China. These included a specific return on investment (ROI) target. IMIGIS' approach is not unique.

As a result of his interviews with US and foreign managers in China, Rosen (1999, 14, n. 13) reported that several of the executives interviewed asserted that an MNC must have specific "paths to profitability" targets already established even *before* signing a contract to invest in China.

With respect to the parent MNC whose affiliates were studied, their objectives are expressed in terms of market share, financial performance, or both. WORLD-WIDE maintains the same objective that has driven its businesses since the 1960s: that each of its business groups must be number one or at least number two globally in their respective markets. MOTORS' objective is a minimum 15 percent return on sales from each of its divisions, although sales growth targets are specific to each division. The last of the three multiproduct parent companies, IMIGIS, aims for global market leadership in its six business groups. There is also a company-wide ROI standard.

In ELECTRONS, with a less diversified product line, the aim of the company is to be the global leader in sales and earnings in its industry.

Parent company organizations

The respective global organizations reflect this market focus. MOTORS, WORLD-WIDE and IMIGIS are all organized around product groups. MOTORS has the most divisional structure, in which functional support units are contained within each of the 40 divisions; at IMIGIS some functional activities, such as manufacturing, are centrally directed from US headquarters. ELECTRONS is also organized along these lines, but as much more of a matrix. Product groups are responsible for developing new products, that are then marketed in cooperation with the marketing group. Manufacturing is centrally directed.

Galbraith (2001) has described these processes as building "customer facing" organizations. Galbraith's research reflects the evolution of a process already evident within US MNC in the mid 1970s: the organization of MNC around different markets' needs (Davis, 1976).

Global Objectives and the Strategies to Implement Them

Targeting high-growth markets

Historically, the international expansion of US MNC has been market driven in an effort to access potential customers (Wilkins, 1975, 219). The MNC parents of the affiliates studied make Asia, and China in particular, the focus of their current global expansion efforts. The annual reports of the companies express a common view that market growth is expected to be most rapid in the Asia-Pacific region. Raj Kumar, the CEO of MOTORS Asia-Pacific, summarized those views:

> *RK:* I think MOTORS' whole objective in the last five or 10 years is to get higher growth. Our base markets grow at 3–4 percent in the US and Europe, maybe slightly less. So we have had to change the mix of our core product markets so that we have moved into things like telecom and electronics applications. The second thing is to invest in higher growth markets, geographic markets, and that's where Asia comes in. Any growth we get in Asia, the market is growing faster, is less saturated, and the infrastructure spending is growing at a rapid rate. The more business we get in Asia the higher our own growth, and as a percent of the business that keeps growing we have a fast growing chunk of our business here.

Developing strategies for China

Within their respective organizations, the locus of strategy development with respect to China does not vary from the locus of strategy development in general. In MOTORS each division pursues an individual "China strategy" consistent with the division's financial targets, which are centrally established by the parent. The divisions are assisted in mergers and acquisitions, legal and governmental relations by the Asia-Pacific headquarters group. As explained in the WORLDWIDE chapter, each business group develops and executes its own China strategy, assisted by Daniel Wen, WORLDWIDE's National Executive for China. At ELECTRONS the strategy development process is more centralized but, as Jim Liu explained, ETCL is expected to furnish recommendations to ELECTRONS management as to China business opportunities and the strategies with which to pursue them. The IMIGIS case discusses the central role played by its current CEO and his predecessor in the company's decision to focus global expansion efforts on China, and the selection of the strategies necessary to achieve those objectives.

Differentiation in strategy implementation

In MOTORS and IMIGIS strategy implementation within China varied from the processes used by these companies elsewhere. This was due to the role of "country/regional manager." John Victors, IMIGIS' Greater Asia Region Vice President for Human Resources, explained this with respect to Henry Peterson, head of both IMIGIS Greater Asia Region and IMIGIS China:

JV: Henry is the General Manager. He is the head of China, the country, and he is the person who clearly represents IMIGIS when it comes to external affairs. The government relations area is a big part of his role and media relations, that's very clear. *And then, in terms of his role in the businesses, that's probably less well defined, yet it tends to be the case that in China he plays a more direct role in the businesses than would country heads in most other countries because of the need to coordinate what goes on in China.* Quarterly, each of the business unit heads would report to his or her global product head. But, and this is true for every country's General Manager, they would also report to the country's General Manager in a matrix reporting relationship, as you called it. *I would say, though, that in the case of China the dotted line to the General Manager is stronger than in any other country in the world.*

STR: That was going to be my next question, which is, based on both of your experiences, taking it from a different direction, whether the type of influence that IMIGIS headquarters has over what goes on in China, if that's different than the kind of influence they would exert say in Singapore or in Europe?

*JV: I would say that to the degree that there are overriding considerations with develop-
ment in China as an overall market for IMIGIS and the importance that China has
strategically across all business units, that the person in Henry Peterson's role probably
has a greater ability to influence what goes on than would be the case elsewhere.*
(emphasis added)

In MOTORS' case Raj Kumar also described his role as being different than his
counterpart regional manager for Europe:

*RK: In Europe businesses are grown by buying European businesses, fully running
companies. So there's not much of a need for a corporate office. So our corporate
office in Europe is smaller, does less development work and then does more of
the treasury, currency, financial functions rather than the kind of things we do
here. I think we do more strategy at the grass roots, building the business up,
which in Europe they don't do because of the nature of the business that we
have there, they are independent divisions who have developed their own
management and their own strategies. So that's the difference here. I am more
engaged in MOTORS business than would be the case in Europe.*

The strategy implementation process employed by WORLDWIDE and ELEC-
TRONS, respectively, did not differ from those of MOTORS or IMIGIS.

Approaching China's Markets

As discussed in Chapter 2, the concept that there is one "Chinese market" is
highly inaccurate for many products, given the continuing regional differences in
disposable income, infrastructure and access to technology.

Marketing is further complicated by lack of the kind of economic and demo-
graphic information available in Europe, North America, Australasia or Japan. On
my first visit to Shanghai several years ago I had the pleasure of speaking with
the then head of the China businesses of an American MNC that is a leading
manufacturer of floor and wall coverings. He had been in Shanghai for almost
15 years at that point, and has since retired. I asked what sort of market research
his company did before entering China in the early 1980s. He answered that
statistics were largely non-existent then, in contrast to the present, when they are
both more available and unreliable. He told me that his company took a calcu-
lated risk that Deng's "Four Modernizations" would result in rapid economic
growth that would, in turn, spur a construction boom. Eventually this risk was
rewarded and the company enjoys healthy market share in several categories of
building products.

Within China, not all variations in product marketing are based on demo-
graphic or geographic factors. Dan Truman, the General Manager of MOTORS'
BRONWYN subsidiary Shanghai joint venture, gave an example of difficulties

encountered in China by Whirlpool, the US MNC that manufactures and sells household appliances:

> *DT*: Just as real short story about Whirlpool. They came over here. Built this huge factory to make washers and dryers. And boy, they're hurting now. They're not making a whole lot of money. Why? Because the Chinese people like to hang their clothes out the window on bamboo poles. They don't buy dryers. So a word of caution when you send your MBAs over to do market research studies of China: you have to really understand what the people want.

Although I have been able to find only one published study that documents this, ergonomic factors also require adaptation of products designed for North American and European physical characteristics so that they can be used by Chinese people (Hougan, Hung and Wardell, 2000).

Yadong Luo (2001) has posited that complex local markets increase the need for local responsiveness on the part of MNC affiliates operating in such markets. Dan Truman's remarks illustrate the local complexity faced by an MNC affiliate, even one that sells to original equipment manufacturers (OEM) rather than directly to consumers:

> *DT*: There is a very large percentage of the market here that buys exclusively on price. The market is stratified. There are the top 10 percent which are your multinationals. These are the Fords, the GEs of the world. And they want top of the line, they want the same as they can buy in New York. And you'll get that. As a multinational you will sell to that market and you're probably going to get 100 percent market share. Then there's second tier which include JVs. They want the best of both worlds. They want rock-bottom prices but they want good technology. And you'll get the lion's share of that. But the 80 percent of the market that is out there and is the volume, is the price consumer market. And unless you have a product toward that market segment you're not going to be successful in China. So to make it real simple, you need a multitiered product offering to be successful in China.

Product offerings are either locally differentiated or undifferentiated, depending on the customer. The aircraft components manufactured by WORLDWIDE's AC division, and the IT products manufactured by ETCL in China, both conform to a global standard, as do the digital imaging products manufactured and sold within China by IMIGIS.

At the Medical Equipment (ME) group of WORLDWIDE, Terence Deng's factories manufacture diagnostic medical equipment according to global standards. At present the "low end" (less technologically complex) machines are sold primarily within China through a local distributor, while "high-end" products are shipped to customers around the world by ME itself.

The most differentiated product offerings that I observed occurred within MOTORS' BRONWYN division. Dan Truman made this point in speaking of the automotive products market:

> *DT*: If you have a car that's all electronic and computerized and has every bell and whistle in the world, it takes a technician of that caliber to support that vehicle. Well, here in China on the other hand, you don't tend to have that. You tend to have very rudimentary vehicles. You have those Santanas which are very basic cars. It probably has a manual choke in it, it's a five-speed stick [gearbox], so we build the product here to match the expectations of the market. We tend not to use cutting edge technology because I can't support it. So, yes, I can sell you the exact same unit in China that we would sell in Detroit and it will have a price point to match. Or I can sell you a highly "de-featured" product – that will do the same thing but not with every bell and whistle, touch screen . . . at a price point that you can live with in a domestic market.

Just as the affiliates' approaches to the Chinese market are differentiated, so are the organizational structures employed by the affiliates. This latter differentiation is driven by the differing objectives of the parent MNC in employing joint ventures globally and within China, and will now be discussed in the concluding sections of this chapter.

Organizing for China

Chapter 1 expressed the intention to discuss the affiliates studied and their parents in terms of the *processes* through which the affiliates' operations in China were controlled and coordinated by their respective parents. The respective organizations are viewed as an interrelated set of actors and processes, rather than simply as a collection of interacting business units (Day, 1994).

The following analysis compares use of WFOE and JV by the affiliates in China, and by their parents globally. The analysis focuses on the business objectives that drive adoption of the organizational forms both globally and within China, and the processes for managing the different entities within China. The analysis thus identifies objectives and describes how those objectives are realized through management of the China affiliates.

Business objectives and entity selection

The choice of entity with which to conduct operations in a foreign country depends both on an MNC's internal management processes and on its external processes for responding to its differentiated markets.

The MNC's internal management processes will influence the choice primarily by consideration whether to have an entity over which it can exercise complete control or one over which it cannot exercise such control (Rudman, 2000). The executives with whom I spoke were consistent in expressing the business objective of fully controlling their China affiliates, and were less concerned about whether the affiliate was structured as a WFOE or a JV.

The market response process involves consideration of several variables. The most important is whether the affiliate can legally operate in the host country as a wholly foreign-owned enterprise. If it cannot, then it must enter that country by means of a joint venture.

Wilkins' (1974, 391) study of US MNC identified host country regulations as the principal reason for US companies using joint ventures with local partners when investing during the 1950s and 1960s in what were then called "less developed" countries. Joint ventures that are created primarily to satisfy host country political requirements have been identified as likely to produce more problems than joint ventures that are formed due to common business objectives (Sender, 1991).

China's accession to the WTO promises to remove most of the few remaining legal barriers to operating WFOE in China. At the same time, however, several important markets, such as that for telecommunications services, will remain closed to WFOE, and will require Chinese joint venture partners for the foreseeable future.

Another important consideration relates to the business objectives for entering into an alliance as opposed to conducting a business without partners. Businesses ally with other enterprises principally to obtain resources that they cannot or choose not to provide entirely by themselves. Examples of such resources include market access, referring here not to the political requirements discussed in the previous paragraph, but to physical resources such as factories and distribution networks. They also include knowledge resources such as a partner's established host country marketing organization, business connections and cultural sensitivity. Other resources include superior partner technology and management process skills. In an emerging economy where the internal political situation may be subject to change that may be both sudden and violent, the capital resources contributed by partners helps minimize the MNC's capital at risk.

The case analyses and the material presented below illustrate the accuracy of the view that MNC engage in joint ventures in emerging markets to pursue object-ives that differ from their objectives in engaging in joint ventures in industrialized markets (Child and Faulkner, 1998, 267–76).

Parent use of joint ventures globally

As discussed in the case studies, the parent companies make extensive use of joint ventures in worldwide operations.

The companies use joint ventures both for market access and for resource acquisition. WORLDWIDE's AC division originally entered into its joint venture with a European components manufacturer as a means of entering the passenger jet components market in Europe. The joint venture has grown far beyond that objective. Each partner has retained its 50 percent interest, and the joint venture has enjoyed considerable success globally. It is managed semi-autonomously, with its own global marketing staff.

WORLDWIDE's ME division entered into a joint venture with a Japanese medical equipment manufacturer through which it obtained market access to Japan. Eventually, WORLDWIDE adopted its partner's manufacturing technology processes for the ME group as well as several other WORLDWIDE business groups. The venture ended with WORLDWIDE acquiring full ownership of the partner.

During a recent five year period, 25 percent of MOTORS' annual revenue came from joint ventures (Bonsignore, Houghton and Knight, 1994). With a 50 percent European partner it operated one of the world's largest hand-held power tools businesses as a joint venture established to counter Japanese competition by combining the partners' technological strengths and financial resources.

ELECTRONS uses joint ventures to obtain market access and knowledge in Internet-related businesses, while IMIGIS uses joint ventures extensively to acquire technology to assist in expansion of its digital imaging and Internet-related businesses.

In general, these ventures appear to be or to have been managed on a collaborative basis. In the situations that I looked at, collaboration was founded on congruent business objectives and mutual respect for partner technological and management skills; the latter was especially true in the WORLDWIDE joint ventures. This respect facilitated trust, a resource that no relationship can do without (Child, 2001). All of these joint ventures shared another important characteristic: all of the partners are or were from industrialized, capitalistic economies. The joint ventures that were encountered during my study of the China affiliates shared none of the above characteristics.

Affiliate Use of Joint Ventures in China

The purpose of this section is to compare the various affiliates' use of joint ventures in China. There is a vast literature on Sino-foreign joint ventures, much of which concentrates on the difficulties involved in managing these entities. The discussion here relates to what I learned from the affiliates studied. Research relevant to the comparisons is discussed, but this section is not intended to be a general review of the literature.

Business objectives: control

Much of the literature on Sino-foreign joint ventures begins with a discussion comparing the advantages and disadvantages of this ownership structure, often with a further comparison to WFOE. Joint venture formation is then discussed, with emphasis on partner selection. After that, there may be some discussion of managing the joint venture, including the control issue.

By contrast, the executives with whom I spoke did not differentiate between management of WFOE and management of joint ventures. The prior chapter and the case analyses all elaborate on a basic theme that was repeated by those interviewed: affiliates in China are managed using the same processes that are used in managing affiliates in other countries, and affiliates in China are managed using those processes whether the affiliate is a WFOE or a joint venture. To achieve these objectives the executives consider full control of the entity to be essential, whether it is a joint venture or a WFOE. Daniel Wen explained why control over an entity rather than the type of entity *per se* was the key consideration:

> *DW*: I would think that the difference is not between wholly foreign-owned enterprises and joint ventures. The difference is between controlled entities and not controlled entities. So joint ventures with majority control and wholly foreign-owned enterprises rightfully should be operated similarly.

Exercise of control was regarded as the essential element in joint venture management, rather than simply obtaining a certain percentage of "supermajority" (over 50.01) percent of equity.[74] John Kelly of MOTORS emphasized this point:

> *JK*: I don't think it's necessarily ownership. It's the responsibilities associated with having majority ownership. The success or failure, I believe, of any joint venture is in the management of the joint venture. What you get by having majority is the opportunity to control the entity. But that means that you have to be engaged in the control. That means you have responsibilities for planning; you have responsibilities for controls, financial as well as legal, as well as personnel. You have to implement them and that means you have to really be engaged with the joint venture. *Majority control in China doesn't get you anything unless you exercise it; unless you actually implement what has been successful for your entities worldwide. I have seen entities where an individual has control or greater, even at 70 percent, and the business is a failure because no one ever brought the management structure or any type of discipline to the business and people stand back.* (emphasis added)

Wally Moon, the General Manager of the MOTORS subsidiary STORMONT's Shanghai joint venture, in which MOTORS holds a 60 percent interest, credited implementation of MOTORS' disciplined corporate culture, along with its management routines, as the cause of the joint venture's success. This observation echoes the suggestion that joint ventures could profit from adoption of the foreign partner's corporate culture (Peng, 1997). In his detailed case study of Coca-Cola's Tianjin bottling plant joint venture, Nolan observed that, in addition to implementing Coca-Cola business processes, the company worked hard "to bind employees into a commitment to [Coca-Cola's] values" (1995, 36–7).

In addition to corporate culture, the importance for joint venture success of adopting the foreign partner's management practices was noted by Newman (1992) more than a decade ago. His conclusion was based on his analysis of the successful manufacturing joint venture between Celanese, at that time a US MNC, and China National Tobacco Company, a large SOE.

Business objectives and reasons for using joint ventures

The most commonly cited reason given by the executives with whom I spoke, for employing joint ventures rather than WFOE, was that joint ventures might provide needed market access. Raj Kumar remarked:

> *RK*: I would say that in a case where we have a clear technology advantage, I say definitely "wholly owned." Because we can protect and leverage that technology advantage. But if it was a case of a market situation and there is a strong entrance barrier for a new company in China I'd go with joint venture because I think it brings you a business base, it brings you a customer base that you don't have.

John Kelly of MOTORS expressed similar views. The same point was made by John Victors and Kirk Tang in discussing IMIGIS' use of joint ventures.

The literature frequently refers to another business objective for using joint ventures in China: the local partner's knowledge of the institutional infrastructure. Two of the companies whose executives did not mention this are IMIGIS and WORLDWIDE. Both of these companies have National Executives whose principal responsibility is to represent their respective companies at all levels of Chinese government. ELECTRONS Technology (China) Ltd (ETCL) is not a joint venture, and it has a Chinese national as Deputy Site Manager for Public Affairs. He is an executive who works almost exclusively on relations with the Shanghai government and local departments of the central government.

Wally Moon of MOTORS' STORMONT division related that his joint venture's local partner has been of no help in marketing, either to Shanghai affiliates of MNC or to SOE. He did say that the partner has provided "some help" in dealing with the Shanghai government. John Kelly provided another perspective in response to my question:

> *STR*: Certainly both management and academic literature repeat quite frequently that it's not wise to try to do business in China through wholly owned entities, if for no other reason than the institutional environment, in particular local, provincial and national government, is so complex that a Chinese partner-guide is necessary. Would you share with me your experience on that?
> *JK*: We fell victim to that same mindset early on. I could give several examples where we created joint ventures and in the initial negotiation we believed our

partners would bring in just that: knowledge of the infrastructure, et cetera. When, in fact, we began the operations of the entities we learned that their "knowledge" was not as originally portrayed to us. Our experience has been that we initially started out with joint ventures and, within two or three years of the startups, realized that it was not difficult to get knowledge about the infrastructure as long as we were committed to the entity.

Problems of joint ventures

Various reasons have been advanced in the literature to account for the difficulties in operating Sino-foreign joint ventures. There are also many studies providing support for the assertion that joint ventures in general have a high rate of dissolution, as well as a short "lifespan" – two criteria frequently used in quantitative surveys of international joint ventures.[75] There are detailed qualitative studies supporting the view that joint ventures between companies from different industrialized countries encounter problems similar to those encountered in joint ventures between companies from industrialized countries and emerging market host country partners (Salk, 1996).

Cultural differences have been assigned a role in the problems encountered by Sino-US and Sino-European joint ventures. At the same time, other studies have shown that joint ventures in which the foreign partner is an overseas Chinese company have encountered many of the same problems encountered by Western joint ventures, despite what is often depicted as a "common" Chinese culture (Shenkar, 1990; Stewart and de Lisle, 1994). These studies have included ventures having partners from Hong Kong (Kim, 1996; O'Connor and Chalos, 1999) as well as Singapore (Tsang, 1999).

The three ELECTRONS executives with whom I spoke who are Chinese citizens had all worked for several years at Sino-US or Sino-UK joint ventures before joining ELECTRONS. Their views of Sino-foreign joint ventures provide important insights into the difficulties involved in operating a Sino-foreign joint venture. The comments illustrate that these difficulties cannot be ascribed to a single source. Each executive offered a different perspective.

Bian Chen emphasized the differences in corporate, more than ethnic, culture:

BC: My observation is that multinational companies are very different than JV in China. The multinationals still keep the global culture. It doesn't matter whether you are in China, the Philippines or the US. The legacy is consistent across the globe. The JV, somehow, they localize a lot. That's why they end up with complicated management structures, or practices, and create a lot of mutual understanding gaps between foreign and local managers. At ELECTRONS, the local managers are totally integrated into the one culture and we are operating all on the same basis. I see this because I used to work in a JV. In the JV, you are seeing two different management concepts, two different systems trying to cooperate. Sometimes they are doing good if there is no conflict, but sometimes they are not doing good, because all the conflicts come out . . . we saw a lot of these problems in the JV I worked for. The problem was that going back 10 years, the management process in China was not very Westernized, so this created a big gap. But as time goes on, local management is better trained, MBA programs and so forth, so the gap may be getting smaller, but even so, if you run two different management systems you still see the gap, and that gap causes a lot of inefficiency in operations.

Gene Ma emphasized the difficulties caused by divergent objectives and expectations:

> *GM*: In my experience the root cause of the problem with the JV was the difference in objectives. AT&T's goal was to obtain market share in China, and the local partners had the marketing channels to make this happen. The local partners wanted to get technology, and at the same time, profits, but an argument developed over "how much profit is proper." The higher profit benefited the Chinese, but most of the components were imported from AT&T in the US, reducing the JV profits, but still allowing AT&T to make money. The fights over this made management of the JV a terrible process.

While the debate over the causes of difficulty in managing Sino-foreign joint ventures continues, events are taking place that may make the resolution of that debate less important to foreign enterprises in China. The latest studies show that new WFOE formations continue to outpace joint venture formations, and that foreign companies are increasingly converting their interests in existing joint ventures into WFOE as the WTO is implemented (Deng, 2001; Xinhua News Agency, 2001). One of the first Sino-foreign joint ventures, established in 1980, was recently converted into a WFOE when the foreign partner bought out the interest of the remaining Chinese partner (Trianto, 2001).

The reasons for the decline in use of joint ventures, a trend in effect since 1997 (Rosen, 1999, 14), were articulately expressed by the third ELECTRONS executive, Shao, the Deputy Site Manager for Public Affairs at ETCL. He attributed difficulties in joint venture management to government policies that have since been changed:

> *S*: Well, let me put it this way. China has realized that in order to implement the Open Door policy, to really attract more and more foreign investment, the government has had to adapt its policies. For example, when you are in the FTZ [Foreign Trade Zone], the government is not going to load you down with a lot of restrictions; the whole idea of the FTZ is to help make it easier for FIE to do business in China. So the environment has changed over time so that the government has made it easier for multinationals to do business here.
> I worked for a JV for almost 10 years. Why did Lucent want a JV? Because sales channels were still controlled by the government. Also, when Lucent established the JV, labor was not free, in terms of ability to hire on the local

labor market. So, if you wanted to get good people you needed a Chinese partner that could help get these problems solved. The market is now open, the labor market is open, universities are open, to hire graduates. All these things are open, and it is much more easy to do business here, for multinationals to have wholly owned affiliates here.

CHAPTER SUMMARY

This chapter has compared the "market-driven" goal setting processes among the affiliates and their parents and the processes used to translate objectives into strategy creation and organizational structure selection (wholly owned versus joint venture) within their respective China operations.

The emphasis has been on the differentiation processes needed to deal with China's markets. The differentiation processes themselves, however, are similar across the affiliates studied. The consistent emphasis was on exercising control over joint ventures, and installing the same management processes used by the parent throughout their respective worldwide operations. Joint ventures were employed only when necessary to obtain or facilitate market access.

CHAPTER NINE

Controlling and Coordinating People: Human Resources Management Policies and Practices

Introduction

Earlier studies of human resources management processes of MNC within China have been influenced by the "global–local" dichotomy. Two detailed studies found "globalized" processes, that is, processes that are globally standardized within an MNC, prevailed in China as well (Bjorkman and Lu, 1999). This might seem surprising, given that HRM processes within MNC in China have been identified as being significantly affected by factors specific to that nation. Such factors include those relating to China's institutional environment such as local labor laws and a centrally directed economy (Ding and Warner, 1998) as well as labor market factors such as shortages of experienced managers and skilled workers (McComb, 1999).

In the companies studied here, HRM processes, when used as means of coordination and control, do reflect global standard policies. When, however, HRM processes are the objects of coordination and control efforts, simultaneous "localization," that is, adaptation to local conditions, is apparent. Finally, whether used to control or as an object of control, the degree of globalization or localization of HRM processes also depends on whether executives or non-executives are the focus of the particular practice (Janssens, 2001).

HRM processes will be considered sequentially. Because it drives all of the other processes, the first subject to be addressed is the actual administration of HRM within the affiliates. Employee selection will be considered next, followed by training and then compensation, and concluding with consideration of managers' career mobility.

Administration of Human Resources Management

"Globalized" policy

The Bjorkman and Lu (1999) study referred to above examined the HRM function inside "China centers" – administrative headquarters established within China by MNC to coordinate and control their various affiliates located there. Three of the companies that I studied use such administrative centers. As with the companies in the Bjorkman and Lu study, the companies' "China centers" handle HRM functions, and, typically, the function involves administering globally standardized HRM processes. There are significant differences among the companies, however. The differences relate to the companies' different organizational structures, and are directly related to the type of global HRM processes that they administer.

Before discussing the companies that use China centers, it is necessary to consider ELECTRONS' use of globalized HRM processes. Jim Liu does have a small HRM staff to assist him at ETCL, but that staff is primarily concerned with human resources management at the factory level, dealing with the local workforce. Executives work for one of two functional groups. Most are from the Technology and Manufacturing Group (TMG), and there is a small cadre from Finance. Both of these groups are global in scope, which facilitates ELECTRONS' deployment of highly standardized HRM processes. At the same time all ETCL employees are considered employees of the parent company and their training is highly standardized. As will be discussed below, selection of compensation levels for the local workforce is the only HRM activity which can be said to be completely localized.[76]

Of the remaining companies, the roles of their respective "China centers" in HRM depend on the organizational structure of the individual company's global operation. IMIGIS' HRM functions for both the Greater China Region (GCR) and the Greater Asia Region (GAR) are led by John Victors who reports to an IMIGIS executive who is head of both GCR and GAR. The two organizations share a common headquarters in Shanghai. Daniel Wen is WORLDWIDE's National Executive for China, with his offices in Beijing; while Corinne Lu is MOTORS' Corporate Director of HRM for MOTORS Asia-Pacific organization, headquartered in Hong Kong, and her responsibilities include HRM for MOTORS' affiliates operating within China.

In the latter two companies the primary purpose of the corporate HRM function in China is focused on providing assistance in the establishment of new affiliates and in implementing some global policies. Daniel Wen discussed this with respect to WORLDWIDE:

DW: [My] function is to have local support for all business development initiatives for WORLDWIDE regardless of which business. Some businesses have a very strong presence in China so they are able to do a lot of things themselves. Other businesses are not as well staffed in China as needed for really understanding how and where and with whom to start their business initiatives. Therefore we provide the local team for those businesses in each functional area so that each business, when they come to China, can be a complete operating entity with and complemented by people from WORLDWIDE International, so that is the concept. And it works very well for us.

In our discussions Daniel Wen also made it clear that one of his responsibilities is "to create a process for WORLDWIDE by which we can develop a pipeline of local leaders." This means recruiting and developing Chinese executives for WORLDWIDE's various business groups. The training of Chinese executives is done pursuant to globally standard WORLDWIDE policies and processes, administered by Daniel Wen's HRM staff organization. Their career development is jointly supervised by the China HRM staff and by the respective business groups in which they begin their careers.

Corinne Lu described her responsibilities at MOTORS in terms of what she called the two types of MOTORS' divisions operating in China. Some divisions relocate directly from the USA in a "startup" configuration. For these divisions her organization provides total HRM support in training, development, hiring and firing and legal compliance. Other divisions, such as those described in the case study, have a long-standing presence in China and Asia. They have developed their own HRM staffs outside MOTORS. For them Corinne's responsibilities are principally to keep them informed of various legal compliance issues as well as overall MOTORS HRM philosophies.

Corinne's remarks focused on MOTORS' divisional structure and its pattern of growth through acquisition of existing businesses that typically retained their existing structures. In her view this resulted in MOTORS being disinclined to compel all of the divisions to adopt uniform HRM policies, with the important exceptions of legal and ethical compliance standards. As was customary with every MOTORS executive to whom I spoke, Corinne noted that MOTORS' strong corporate culture and focus on communicating with every employee were major influences on global uniformity within what is a very decentralized MNC. Part of her organization's responsibility was implementing communication throughout Asia-Pacific so that employees at every level are acquainted with MOTORS' HRM philosophies.[77]

Corinne's observations on two issues illustrate the absence of globally standard HRM policies at MOTORS. In her words, the current "hot topic" among senior managers at MOTORS and its divisions in Asia is the issue of management localization. Yet she emphasized that MOTORS does not have a corporate policy mandating or discouraging use of either local managers or expatriates. The divisions themselves are responsible for selecting and assigning managers.

Corinne related that HRM managers from the divisions as well as from her Asia-Pacific headquarters group held regular conferences as part of the MOTORS global planning process. As a newly hired senior regional HRM executive she had also been invited to participate in a conference held at MOTORS' US headquarters and attended by headquarters HRM staff from MOTORS and from the divisions (all of which are themselves headquartered in the US). Corinne was struck by the fact that the respective conference agenda were almost totally different. The Asian conference focused on management localization, while the principal topics at the US conference were "lean manufacturing" and workplace diversity.

The absence of many globally standardized HRM policies at the corporate level of MOTORS is not reflected by divisional practice, however. The divisional executives with whom I spoke, whether joint venture general managers or regional HRM directors, all related that HRM processes within China affiliates were the "mirror image" of their respective division's global HRM processes, with the exception of modifications necessary to comply with Chinese law.

IMIGIS represents an approach that falls between those of the first two companies. John Victors explained that management development and executive compensation were areas in which global processes predominated. IMIGIS is also trying to broaden job opportunities within both the GCR and the GAR by developing a corporate intranet through which the affiliates of the six different business groups are supposed to post available jobs. John described this as an effort to overcome "parochialism" by business group managers who are eager to hold on to talented employees. MOTORS has instituted an intranet for job postings within its Asia-Pacific organization for the same reason.

As with the MOTORS divisions, some of the IMIGIS business groups, for example William Lobashevski's China manufacturing organization, have fully developed HRM staff. These are responsible not only for localized functions such as recruitment and compensation of non-executive employees, but also for hiring Chinese citizens for executive positions with the group's JV and WFOE. They are also responsible for implementing global policies relating to legal and ethical standards.

Within the HRM organizations of all of the affiliates there are reporting processes followed that consolidate personnel data provided by business groups or divisions within China, or elsewhere in the respective regions, for presentation to the regional executives and the US headquarters.

"Localized" people

Before reviewing HRM selection processes it is appropriate here to consider the people who execute HRM functions at both the regional and the operating unit levels.

Daniel Wen's staff at WORLDWIDE in Beijing almost totally comprises Chinese citizens. Corinne Lu of MOTORS is a native of Hong Kong and directs an eight person staff. Five of the eight are Chinese citizens working in teams located in either Shanghai or Baoan. Her three associates in Hong Kong are Hong Kong residents. IMIGIS' Greater Asia Region HRM staff is the most "non-local." The small senior staff, in addition to John Victors who is a US citizen, include several expatriates. Under IMIGIS' definition, citizens of Hong Kong and Singapore as well as US citizens who were born in China or Taiwan are considered "expatriates" with regard to working in China.

Within the operating companies themselves, however, HRM staff working in the affiliates that I visited are all Chinese citizens. The two basic reasons that were offered in the interviews can be summarized thus: expatriates are expensive, and local people know China better, in terms of both culture and regulations.

The affiliates studied do not confine localization of staff to the HRM function alone. Localization is the policy pursued in employee selection throughout their organizations.

Selection Processes

Selecting executives

Chapter 1 reviews the many studies of use of expatriate managers as a normative control device by MNC. That review will not be repeated here. In contrast to those studies, the following comparison of executive selection within the affiliates studied focuses on which executive positions are held by expatriates and which by local managers. "Local manager" is used here as it is used by the companies studied, that is, to signify a manager who is a citizen of the People's Republic of China. "Expatriate" refers to everyone else, including managers from Hong Kong.

Within the affiliates studied, the most common criterion for executive selection was "localize if at all possible." This policy was carried out at all levels throughout the respective organizations except at the very top. None of the affiliates was headed by a local executive, and of the operating companies within affiliates that I visited, only one operating company had a Chinese general manager.

With respect to leadership at the affiliate level, the head of IMIGIS GCR/GAR is a French national; the head of ETCL is an American citizen of Chinese descent, as is the National Executive of WORLDWIDE in China. The executives who are the closest to being "local" managers are the co-heads of MOTORS Asia-Pacific. Sterling Luo was born and raised in Hong Kong and Raj Kumar was born and raised in India.

At the operating company level almost every business unit head is an American citizen, although many were born in either China or Taiwan. I interviewed only one local executive who heads a business unit: the General Manager of a Shenzhen-based manufacturing WFOE within MOTORS' MAYAN division. MAYAN itself was originally an Australian company that MOTORS acquired several years ago; the executive in question has worked for MAYAN for many years and has headed the Shenzhen operation since it was established in the late 1980s.

The most important limitation on the localization of top management is the well-documented shortage of local managers capable of assuming these responsibilities (Wong and Law, 1999).

The training and development of local managers will be considered throughout the remainder of this chapter. Training and development are directly related to the localization of management at all levels. Terence Deng noted that there was only one expatriate besides himself in the WORLDWIDE Medical Equipment factory near Beijing:

> *TD*: We are very local. I think that's another success factor, at least in my opinion, for WORLDWIDE Medical Equipment being successful in China because we localize people. We don't rely on outside people. Yes, at a certain stage you do need someone from outside. But only really senior leaders, and anyone after that it is my responsibility to find and to train.

At this point it is fair to ask how the US MNC affiliates' practices in using expatriates differ from those of European or Japanese MNC. European MNC executive staffing practices have been characterized by both academic researchers (Hulbert and Brandt, 1980, 143–4; Bartlett and Ghoshal, 1987) and practitioners (Maljers, 1992) as embodying employment of a corps of mobile executives dispatched from headquarters to constitute the foundation of management at foreign affiliates. These executives are rotated through various assignments outside the home country, interspersed with assignments at headquarters.[78] The traditional view of Japanese MNC has emphasized their extensive use of expatriate executives on long-term foreign assignments (Gamble, 2001). Some recent studies of Japanese MNC, however, indicate that use of expatriates depends on the nature of the business being operated (Anand and Delios, 1996) and that the overall trend is for reduced use of expatriates in general (Beamish and Inkpen, 1998), and in China in particular (Taylor, 1999).

The US affiliates' use of expatriates differs from European or Japanese practice. Outside the top level of management, that is, the level of general manager of a WFOE or JV and above, few expatriates are employed. In the six WFOE and JV that comprise William Lobashevski's IMIGIS manufacturing organization there is only one expatriate in each operating company. Dan Truman is the only expatriate in the BRONWYN joint venture in Shanghai that he heads. Besides Terence Deng there is only one expatriate in the WORLDWIDE Medical Equipment manufacturing joint venture in Beijing. This individual is an American who is married to a Chinese woman, and who is paid a non-expatriate salary. The only expatriate in Wally Moon's joint venture in Shanghai, other than Wally, is an Australian who is the controller. The use of expatriate chief financial officers to insure parent financial control of foreign affiliates is a characteristic of MNC globally (Peterson, Napier and Won, 2000).

American MNC's preference for employing local managers in foreign affiliates is not new, nor is it confined to China. Case studies done more than 20 years ago in Brazil (Hulbert and Brandt, 1980) as well as more recent case research in Thailand and the United Kingdom (Richards, 2001), among others, describe the localization preference, although Richards found a positive correlation between use of expatriates and the size of the affiliate. Recent broader surveys confirm the continuing trend of US MNC to reduce expatriate use in their foreign affiliates (Peterson, Napier and Won, 2000).

The reasons for localization of management within the affiliates that I studied deserve some consideration. The localization efforts exemplify both the "internal face" of the affiliates, that is, the unity of their management processes, and their "external face," that is the adaptation to the Chinese environment.

Transfer of management processes and shared values: "internal face"

As I showed in Chapter 7, management of the affiliates studied involves incor-poration of management processes and shared values common to the parent and its other affiliates. This is done by transmitting the processes and values from the parent to the affiliate and implanting them in the affiliate by means of the res-pective parent's corporate culture.

Previous researchers, from Edstrom and Galbraith through Harzing, have iden-tified the transfer of expatriate executives from home country headquarters to foreign affiliates as the principal means used by non–US MNC by which corpor-ate culture is transferred to and implanted in the affiliates. In the affiliates studied here, however, management within business units has been almost completely localized below the very top level. At the same time, however, the affiliates of three of the four parent companies clearly show the presence of a strong corporate culture within the affiliate organizations. How to account for this? It can be accounted for by considering the objective of the parent companies.

The parents' objective is to manage the affiliates internally in a manner similar to the way in which both the parent and its other worldwide affiliates are managed. To do so requires transmission *and* implementation of shared proc-esses and values. Expatriates cannot be depended on as the principal means of both transferring and implementing. By definition expatriates are sent from some-where else, and, at some point, return there or go to a third destination. Within some companies executives are constantly rotated among assignments throughout the world.[79]

Yet the successful implementation of shared processes and values requires that they be *shared* among people who are likely to be in different places and to have different ethnic and cultural heritages. Researchers who have identified corporate culture as an effective means of control are not incorrect. Yet corporate culture, like control, has a volitional element (Lebas and Weigenstein, 1986), a point pre-viously discussed in Chapter 7. Corporate culture can be successfully implemented when, as in the case of the affiliates studied here, it is accepted by and becomes a part of the work life of the local workforce, that is, by people who are working in the affiliate every day, and likely to continue to do so.

Expatriates can help bring corporate culture to the affiliate, but for the culture to take hold it must be accepted and acted upon by local people who will manage and staff the affiliate long after the expatriate is gone. Thus it is better that affiliate management be localized to the greatest extent possible, as soon as possible.

Adaptation to the Chinese environment: "external face"

At the same time, localization of management also addresses the need to adapt the affiliate to the Chinese environment. As Daniel Wen explained, "WORLDWIDE believes that local leadership should be people who understand China very deeply because this is where they come from."

Understanding China very deeply also involves knowing how to do business in China. Recent works on tacit knowledge, learning and competitive advantage have depicted the knowledge necessary to operate a business as almost ephemeral (Lubit, 2001). It is not.

I asked Dan Truman what he had found to be the best source of the market knowledge that he needed to manage MOTORS' BRONWYN JV in Shanghai, given his earlier comments that Chinese statistics were unreliable, and that market conditions changed rapidly. He gave his usual straightforward answer: "Out in the street . . . just go out and pound the sidewalks with the salespeople. Get to see what they are up against every day." The salespeople in his JV are all Chinese; Dan is the sole expatriate in the 800 person JV that he manages.

Earlier research that surveyed a number of Western companies in China found that most of the companies with their own affiliates in China gave marketing responsibilities to local Chinese employees. One Western manager quoted by the study observed that "It's absolutely mandatory to have [Chinese employees]. We were silly not to understand that" (Bjorkman and Kock, 1995).

In addition to their understanding of Chinese cultures and institutions, Chinese executives also have a considerable advantage over expatriates in gaining the specific knowledge to understand China's markets, and to adapt parent company business strategies to meet the demands of those markets. Thus both the "internal face" and the "external face" require localization of management.

Selection of non-executive staff

"Expatriate versus local" is not an issue in selection of non-executive staff since in no case did I observe any non-executive staff in China who were not local. Also, I did not see any expatriates working in non-executive positions in the Hong Kong offices of the affiliates that I studied.

Liberalization of employment laws in the People's Republic of China has greatly increased the amount of freedom that foreign-invested enterprises have to hire the employees that they want for their businesses, whether WFOE or JV. At the same time, however, the affiliates must deal with the consequences of acquiring or expanding their investments in existing JV that have or had SOE as local partners. One of the consequences of operating with SOE partners is the *danwei* system.

Danwei (literally, "work unit") is a system that originated in government units and SOE during the Mao era. *Danwei* are generally responsible for personnel decisions within an organization, including hiring, firing and transferring employees, and control of employee personnel files. *Danwei* also have important social welfare responsibilities. They provide housing, medical facilities, transportation and other social services for work unit members (Li and Kleiner, 2001). The Mao-era "iron rice bowl" system of job security and cradle-to-grave welfare coverage within SOE was centered on *danwei* (Warner, 1997).

Dan Truman of MOTORS was quite direct about the effects of the "iron rice bowl" and the *danwei*. He related that the largest single staff problem with doing a joint venture with an SOE was that "you get a lot of baggage. You've got people who do not have leadership skills. They are not willing to accept responsibility. They have no initiative . . . when you've got 75–80 percent of your staff not exhibiting any one of those characteristics, you have got some severe problems."

The issue of freedom to hire and fire has a direct bearing on affiliates' choice of entity. The comments of William Lobashevski are representative of the views of every operating company head with whom I spoke:

> *WL*: First of all, to contrast setting up a wholly owned operation, versus getting involved in a JV, where you are inheriting a workforce from an existing operation, there is a fundamental difference because of the people who show up in terms of your job solicitation. The people who show up looking to work with a wholly foreign-owned enterprise are there because they want something different. The old security that used to be acquired by working with an SOE, well, I think that they like the idea of being able to be a bit more creative in their career. That is something that we have really embraced here; trying to tap into the power, particularly in the Shanghai area, of the professional workforce. We have found that this workforce has a lot of creative ability.

Large scale changes in staff are often accomplished through acquiring additional equity in an existing JV. Terence Deng commented that he didn't feel HRM processes in his medical equipment manufacturing JV were still influenced by the legacy of the *danwei* system that prevailed when two Chinese SOE together held a 35 percent interest in the JV:

> *TD*: No, not really. In this joint that is almost gone. I don't see that. I don't feel that; maybe I'm dumb, but I don't feel that. It used to be, but last year or the year before last, my predecessor went through a massive house cleaning before and after we bought off the 25 percent share from aerospace department. Because the people with more seniority, they came from that family. A lot of them are not there anymore.

As noted above, selection of non-executive staff is handled by operating company HRM staff who are all local. The selection processes used are, to the maximum extent permitted by Chinese institutions, globally standard HRM processes employed by the parent throughout the world.

Thus while the question of "who to select" reflects a desire for staff localization, the process of deciding which candidates to select from among local applicants uses global HRM selection processes. Employee training also reflects the implementation of parent company global practices. Training is discussed next.

Training Processes

Without exception, the affiliate heads that I interviewed identified their major challenge within the next five years as hiring, training, developing and retaining Chinese staff. Who to train and what skills and knowledge to impart varied among the parent companies whose affiliates I studied. Therefore, training processes will be described individually for the affiliates of each of them. At the same time, the companies' training objectives and methodology were noticeably similar. Daniel Wen's remarks provide a fair summary:

> *DW*: [W]e do not have a different way of dealing with it [training and development] in China than anywhere else. So we deal with developing leadership in China by focusing on what the needs are, the gaps that we need to fill, and then developing a path of classroom training and networking and succession of work experiences to achieve that objective. This is the same process that we have used in India, as well as in the United States. So, many of our training programs are actually the same ones. Chinese folks participate in global training programs that we have. On account of the fact that China has a bigger gap than some other countries in both commercial culture and language, we may provide specific help on [English] language, for instance to Chinese employees . . . but the methodology is exactly the same. There is no difference.

WORLDWIDE

Daniel Wen's remarks were made in answer to my specific question about training within WORLDWIDE's China organization. As discussed in Chapter 6, WORLDWIDE's long history has emphasized learning, including foundation of the first research laboratory and the first formal management training program with its own campus.

As explained earlier, the company's "initiatives" are implemented globally, and involve all employees. Terence Deng's explanation of how Six Sigma was put into effect within his Beijing Medical Equipment manufacturing JV has been previously quoted at length and the quotations will not be repeated. It is important to recall that Six Sigma was installed through training that did not vary in methodology from that employed at other WORLDWIDE sites. Also, according to Terence, there was no consideration given to the idea that his JV might not be ready for Six Sigma, or that Six Sigma simply could not be implemented in China.

To some observers this may smack of some sort of politically incorrect "cultural imperialism." The executives with whom I spoke had different views, however. In the opinion of one executive with considerable experience in foreign assignments, the idea that "X can't be done in China right now" or that "the Chinese aren't ready for X" simply represented a not very subtle form of racism.[80] The prevailing view within the parent companies of the affiliates that I studied is that internal management processes need to be globally standardized. The training that is required so that these processes are standardized must be delivered in every geographic location where the company has operations.

At the same time, the companies understand that training in China represents a special challenge. Terence Deng was speaking of his WORLDWIDE JV but his comments were echoed by those of executives from other affiliates. At the end of our interview I asked Terence whether he wished to ask me anything or add anything about issues that I had not covered or had not fully followed up. He said that people were the most critical part of his operation:

> *TD*: As far as how to keep them, how to grow them, and more importantly, how to make them part of the global operation, we find this very challenging. Chinese tend to have different ways of thinking, different ways of communicating, compared with Americans and compared with Europeans. They [the Chinese] are very subtle, very humble, most of them. That's the way they are brought up. So because of this, we found it particularly hard, and of course hard because of the need to cross the language barrier, we found it particularly hard for them to get used to this type of environment and to be very process oriented. But this is the way it has to be. This is the challenge for every employee I have here, to open themselves up, to become understood by the global team, to be known by the global people . . . I believe that the same challenge applies to all the multinational companies here in China.

In addition to implementation of its global initiatives, WORLDWIDE conducts both China-task-specific and business-group-specific training. The first type is given to all employees within China; the second is part of global executive training programs.

MOTORS

MOTORS' 40 divisions operate in a decentralized manner and this is reflected in MOTORS' approach to training. With two important exceptions, MOTORS does not have a corporate-level training policy. Training is conducted by the divisions, and individual operating company heads within the divisions (heads of JV and WFOE in China, for example) exercise discretion over training, except in cases where the division mandates job-specific or process-specific training. An example of these would be training programs to enable a factory to qualify for ISO 9000 series or ISO 14000 series certification.[81]

MOTORS does have two corporate-level training programs. Both originate at MOTORS' headquarters and both are delivered to everyone in all divisions of MOTORS. Both serve to disseminate MOTORS' corporate culture in a similar manner as WORLDWIDE uses "initiatives" to disseminate its corporate culture. These programs deal with corporate ethical standards and corporate human resources philosophies.

In response to my question, John Kelly explained the corporate ethical standards training process:

STR: Are there particular published guidelines that are disseminated? You mentioned ethics, business ethics.

JK: Yes, we have a business ethics handbook that is disseminated to every employee at every level.

STR: Is this handbook prepared in many different language versions?

JK: Yes.

STR: What sort of reporting responsibility do you have as far as advising MOTORS headquarters that everybody has received this handbook?

JK: We now have included the dissemination of those books in our annual audit process. Employees must attest that they have read the ethics handbook by signing a page at the back of the book. This signature page is then filed in the personnel files. During our annual audit our external auditors are required to do a random search of the personnel files to make sure that employees have signed this signature page. Because this is a one-time signature, my office conducts refresher seminars at various locales throughout Asia. I've been routinely invited to make ethics presentations at sales and distributor meetings. I think people genuinely want to comply. Sometimes there is confusion as to what "compliance" means and they want their people to comply. So I'd like to reiterate my comment about our ethical standards coming from the top down. Management is engaged in proper conduct because it shows who we are as a company. It is very disruptive if you have a deviation that results in an investigation, either internal or external. It's very disruptive and it could be costly. However, the reputation of MOTORS is such that people do believe that we have to protect the assets of our shareholders and that one of the ways to protect those assets is to conduct ourselves legally.

MOTORS' human resources philosophies are set out in note 77. In discussing these philosophies Corinne Lu emphasized the importance that MOTORS attaches to frequent communication with all employees through something called the "communications pyramid." In addition to reinforcement of the company's human resources philosophies and ethical standards, the communications pyramid is also devoted to making every employee aware of four issues. These are: who are our competitors, what is the nature of the competitive environment, what can each employee do to make MOTORS more competitive, and the means by which each employee's performance is measured in relation to making MOTORS more competitive.

The "pyramid" refers to the frequency of each type of meeting. The base of the pyramid comprises "tool box" meetings, which are held every week or every fortnight. As the name suggests, these meetings deal with issues specific to basic work units. Departmental meetings involve meetings of all staff of functional departments, and take place monthly. "All employee" meetings, involving all employees within a division's operating companies (such as JV or WFOE in China), are held quarterly. There is an annual "state of the business" address by MOTORS' CEO, with supplemental remarks by divisional and operating company heads.

Finally, the detailed planning processes described in Chapter 3 serve to further train managers in MOTORS' corporate culture, just as similar meetings at WORLDWIDE and its business groups serve the same function at that company.

ELECTRONS

ELECTRONS is more centralized than either MOTORS or WORLDWIDE and its training processes reflect this. The following summarizes material presented in detail in Chapter 5.

Every ELECTRONS employee throughout the organization goes through the same training within a short time after being hired to introduce them to the company. In the case of ETCL, which is part of the Technology Manufacturing Group (TMG), continuing training is provided through the work unit. Kyle Urban explained this with respect to the software designers that he manages:

> *STR*: What about training. Do you provide that here, at other ELECTRONS facilities? Elsewhere?
> *KU*: I do both. My job is to technically train, because we are bringing on new staff. Training in how we do design work at ELECTRONS, what our methodologies are. We do this by using a real product so that the design engineers had a good intuitive model of the building blocks of a flash memory.
> *STR*: And this is based on standardized ELECTRONS processes, basically introducing them to how ELECTRONS designs products.
> *KU*: Every ELECTRONS division has a development plan template for each job. Every ELECTRONS employee has a development plan; there are a set of internal classes as far as ELECTRONS culture, how we do work here, how you are expected to behave, legal aspects such as safety. All of that is standard anywhere that you go. Then, for the job itself, that is where my training comes

in. I prepared an introduction to flash memory that has been codified within the division. Basically, it says "You need to understand these things." Here, we don't have senior people to do the mentoring yet, so I was mentor, ran an intense training course, doing in three months what takes a year otherwise. You provide them with enough comfort as to how flash memory is built, and how it works, so that they can go to Folsom [a chip design center in the US]. Then they are put on a design team at Folsom to produce a part of a design. We make sure that the product that they help design there will be a "parent" of a product that will be manufactured in Shanghai. After six months at Folsom, they have had a chance to get integrated into the team, and get to know the Folsom experts who they can contact if they need additional help. After we have run products here for several years, we will be able to do initial training in design at this facility. Until then, we found out through our experiences at the Manila site, that integrating them into a project team of designers at Folsom for training is the best way to proceed. This is in comparison to using visiting lecturers and external training, both of which we have also done.

Training also takes place through the "Copy Exactly" process described earlier. Finally, the numerous cross-organizational meetings serve to disseminate "best known methods" and constitute another training process. This is due both to the nature of the "Copy Exactly" process and to the extensive use of cross-functional teams.

IMIGIS

IMIGIS' Greater China Region (GCR) organization contains a fully developed HRM functional staff, led by John Victors, with broad responsibilities for HRM within China. The business (product) groups, however, have the most influence on training at the operating company level.

As described in Chapter 4, institution of the Six Sigma process along with the accompanying methodology throughout IMIGIS was initiated by the then CEO, Jack Hunter, from US headquarters. The training for and actual implementation of the process takes place within the business groups, however.

William Lobashevski was justifiably proud that the first product produced by IMIGIS anywhere in the world that meets Six Sigma standards was produced by the Shanghai factory that is part of the GCR manufacturing group that he heads. This was accomplished more than four years ago, and since then all IMIGIS products produced in the GCR have achieved that quality level.

Compensation

Among the affiliates studied, the principal factor determining whether compensation policies are globalized or localized is whether executive or non-executive compensation is involved. Before addressing these issues, however, it is necessary to examine an area that has been overlooked in prior research, but directly relates to American MNC preference for using local managers whenever possible. This is the subject of taxation of American expatriates.[82]

US taxation of US citizens working in foreign nations

The greater expense of employing expatriates versus local personnel has been considered in virtually every study done regarding utilization of expatriates by MNC. Additional expenses include salary premiums, home leave expense, housing, children's educational expense, as well as a myriad of other factors involved in trying to replicate, in different host countries, expatriates' home country lifestyle. There is a sizeable additional obstacle to American MNC using US expatriates, however. This obstacle is caused by US tax laws.

Unlike citizens of most other countries, US citizens, whether individuals or corporations, are taxed on their worldwide income (Schenk, 1998, 613). Thus, in the absence of treaties mitigating or removing application of host country taxes, Americans are subject to "double" taxation on the same income. This is partially dealt with in the US Internal Revenue Code by allowing a tax credit (that is, a dollar for dollar reduction), up to certain limits, against the net federal tax liability of US citizens for qualifying taxes paid to foreign countries. Section 911 of the US Internal Revenue Code also provides, for individuals who reside outside the US full-time, an exclusion from US taxable income for up to $US70,000 in salary and an adjusted exclusion for portions of amounts paid to expatriates as reimbursement of foreign housing expenses.

In addition to the unnecessary complexity that afflicts all US citizens, US tax law thus poses a particular HRM problem for US MNC utilizing US citizen employees in foreign countries. Briefly, the problem is this: how does the MNC establish a global expatriate compensation system that is fair to all employees, whether they work in high-tax or low-tax host countries? Due to complexities of US tax law, discussion of which is beyond the scope of this book, neither Section 911 nor the foreign tax credit provision provide complete answers. US MNC have had to develop their own answer. Unfortunately the answer itself has created major HRM problems.[83]

The most commonly employed means of dealing with the problem is to create a system of "tax equalized" compensation. Employees on foreign assignments are compensated as if they are employed in the US headquarters of the MNC. The result is that expatriates in high-tax host countries receive additional compensation, while those in low-tax host countries have their compensation reduced, so that the "after-tax" effect is that everyone will receive the same amount of compensation, regardless of foreign assignment, that (s)he would have received if working at US headquarters. By paying expatriates through the US headquarters payroll, employees are also allowed to participate in company stock option programs and company pension and profit-sharing programs, and also to continue to accrue benefits under the US Social Security (government-administered retirement) system (*The Tax Advisor,* 2001).

In addition to HRM problems with this approach, to be discussed below, the use of tax equalization causes US MNC to incur substantial out of pocket costs. The first cost, which is not insubstantial itself, is the cost of maintaining and administering the program. Although the tax computations are usually "outsourced" to the company's outside auditors, this is not inexpensive. Further, additional internal HRM staff are required to administer the program and interact with the expatriates.

The next area of increased cost is the increased expense of maintaining expatriates due to the need to pay additional compensation to expatriates working in high-tax host countries. If the number of expatriates working in such countries is significant relative to the number working in low-tax host countries, the additional expense can be considerable.

While the tax equalization system has a disarming mechanical simplicity, human nature creates problems. Employees in high-tax host countries that are otherwise desirable places to reside are generally happy to have their visible compensation "grossed up" (to use US tax accounting jargon) to reflect high local tax liabilities. Employees whose visible compensation is reduced because they reside in low-tax host countries are less happy. The degree of unhappiness depends on whether the low-tax host country is an otherwise desirable venue.

The problems created by the tax equalization system for expatriate HRM in US MNC are twofold. First, some employees would rather not accept a foreign assignment if they feel that they will be financially penalized for doing so. Expatriate compensation usually includes reimbursement for expenses such as primary and secondary school education for children and home leave for the entire family. Depending on the size of family and age of children these amounts can sometimes approach the amount of the expatriate's base salary. *Only* salary (to a maximum of $70,000 annually) and, to some extent, housing expenses, are excluded from US taxable income, however.[84]

Second, transferring expatriates between foreign assignments is made more complicated. Employees going between host countries where the local tax rates on individuals are very dissimilar, especially if going between locations that also differ in terms of lifestyle, may resist transfer. Thus the fiscal and psychological consequences resulting from the compensation of US expatriates are an added complication, and expense, of their utilization by US MNC.

Executive compensation

Three of the four parent companies administer executive compensation programs globally. In part, this is due to the aforementioned complexity of compensating US expatriates. At the same time, all of the parent companies also employ "third country nationals," that is, non-US citizens who work in countries other than their home country. US MNC compete with non-US multinational enterprises for executives, and their compensation is set according to generally known regional or global standards.

IMIGIS executive compensation policy is representative. John Victors explained the process:

> *JV*: Things like executive development and executive compensation are very much done on a worldwide basis. In fact, our executive compensation system operates globally and ignores both market practice, and, to some degree, market competitiveness on a country-by-country basis. We just have one variable pay program and the percentages of variable opportunity don't vary based on what is normal practice within a particular country.

The one exception to this pattern among the affiliates I studied is MOTORS. Corinne Lu was emphatic that, just as there was no MOTORS policy on use of expatriates, there was also no MOTORS company-wide expatriate compensation policy. Both employment and compensation of expatriates were matters for the individual divisions to determine. MOTORS does set policy and standards for compensation of expatriates employed by MOTORS itself, of which Corinne, Raj Kumar and Sterling Luo would be examples within MOTORS' Asia-Pacific regional headquarters in Hong Kong.

Also, there are MOTORS policies for both executive compensation and executive development that apply to the top 1,000 corporate and divisional executives. These apply, however, whether the individual is stationed in the US or is an expatriate. Corinne explained that within the divisions themselves there was considerable variation in HRM policies towards expatriates. For example, in some divisions there are a large number of long-term expatriates, by which she meant individuals who were serving beyond the terms of their initial foreign assignments contract.

Non-executive compensation

Within China all of the affiliates studied maintain localized compensation policies for non-executive staff. This is similar to the manner in which American MNC deal with non-executive compensation in other foreign countries.[85] In China, however, non-executive compensation policies are highly localized, in the literal sense of the word. Non-executive compensation varies considerably depending on the location of individual facilities. This is partly a consequence of the absence of a single "Chinese labor market." It is also due to the variability, among China's large, autonomous cities and provinces, of the laws and government regulations applicable to wages and benefits.

According to Corinne Lu, in some areas in China government mandated employee benefits equal almost two-thirds of base salary. For example, in the coastal provinces and in the Beijing and Shenzhen autonomous regions, the typical situation was that total compensation included both base salary and benefits equivalent to 60 percent of the base salary. She also mentioned that in the more underdeveloped inland provinces, base salary plus benefits equal to 35 percent of base was much more commonplace. She repeatedly emphasized the challenge in China of following legal requirements. However, she also emphasized that these requirements, as was just illustrated with the question of the size of the benefits package, tended to vary by province, so that uniform HRM policies, for example compensation policy within the People's Republic of China, simply could not be implemented.

Jim Liu indicated that even as highly centralized an organization as ELECTRONS left compensation to be localized:

STR: In terms of compensation structure, is this set centrally someplace within ELECTRONS, say at headquarters, for overseas operations, or is this something that you have authority to vary, or is there some intermediate person?

JL: That's a good question. We have a central group at ELECTRONS called C&B [compensation and benefits], and we have a C&B philosophy, which is too complicated to get into, but our C&B policy is basically to be competitive with the market. If you asked, "How do you determine your C&B policy?," the simplest answer is "the market." Every geographic location has a different market, so every site has a different C&B. The central C&B group has the expertise, and works with consultants who are doing surveys to establish C&B. Every year, the C&B group proposes to us changes, increases, etc., which I, as site manager, have to approve. At the same time, I have to be "in sync" with it, and to champion it.

John Victors of IMIGIS explained that the localization could also be specific to individual operating units, as well as to geographic locations:

JV: Each business or each factory has a different history. Many of the workers used to work for different state-owned enterprises which had different pay scales and different practices. It is evolving toward more common practices but there are still quite a few legacies that are a little bit different. The other thing is, within China, and again it's starting to change, but you know I could talk about the Philippines and I could talk about the Philippines labor market. However within China I have to talk about the Xiamen labor market, I have to talk about the Shanghai labor market, I have to talk about the Beijing labor market, I have to talk about the Chengdu and the Xian labor market, and what is competitive practice is different. At this point in time, pension programs, social security systems are separate or run by the city, those things are very different. Pay scales between Beijing, Shanghai and Guangzhou seem to be comparable now, such that we're operating under a single pay scale for those three primary cities. But beyond that, we have different pay scales for different cities because they are very different. In China it's basically competitive practice, city by city or municipality by municipality, which sometimes I try to make people [at US headquarters] understand that you have to take a little bit more resources to do these things because everything you do for the whole country in the US we have to do for every city in China.

Managers' Career Mobility

In the affiliates that I studied no other HRM issue was more directly affected by the size and structure of the affiliate's operations in China than the issue of managers' career mobility. All the affiliate heads with whom I spoke mentioned that finding and retaining competent local people is the biggest or one of the biggest challenges that they face. Without exception "finding" and "retaining" were always used together.

Large affiliates have a clear advantage in retaining managers by virtue of their size. They offer more opportunities for advancement within their operating companies in China because they have more managerial jobs to fill. Daniel Wen pointed out that WORLDWIDE has a justifiably excellent reputation for developing managers, and he is absolutely correct. At the same time, WORLDWIDE is one of the largest industrial companies in the world. There are a number of WORLDWIDE business groups operating large businesses in China. Size is not the only organizational design factor that bears on the capacity to retain and develop managers, however. Organizational structure, in conjunction with size, plays an important part as well.

MOTORS is the most decentralized and "divisionalized" company that I studied. Raj Kumar made it clear that "divisionalization" was not an advantage when it came to management development:

> *RK*: When you don't have critical mass in every division then you have problems with human resources . . . where it comes to not having enough human resources, there are problems with divisionalization in Asia. Now once you get to a large enough size, if you have 400 people in your company, then you can move your people around, you can train your people. You have enough mid-level career positions to get good people who can grow up to senior positions. But if you have only 20 people then you have only so many positions. Where will they go?

It should be noted here that while MOTORS has almost 10,000 employees in China, they are spread out among several dozen joint ventures and wholly owned subsidiaries. To open up more job opportunities within the total MOTORS Asia-Pacific operation, Corinne Lu has established a website on which are posted all available management positions within MOTORS Asia-Pacific. Raj Kumar has stressed to division and operating company executives that they should use the website to post their management openings. Yet the divisional structure may continue to be an impediment to the kind of management development process used at IMIGIS. This process was described by John Victors of IMIGIS:

> *STR*: And with respect to taking people across boundaries, whether they are business unit boundaries or geographic boundaries, for example, would business units who are looking for a controller or a factory general manager, would they consult with you about hiring or bringing somebody from a IMIGIS organization outside China?
> *JV*: Yes, certainly at a senior-level position we would look across the organization for opportunities. We have a process called the "gold process" in which people we feel have potential and promotability in particular are kept on a database. We keep online their résumé, their whole background, the assessment of their strengths, and again, their set of competencies, their educational history, their job history is all on a database on which we can do searches for open positions. And for senior-level positions we would do that, for more junior-level positions the HR organization – we just started doing this about six months ago – we post within the sales and marketing and administrative areas, we post all positions across the country so that it is transparent, that there's openings and people can self-nominate. One of the reasons we did that, quite frankly, is because there was a bit of parochialism among some of the business unit leaders and in spite of best intentions, sometimes people are not very willing to give up their best people. I don't know if we're unique in that regard but we try to deal with that.

All of the companies, regardless of size or structure, are already implementing one key process that will provide more career mobility for executives within their respective China operations. They are hiring local managers to the maximum extent possible, and minimizing the use of expatriates. This will create more career advancement opportunities for Chinese managers. These opportunities will also grow concurrently with the growth in China's economy.

CHAPTER SUMMARY

The HRM processes described in this chapter provide clear examples of the basic finding of my research, that is, that the affiliates studied employ management processes that their respective parents employ throughout the world, but that the affiliates simultaneously adapt both strategies and organizational structures to meet the particular needs of doing business in China.

178 HUMAN RESOURCES MANAGEMENT

Within HRM, for example, I have shown that the American global preference for management localization is implemented in China, but with limitations imposed by the need to retain limited expatriate management to lead operating companies until sufficient numbers of local managers are available.

I have shown that training methodologies for introducing processes such as Six Sigma do not vary from methodologies employed in other countries. Yet, at the same time, additional training is provided to bolster language and business skills that Chinese staff may lack as a result of China's institutional legacy.

CHAPTER TEN

Control and Coordination of Money and Factories: Finance and Manufacturing

Introduction

This chapter explores control and coordination of the relatively tangible processes of recording and transmitting financial data and transferring money, as well as designing and manufacturing products. Both functions represent a high degree of parent–affiliate integration. This integration is in terms of parental specification of standards used in the respective processes, whether it be use of generally accepted accounting practices (GAAP) in the preparation of financial statements, or the employment of Six Sigma, ISO or "Copy Exactly" standards for manufacturing operations. The chapter contrasts the finance function, representing the least degree of differentiation in terms of adapting financial processes to the Chinese environment, with manufacturing. The analysis distinguishes between manufacturing process standards – those used by the parent globally (the "internal face") – and manufacturing strategies exemplified by content localization and product development that are adapted to the needs of China's markets (the "external face").

Finance

Control of acquisition and disbursement of capital

Regardless of the structure of the individual affiliates and their respective parents, acquisition and disbursement of capital are centralized and controlled at the headquarters of each parent. All of the parents are publicly held (that is stock exchange quoted) corporations. Given the legal and financial realities of operating such companies in America, the acquisition and disbursement of capital must be centrally managed and controlled, even in an otherwise decentralized organization such as the MOTORS divisional structure.

Yan, Child and Lu (1995, 21) observed that the traditional concept of business ownership is that of a legal right, obtained by the provision of capital for the enterprise being financed, that carries with it the further right to determine the policies of the business being financed, and how it is managed. The financial structures of the affiliates studied here reflect this concept.

In each of the affiliates studied, the US parent provides the capital and controls its allocation, thus effectively controlling the affiliate. William Lobashevski gave a concise explanation that, although related to IMIGIS, applies to all the affiliates studied: "Whoever controls the cash, controls the decision making process." In IMIGIS, as with the other parent companies, capital is centrally controlled from headquarters, and disbursed through either the product groups or, in MOTORS' case, the divisions.

William Lobashevski's remarks are similar to those offered more than 25 years ago by a former financial manager of British Ford. When asked whether the English subsidiary was controlled by the US parent, he answered that one controls a company through control of its capital expenditure, and that, in British Ford's case, this was controlled by the American management in Detroit through American managers in the UK (Tindall, 1975, 166).

The control of capital by the parents has also involved provision of working capital, usually direct from the US. This has been a practical necessity as well as a control mechanism, however. In the past, home country originated short-term lending by the parent has been necessary for many foreign-invested enterprises (FIE) in China. This was due to both legal and practical obstacles that restrict FIE lending to other China affiliates, obstacles to use of the domestic banking system, as well as by the undeveloped nature of the institutional infrastructure needed to support business lending.[86]

Accounting for and reporting of transactions

The respective parent of each of the affiliates studied has shares that are traded on the New York Stock Exchange or on the NASDAQ. Thus the parents are all subject to the US securities laws. Their financial reports must be filed with the US Securities Exchange Commission (SEC), and must be prepared and presented under the GAAP format. The processes used to account for and report transactions by the affiliates to the parents are almost identical for all of the affiliates studied. The common elements are summarized as follows:

- Company accounts are kept pursuant to GAAP supported by the parent's globally uniform accounting system.
- Accounts required for reports to Chinese fiscal authorities are kept according to regulations established by the respective local, regional and national tax administrations.
- Outside auditors are selected by the parent company headquarters. The affiliate has no authority to independently alter that choice. Outside audit services are

provided by the China offices of one of the "Big Five" US multinational public accounting firms. Usually the same Big Five firm will have a global engagement to provide auditing on a worldwide basis for the parent.

- Regardless of whether the structure is divisional, business/product group or "stand alone," each affiliate produces detailed financial reports on at least a monthly basis to the affiliate management as well as to the parent's headquarters financial organization.
- In addition to review by outside auditors, China affiliates are visited regularly by parent company internal auditors to review compliance with company auditing standards, as well as compliance with the reporting requirements of US laws such as the Foreign Corrupt Practices Act. Outside auditors also review compliance with reporting requirements imposed by US law.
- Preparation of budgets, financial plans and capital expenditure requests are also part of the duties of affiliates' financial officers.

Processes for controlling and coordinating manufacturing processes display a similar uniformity among the affiliates studied. Manufacturing strategies vary among the affiliates studied, however.

Manufacturing

The global standards successfully applied by the affiliates in their manufacturing operations in China, such as Six Sigma, "Copy Exactly" and ISO 9000 and ISO 14000, have already been discussed in detail in the case studies and will not be repeated here. At this point it is only necessary to recall that these global standards have been applied successfully, in full, without adjusting the processes for the notion that "this is China and we can't do that here."

Analyses of the necessity of making adjustments in global strategies, for example management localization, have identified shortages in Chinese resources such as the shortage of trained Chinese managers as causing the necessary adjustments within China. Manufacturing represents a different situation.

The parents of the affiliates studied have adjusted their global manufacturing strategies with respect to China. The adjustments, however, have principally been to take advantage of Chinese human resources. Contrary to popular belief, the human resources in question are not millions of unskilled laborers working for pennies or pence a day.

Rather, the human resources are an abundance of technically trained engineers and skilled factory workers, whose compensation levels are very low relative to those for similarly qualified people in industrialized nations, although not low by Chinese standards (Wonacott, 2002a). The affiliates have been successful in taking advantage of relatively low-cost engineering and technical staff to build manufacturing capabilities within China that have changed the global manufacturing strategies of their parents. To understand the process it is first necessary to discuss changes in MNC manufacturing strategies, and the effects of those changes on MNC manufacturing strategies in China.

Global manufacturing

Following the end of the Second World War, worldwide improvement in living standards and high tariff barriers encouraged MNC to build factories outside their home countries to supply growing foreign markets. For many MNC from industrialized countries, factories in foreign countries or "international production" replaced the "manufacture for export from the home country" manufacturing strategy.

By the 1970s two developments drove the change to what became known as multinational production rationalization. Gradual removal of trade barriers made it financially possible for MNC to move components among factories in different countries, and to centralize assembly of particular products at factories specializing in that product. Containerization of ocean freight shipping made the process physically possible. Yves Doz (1978) gave the process a name: "manufacturing rationalization."

Doz's research indicated that rationalization was needed where the product produced was subject to price competition, and where the product was standardized on a global basis. Thus the impetus for rationalization was to find the lowest-cost host country to site global production facilities, provided that the host country had the necessary infrastructure to support such factories and their communications and logistics requirements.

Manufacturing rationalization is still a valid concept. It is, however, no longer restricted to price sensitive, globally fungible products. Thanks to electronic data interchange, first over private networks and now over the Internet, almost any product can be designed at a location, or collaboratively at several different locations throughout the world. Thus, finding the most cost-effective site now involves more than just finding the lowest-cost manufacturing site. The ideal location is one that combines low production costs and technical staff who are competent to design products and whose compensation is low relative to comparable home country or third country personnel. Enter China.

Changes in the affiliate's manufacturing strategies in China

Although he was speaking only of the WORLDWIDE ME factories that he now leads, Terence Deng's description of the evolution of the manufacture of CT equipment in China represents the process that other affiliates also went through in adjusting their China manufacturing strategies. He explained that his factory was originally established to avoid the institutional and tariff barriers to importation of medical equipment into China in the early 1990s:

TD: CT is a controlled item for importing into China. So for these many years we mainly did what we call the SKD. SKD means "semi-knockdown." Semi-knockdown means you assemble machine 100 percent somewhere in Japan or US, most of them actually in Japan. Then we tear it apart, not in detail, but some big portion, bring it back to China, we screw them together, send them to test, put on a new label, sell it in China. That gives us mainly, not necessarily a tax advantage, that is not really the one we are looking for. It gives us the flexibility of being able to participate most particularly in a tendering system. After all, government in China they favor local factories, local people, local joint venture compared with 100 percent import and so there's a reason these places exist. Very limited engineering competency except try to do a small scale modification of the product to make it a little more localized. That's a small scale of localization in terms of material. That's what we've been doing for eight and a half years. Starting in 1999 we changed. All of a sudden this place became part of the global organization.

I asked Terence whether, after the change to what is known within WORLDWIDE as the "global product company" or just "GPC," his JV did more manufacturing rather than assembly:

TD: I don't know how you classify manufacturing or assembly. We are considered manufacturing from our perspective, but you're looking at the operations from more a production management point of view, from the business school's point of view. [Terence holds a PhD in industrial engineering from a leading US university.] We are an assembly plant. We are a high-level assembly plant. We rarely do any low-level assembly here. There are parts that come from all over the place, for example I have one machine which is an X-ray system – 712 parts in that particular machine. How many do we make? We make zero. WORLDWIDE makes zero products. I have a generator that comes from India made by a WORLDWIDE plant, but that plant, they make nothing, they buy everything and put it together, and make it a generator and send it to me. I purchase 122 parts from China and I purchase the rest of the parts from all over the world. It can be anywhere. Then we put it together here. Because I am, what we call the system plant. The system plant being the last people, the last people to touch the system. From here it goes directly to the customer.

Terence used WORLDWIDE nomenclature when describing his factory as a system plant. The concept includes factories that are called "server," "contributor" and "outpost" in Ferdows' (1997) typology of global manufacturing facilities. Ferdows identifies six types of factory: offshore, established to gain access to low-wage labor, or other factors integral to low-cost production; source, established for the same reason as the offshore but with sufficient resources and expertise to produce a component or product for global markets; server, which exists to serve a particular national or regional market; contributor, which is a server that has the capability to develop, modify or customize products; and outpost, established primarily to gain access to knowledge or skills that the MNC needs. Finally, a lead factory has the ability and knowledge to create new processes, products and technologies for the parent MNC.

Terence described his factories' role in the ME "global product company" concept in reference to localization of components as well as product design:

> *TD*: We have 37 factories globally. Fifteen of them, I think it's about 15, are system plants, like the two I have here in Beijing. The rest of them are what we call a feeder plant. Feeder plants they make large components, not small components, large components like a generator, all that kind of stuff. And they send it to us, and so that part I have no decision at all. For other parts, I get to make decision and we get to decide on whether we want to do it locally or not, and that, it depends on the local supplier and we try to localize as much as possible. Some of my products they are 100 percent localized. That means everything is purchased in China, put on the label, then send it out globally. That tends to be more low end on the technology side. For the system, it also depends. Some of them can go all the way up to 60 percent localized, 60 percent means everything except the major component, which would come from Japan, India, France, US.
>
> But some of the newer developed equipment, they can start with maybe 25 percent. The target is 50–60 percent and that is what we call localization from the system point. But my sourcing operation has separated into two different kinds, or styles. Part of my sourcing, after we put together the GPC, we started to grow our engineering capability. So right now we are designing, not only transferring. There are four stages, really. You transfer the product, you localize the product, you "value engineer" the product, and you design the product bottom up. Some of this, like my X-ray operation, we are able to do the bottom up design, we design everything here; sourcing will be a big part of it because design is such a tedious operation so you need sourcing to be a big part of this because you have to get whatever component that you have to have in order to put the product together, to test it, and then to go. So I have a whole team of sourcing people who do that part. And when the product becomes mature, that means starting mass production. These sourcing teams will turn this prototype supplier into the logistics department and then they become, say, a regular supplier. So these are the results of our efforts from the sourcing side.

I followed up by asking Terence whether, by design localization, he was referring to design to meet the demands of the local Chinese market:

> *TD*: No, *we design for global*. Like one of my X-ray machine design teams started the work in the beginning of last year and by the fourth quarter, we shipped about 220 pieces of equipment. None of them in China, because at that time WORLDWIDE China did not even have a license to sell. Seventy-five percent

of the machines were sold in the US. The rest of them went everywhere, Europe and particularly in South America. This year for only the first quarter we produced 150 of the machines. Total yearly plan is 550 to 600. It will be about the same percentage shipped out. China, now that we started selling, we're looking at 12 machines of that kind for the China market this year because we just got a license about two weeks ago. And that's what we talk about. Good engineering means they learn, they know, and of course with the help from the global team. (emphasis added)

Terence's remarks were echoed by Dan Truman of MOTORS' BRONWYN Shanghai joint venture:

STR: Does this JV manufacture for export?
DT: Yes it does.
STR: And does that go to other BRONWYN or MOTORS companies?
DT: It goes within BRONWYN worldwide. *That was not the original charter of this operation. The original charter was to be a domestic manufacturer for the Chinese market. It has all changed because the quality level that we're producing now is up to world class standards and now you can export to Japan and they'll accept. Or you can send it to the US and they'll accept it . . . We're currently designing product for BRONWYN North America here, from scratch . . .*
[T]o get a CAD mechanical engineer in the US you're going to have to pay him a minimum of $50,000 and he probably won't even stay. It's more like $65,000–$75,000 to get someone that's even fair. Here you can get someone for a fraction of that who is outstanding and wants to be here and loves it. It's air-conditioned, it's run by Americans, this is a great company, life is good. So that being said, where does it make sense to do your engineering? In the US or perhaps here? Or India? Or wherever you can get it done. I mean, the Internet is great. I can send a CAD file back to New Jersey in about 14 seconds. And it really makes a big difference. Time to market and cost are the two real advantages that working here give you. That's providing you have the quality matrix in place to ensure that the work that's done here is done to standards that are going to be accepted on the receiving end. And fortunately we do. (emphasis added)

Terence Deng has similar views on the professional resources available in China:

TD: In our industry, except for some of the feeder plants, in some components, labor cost is not more than 10 percent of total cost. Labor is nothing. And so moving to China, if we only consider labor, we're kidding ourselves. We are moving here because we want the people. We want the people who are engineers. We have the best engineers in the world and with a very competitive salary, abundance of materials, abundance of qualified good suppliers here in China, and that is where our hope is.

Chinese universities annually grant engineering degrees to 37 percent of their graduates. In the US the comparable figure is 6 percent (Wonacott, 2002a). Jim Liu explained ELECTRONS' reasons for building the Pudong factory this way:

> *JL:* And, if you look at ELECTRONS, the reason that we're here [in Pudong] is the China market, and then you ask, "How do you know that you're maximizing your presence here?" And another reason that we're here, that I didn't mention before but that I want to mention now, is that we are facing a worldwide shortage of very competent high-tech people, and we can get our share in China. China certainly has very good universities that can produce such people, so . . . we are expected to help ELECTRONS deal with the crunch in high-tech resources.

Manufacturing in China and protecting intellectual property

There is one important aspect of the Chinese institutional environment that works against implementation of global manufacturing strategies in China. This is the lack of protection for intellectual property, including proprietary manufacturing technology. Wally Moon, the General Manager of MOTORS' STORMONT affiliate in Shanghai, explained how concerns over protection of proprietary technology affected his joint venture's operations:

> *WM:* As I said earlier, the joint venture was originally envisioned as being STORMONT's single window into China and it has now evolved into a couple of different STORMONT divisions. One of those is the Flow Control and there's a fine line that this division is not really willing to go over. That has to do with supplying technology and intellectual property that cannot be protected in China, so [here] we do some assembly, some light manufacturing, we weld flanges, and we do all of the high-accuracy flow calibration. But the core technology of that product has not been transferred to the JV. Instead, it is still actually manufactured in the United States.
> The Beijing JV, on the other hand, produces the STORMONT transmitters. The only place [in the world] that this transmitter is manufactured today is in that JV in Beijing. But it is an older technology. The newer technology is not manufactured in China. There remains a great deal of risk in the choice of technology that you bring into China. What you can afford to have cloned or stolen. Can you protect it?

According to Wally and several other executives with whom I spoke, changes in Chinese law contemplated as necessary for WTO entry would actually have to be implemented and enforced before changes were made in MNC policies that militate against transferring advanced technology to China. As shown in Chapter 2, enforcement of intellectual property protection in China continues to be a serious problem for MNC.

CHAPTER SUMMARY

In both the finance and manufacturing functions of the affiliates studied, global standards dominate how processes within these functions are done, in other words "how to do it." In finance, "what gets done," that is, the nature and extent of financial reports, as well as the identities of those within and outside the affiliate who prepare and review those reports, is also globally standardized. It is fair to say that the finance function within the affiliates studied is the least affected by the fact that the affiliates operate within China. This is also true of the national origin of chief financial officers of the affiliates' operating companies, almost all of whom are expatriates.

In contrast, "what gets done" in the manufacturing function, that is, the manufacturing strategies of the affiliates within China, is very much affected by China's markets, and resources. The affiliates have gone from using their Chinese factories solely to serve local markets to integration of these factories into their respective global production networks.

This has been facilitated by the presence of technically educated, highly motivated Chinese, whose services can be obtained at a much lower cost compared with compensation in industrialized countries. It is not my intention, however, to portray contemporary China as a "workers' paradise" for engineers and technicians. It is not.

The same edition of the *Wall Street Journal* that reported on the abundant numbers of and employment prospects for Chinese engineers also carried a story, by the same journalist, reporting a siege of the offices of a subsidiary of PetroChina, a large SOE, by workers angry over being discharged (Wonacott, 2002b). In addition to the redundancies caused by restructuring, the relative decline of the SOE sector has weakened the entire *danwei* concept (Eckholm, 2001).

China's institutional environments are markedly different from what US MNC have encountered in other countries. The final cross-case comparison chapter discusses control and coordination of the affiliates' respective responses to those environments.

CHAPTER ELEVEN

Control and Coordination of Responses to China's Institutional Environments

Introduction

The scope and nature of the interaction between the affiliates studied here and China's institutional environments are governed by the affiliates' respective globally uniform policies establishing standards for the ethical conduct of business. These policies are internal standards to which the affiliates' officers and employees must comply. Yet, although internal, they control what staff may and may not do in the external environments.

The strategies used by the affiliates for permissible interaction with China's institutional environments are highly localized, however, as are the executives who bear primary responsibility for daily interaction with these environments. The globally uniform policies will be discussed first, followed by consideration of the local strategies used for permissible interaction. Local strategies will be illustrated by discussion of the affiliates' manner of interacting with *guanxi*.

Standards of Conduct

The US Foreign Corrupt Practices Act (FCPA) has been described earlier. The focus in this section is on how observance of its requirements is implemented by the affiliates. Each of the affiliates studied has processes in place whereby compliance with both FCPA and company standards of business conduct are monitored, and periodic, continuing education in FCPA and company business standards is supplied. John Kelly's explanation of the processes for MOTORS, also discussed in Chapter 3, is representative of the affiliates' practices. The affiliates do not limit their efforts solely to their staff, as John Kelly explained:

> *JK*: When we initially begin our negotiations for these joint ventures, part of the contract contains provisions dealing with how or what laws and regulations

and type of ethical standards we are going to engage in. We spend a considerable amount of time explaining those to the partner so that they are never uncomfortable with, or at a loss for, what we will or will not do. We actually have ethics handbooks that we present to them at the initial negotiating stage that show the standards that we will hold the employees to. And it's always an entertaining conversation when trying to explain to them how the US Foreign Corrupt Practices Act or import/export laws govern their activities, for instance, in places as remote as Luding or other places. But it is an educational process. We do set the standards early and then we monitor them to make sure that they do comply with the standards. Under no circumstances do we ever leave it gray or in any way encourage any type of deviation from that.

Dan Truman described how MOTORS' policies worked in practice:

DT: To this day it is not uncommon to have a purchasing agent ask for a commission from you, the manufacturer, in order to place an order with your company. Now, that is illegal for us to do . . . there are laws that say you can't do that. Consequently, when we find ourselves in a position like that we walk away from that business. And it's a conscious decision we've made.

STR: And certainly a wise decision and there are lot of examples. [Naming a European MNC] the most recent, was not following ethical practices . . . very damaging.

DT: You'll find that there are Europeans who tend to disregard that and will play that game. American companies won't do it. I don't believe General Motors does that. I know Ford and Chrysler certainly don't do it. There's a variety of market segments here. There are your multinationals which GM and Ford would certainly be. And then there are your Chinese state-run factories. Well, if you sell to a state-run factory you're not going to get paid anyway. So we don't target those people. And they don't have any money. So not only are they not going to pay you, they're not going to buy at the beginning. Who do you sell to? You sell to either privately owned companies or multinationals. And those [companies] play by the rules.

Osland and Bjorkman (1998) have observed that Chinese officials, just as those in other countries, seem to respect MNC that fulfill their promises and act with integrity. John Kelly's remarks support that view:

JK: I can only speak for MOTORS but I've heard people talk about having to provide bribes or kickbacks, as harsh as those words may sound, in order to do business in China. Candidly and honestly, although corruption is rampant in China, we have not experienced that. We are a multinational that has a reputation for not engaging in those activities. Luckily, to date, we have not experienced any type of overt or covert attempts at bribes or kickbacks. *We may have the advantage of being a US company, in that PRC nationals realize that there is a Foreign Corrupt Practices Act and they understand that bribes and kickbacks are not acceptable types of business conduct for American companies.* So when people ask me about providing bribes and kickbacks in order to do business, I answer that we don't. To date we haven't experienced these types of transactions, so, knock on wood, I consider ourselves quite fortunate. (emphasis added)

While the interactions between the affiliates and China's institutional environment are governed by globally uniform policies, the strategies for permissible interaction with those environments, and the executives responsible for interaction, are both localized. These areas are considered next.

Interacting with Institutional Environments

The strategies for interacting with institutional environments, as well as the executives responsible for those interactions, are localized with respect to all of the affiliates studied. The focus of the interactions varies, depending on the business needs of the individual affiliate. Each affiliate will be briefly considered in turn.

ELECTRONS

Shao is Deputy Site Manager for Public Affairs at the ETCL WFOE in Shanghai. He reports to Jim Liu, the General Manager. He is a Chinese citizen, as are all of his six staff. The Beijing office of ELECTRONS China, Ltd, the holding company for ELECTRONS' China investments, is responsible for dealing with the central government. Shao is responsible for all government relations work for ETCL in Shanghai, with both local government and the Shanghai offices of central government agencies. According to Shao he has very little interaction with ELECTRONS China, Ltd., unless Beijing asks him to help with something that involves Shanghai. He gave an example of assisting Beijing:

S: ELECTRONS, when we do manufacturing, we will ask our subcontractors to do some processes for us; let's say for the flash, we have some people doing subassembly for us, then these are shipped back to us in Shanghai for assembly and test, and then exported. Well, one of these subcontractors is not in the Pudong Foreign Trade Zone, but outside of it. This is a long time, high-quality, low-cost, supplier for us. But Shanghai tax people stepped in, and said "Hey, you are getting material duty free, conditional on you using the material to manufacture for export, but you aren't exporting, so we have to charge you sales tax." I got a request from ELECTRONS Beijing to work with the local government to see what we could do. Well, we had to follow local policy in the short term, and this involved the subcontractor shipping to Hong Kong and then back to Shanghai! Later, we were able to get the whole question referred to a different tax office, and things were resolved in a satisfactory manner.

WORLDWIDE

Daniel Wen is National Executive for WORLDWIDE in China and Daniel's job involves, in his words, "being the executive on behalf of WORLDWIDE facing the nation." Daniel is a US citizen of Chinese ancestry. He has several WORLD-WIDE executives working in government and public affairs in Beijing reporting to him; all of them are Chinese citizens. The government and public affairs function is centralized at Beijing and, as National Executive for China, Daniel Wen reports directly to the Vice Chairman of WORLDWIDE responsible for WORLDWIDE International.

As discussed in the case analysis, China is regarded as critically important to WORLDWIDE's global success. James Walls, the now retired CEO of WORLD-WIDE, was a frequent visitor, and his successor visited many times while head of WORLDWIDE Medical Equipment (ME), the position he held just prior to being named CEO. Daniel, however, made it clear that he was the first and principal resource that WORLDWIDE management looked to for counsel on the company's relations with China's institutional environments.

IMIGIS

The CEO of IMIGIS' Greater China Region (GCR) as well of the Greater Asia Region (GAR), of which GCR is a part, is Henry Peterson, a European. He is also IMIGIS' National Executive for the People's Republic of China. Henry's responsibilities as National Executive are quite similar to those of Daniel Wen, but with a historical difference.

IMIGIS' entry into China was personally directed and led by Jack Hunter, its then CEO. It was he who negotiated the agreement with the central government, discussed earlier, that resulted in IMIGIS investing over one billion US dollars in China. He continued to be directly involved in interaction with Chinese officials through frequent visits to China, and his successor has maintained this close involvement. Henry Peterson and his staff are directly responsible for day-to-day contact with all levels of Chinese government and media. At the same time, John Victors remarked to me that "China is the most visited country in the world" in terms of visits by IMIGIS' top management, so the tradition of direct involvement by senior headquarters executives, begun by Jack Hunter, has continued. By the same token, however, local executives in China are responsible for day-to-day interaction, and advising headquarters and local business units on strategic issues.

MOTORS

The interaction between MOTORS, its subsidiaries and their operating companies in China, on the one hand, and China's institutional environments, on the other hand, is the most centralized business function in what is otherwise a decentralized organization.

Sterling Luo and Raj Kumar have direct personal involvement in and responsibility for this activity, and, as noted in Chapter 3, John Kelly is responsible for all MOTORS' units complying with the FCPA as well as with MOTORS' standards of conduct. Assisting Sterling and Raj with respect to China is a MOTORS executive who is a Chinese citizen, residing in China, who travels throughout the nation and maintains daily contact with all levels of media and government.

The accession of China to the WTO does promise dramatic changes to China's institutional environments. At the same time, institutions of ancient origin may be less affected. One of these institutions is *guanxi*, which is the subject of the last section of this chapter.

How the Affiliates Deal with *Guanxi*

Discussion of *guanxi* here is in terms of its meaning to the affiliate executives with whom I spoke, their perceptions of its effects on their businesses, and what they did in response to those effects.

Guanxi *and geography*

As described in Chapter 2, the meaning of *guanxi* is subject to geographic differences in interpretation between rural and urban regions of China itself (Yang, 1994, 76–8). Daniel Wen illustrated how he perceived the differing influence of *guanxi* in the latter case:

> *DW*: [W]hen you go to one part of China sometimes folks from another part of China are regarded as "foreigners" and so it's very difficult to generalize about China. [But] I would think that in areas with a high degree of local protectionism *guanxi* is very important. In areas with very open economic thinking, it becomes less important.

How executives define guanxi

The lack of a Chinese language definition of the term has not stopped either academics or business journalists from supplying their own definitions. An American executive who has worked in China for many years defines it as "connections" (De Mente, 1994, 218). Another US executive defined it in terms of "grease" (Seligman, 1999). This word has two meanings in American slang; applying lubrication so that something goes smoothly, and "greasing the palm" which means giving a bribe.

Guanxi, as understood by the executives with whom I spoke, does *not* involve bribery. Shao, the Deputy Site Manager for Public Affairs at ETCL, provided one definition:

STR: Please give me your views on *guanxi*, how important is it now, to do business.

S: It is important but it cannot do everything for you. For example, if we don't know each other, the first time contact is difficult, to trust each other is difficult. But if I already know you, there is some kind of *guanxi*, so, you have to maintain *guanxi*, but you have to define it properly. It is not money; specifically, when the PRC really realized that things are wrong with doing business in *guanxi*, now there are all kinds of written law to prohibit what we call "power and money trading"; to use money to buy power. *Guanxi* means that we trust each other, and help each other, but that help is not based on money. It is based on achieving a "win–win" situation; doing things that are to both parties' benefits. When I call somebody, they recognize my voice imme-diately. This is a big help. But even if you have good *guanxi*, if you are ELECTRONS, you still don't violate the law.

When I deal with local government, I do so on a basis of trust. I want them to know that I trust them, and to let them also trust me. Because if there is no trust, then you are in big trouble. (emphasis added)

Shao provided what I call the "businessperson's definition" of *guanxi*: the concept of reciprocal assistance based on trust, established through direct, personal inter-action. Daniel Wen provided another:

DW: But if you think about what *guanxi* is, it is the Chinese equivalent of what we would call networking and therefore, graduating from a certain school sometimes can be a key factor of success because of the people you know and the access you have. And I think that's similar in China. And it is a very involved thing, that. Chinese businesses tend to want to do business with entities that they know and trust. The same applies to British or American businesses. From that principle, what is perceived as *guanxi* becomes very important for foreign companies that do not in themselves have the ability to establish a very local level of trust with the businesses that they are dealing with. I think that if companies are able to overcome this gap then it should become easier for them to actually better determine what pieces of *guanxi* are still more important, is more important for that business, meaning the relation-ships that it, as a corporate entity, does not yet have. But should be developing by itself. And what they have acquired from the outside from what pieces they already do have as a local operating entity. I think all entities, regardless of how much share is owned by foreigners, ultimately work in a local environment in China. And so how successful they are depends on how much they are sensitive to the local environment.

The continuing importance of guanxi

The comments of Shao and Daniel Wen reflect the view that *guanxi* is still important to the conduct of business in China. Part of this continuing importance is that having *guanxi* avoids complete reliance on uncertain institutional environments. As noted earlier, in the PRC *guanxi* often acts as a defensive mechanism to replace or substitute for the legal relationships that structure Western business transactions as well as the interactions between Western businesses and government regulators (Yang, 1994; Xin and Pearce, 1996; Luo, 1997).

Dan Truman reflected a view of *guanxi*'s importance different from that of Shao and Daniel Wen. His perspective was that of someone not born in China, or of Chinese ancestry, but who had worked in China for some time. He provided a detailed answer to my question:

DT: Years ago, and when I say years ago, it could've been 20 minutes ago, I mean, [things] here are very, very dynamic and they change so quickly. You probably needed it five years ago. You certainly don't need it today in order to run a profitable business here.

STR: Does that reflect, I don't know how you would put it, that a real market economy is developing in China?

DT: I think it always had a market economy. Even back during the darkest throes of communism . . . the economy was really, really entrenched, honestly it had Chinese characteristics but these people are very, very much money oriented. You've probably seen it yourself. You give someone one square meter here and they'll open a business. They'll throw a blanket down . . . and on a table they'll have a couple of broken batteries and a couple of used batteries and they'll be out there trying to hawk them. And my hat's off to these guys. But it very much is a capitalistic society and the government will do whatever it takes to get foreign investment here. In the past they were very protective of their industries but now I think they realize that they really don't have a heck of a lot of choice. Maybe there are a few industries, i.e. telecommunications and perhaps automotive, to a lesser degree, that they're still somewhat protective of. But as for the rest of them I think they'd rather have you than not so they'll welcome you with open arms. If you were to come here with $500 million and want to open a factory, you can get land for free in western China and they'll probably give you tax abatements for 100 years. They so desperately want western China developed.

CHAPTER SUMMARY

We have seen that the affiliates studied interact with China's institutional environments pursuant to globally standardized codes of conduct. At the same time, the strategic management of those interactions, as well as the people responsible for managing those interactions, are both localized.

This research took place prior to China's accession to the WTO. Some of the quoted interviews with executives touched on what the WTO might mean to China's institutional environments; however all of the interviewees denied any predictive abilities.

Peter Drucker has observed that:

> It is possible – and fruitful – to identify major events that have already happened, irrevocably, and that will have predictable effects in the next decade or two. It is possible, in other words, to identify and prepare for the future that has already happened.

> *(in Ireland and Hitt, 1999, 43)*

With those words in mind, it is appropriate to conclude this chapter with Shao's observations concerning the changes over the last decade in China's institutional environments, as those changes affect foreign enterprises in China. His remarks reflect trends in Chinese institutional attitudes towards foreign investors noted in earlier research (Pearson, 1991; Yan, Child and Lu, 1995):

> S: Well, let me put it this way. China has realized that in order to implement the Open Door policy, to really attract more and more foreign investment, the government has had to adapt its policies. For example, when you are in the FTZ [Foreign Trade Zone], the government is not going to load you down with a lot of restrictions; the whole idea of the FTZ is to help make it easier for FIE to do business in China. So the environment has changed over time so that the government has made it easier for multinationals to do business here.
> I worked for a JV for almost 10 years. Why did Lucent want a JV? Because sales channels were still controlled by the government. Also, when Lucent established the JV labor was not free, in terms of ability to hire on the local labor market. So, if you wanted to get good people you needed a Chinese partner, that could help get these problems solved. The market is now open, the labor market is open, universities are open, to hire graduates. All these things are open, and it is much more easy to do business here.

Conclusion: Informing the Theory and Practice of Control and Coordination in the Multinational Corporation

The evidence from the Chinese affiliates of the US MNC studied here shows that the affiliates are managed so that they are simultaneously integrated into the MNC global organization and also responsive to the needs of China's unique markets.[87]

The affiliates studied are managed internally (their "internal face") using management processes developed by their respective parents through prior global experience, and transferred to and implemented within the China affiliate in ways that result in the processes not meaningfully varying from the processes used by the parent's other affiliates worldwide.

At the same time, the processes by which the affiliate deals with China's markets[88] (the affiliates' "external face") involve adapting organizational forms and strategies to meet the demands of those markets.

The research findings reflect knowledge gleaned from many hours of interviews with MNC executives. In summary: "We manage in China the same as we do in other countries, but approach China's markets using strategies and organizational structures differently than we might in other countries."

We will first review the issues that were presented for analysis in the Introduction, and summarize the findings presented. We will then address the question "What is likely to change?" in terms of both MNC internal management processes (the "internal face") and the processes by which MNC deal with China's unique institutional environments (the "external face"). This will involve consideration of developments within and outside China from now until the end of the decade.

The Issues and the Findings

- *What are "control" and "coordination," and how do they interact in the management control process?* The precise definitions of the terms "control" and "coordination" lay the groundwork for development of a new theory of management control built on a meaningful distinction between the two terms. Management control has two elements: one of direction, represented by control, and the other of volition, represented by coordination. Both are needed for management control processes to be effective within a global organization, as the example of MNC compliance with the US Foreign Corrupt Practices Act demonstrated.

- *How are control processes used to control and coordinate the operations of the China affiliates of US MNC studied here, and how, if at all, does their use vary depending on the nature of the control process?* As demonstrated in the case studies and Chapter 7, management control processes are used to enable MNC to simultaneously integrate their China affiliates into the parents' global operations, while permitting the affiliates to remain responsive to China's unique economic, political, social and business environments. Both the control processes that prior studies have categorized as "bureaucratic" and which I refer to as management "routines," and the "normative" control processes which I subsume under the rubric "shared values," are employed. Management routines are exemplified by the parents' global management processes, and shared values are exemplified by the parent MNC's corporate culture. Corporate culture was revealed as a significant contributor to the successful implementation of the respective parent's global management processes, without relying on a large staff of expatriate managers.

- *Do the control processes vary among the four different business function areas studied within each affiliate, that is, human resources management, financial control, manufacturing, and governmental relations?* As explained in Chapters 8 through 11, employment of management control processes does vary depending on the business function. At the same time, these chapters and the case studies both describe the common elements present across business functions – elements that have not been identified in earlier studies. The common elements may be understood in terms of the differentiation developed in this thesis, between the "internal face" and the "external face" of the China affiliates studied. With regard to the "internal face," the affiliates are managed internally using management processes, including management control processes, that do not meaningfully vary from the processes used by the parent's other affiliates worldwide. At the same time, the processes by which the affiliates deal with China's markets and social institutions, their "external face," involve adaptation of organizational forms and strategies to meet the demands of those markets. As part of the adaptation, management control processes are employed differently across functions and within functions.

- *Do the parent MNC utilize the same control processes for their China affiliates as they employ to control and coordinate the activities of affiliates in other foreign countries?* The four companies use the same control processes for their China affiliates as for other affiliates worldwide. Evidence for this is presented in the case studies in Chapters 3 through 6, and in the cross-case comparisons.

- *If they do, how are these control processes transmitted to and implemented within the China affiliates?* They are transmitted to and implemented within the China affiliates through the parents' respective corporate cultures. While corporate culture is the common means of transmission and implementation, the case also reveal considerable differences between the respective corporate cultures. The cases also reveal that corporate culture can be transmitted and implemented within local affiliates even where executive staff are almost totally localized.

- *If different control processes are used in China, how do these vary from those that the parent MNC employs elsewhere?* For the affiliates of the parents with standardized worldwide control processes, the evidence shows that the same control processes are used, and no variance was established.

- *Do control processes differ depending on whether the affiliate is a WOS or an IJV, and if they differ, in what respects?* As demonstrated in the case studies and further explained in Chapter 7, the companies make no distinction between management processes employed within WOS and IJV in the affiliates studied, where affiliate operating companies were organized using both structures. The expressed objectives of the affiliates who operated both WOS and IJV was to manage using similar processes, regardless of organizational form.

- *Does the extent of equity ownership of an affiliate affect employment of management control processes within the affiliate?* The evidence from the case studies showed managers' objective of achieving total control of the management of affiliates, regardless of whether an individual affiliate was structured as a WOS or an IJV. As explained in the case studies and in Chapters 7 and 8, possession of majority equity control (a mechanism) was regarded as only one of the necessary preconditions to achievement of total control through processes. Regardless of extent of majority ownership, the clearly expressed intention was to achieve total control through implementation of the parent's worldwide management processes, including control processes.

- *Do affiliates' interaction with the Chinese institutional environment differ depending on whether an individual affiliate is a WOS or an IJV, and, if differences exist, what are the differences?* The affiliates' interactions with China's institutions do not differ depending on whether the affiliate is a WOS or an IJV. Given the heavy use of local (Chinese) managers by US MNC, public affairs duties within affiliates, regardless of organizational form, are typically handled by Chinese managers.

- *Do the parent MNCs employ different business strategies in China depending on the form of ownership of their respective China affiliates?* As demonstrated in the case studies and elaborated on in Chapter 8, the affiliates are governed by corporate objectives set by their parents. At the same time, the affiliates are expected to adapt strategies appropriate to China to implement those objectives. The objectives drive strategy selection, which in turn drives the choice whether to employ WOS or IJV ownership structures, or use both types of structures for the affiliates.

What May Change, and Why

The "internal face"

The management processes that multinational corporations have successfully employed in worldwide operations have been implemented in China with generally favorable results. The American Chambers of Commerce *2004 White Paper* reports that, of 1,800 multinationals surveyed, 75 percent reported that they are profitable (2004, 10). This is a marked improvement from earlier results, such as the 1999 A.T. Kearney survey of 70 large MNC in China, that reported two-thirds of the 70 companies surveyed were unprofitable, and another 25 percent were only "breaking even" (*China Business Review*, 1999).

This improved profitability is attributable in part to successful implementation of global management processes, and it is likely that foreign MNC in China will continue that implementation. At the same time, however, China's institutional environments have evolved in ways that have been largely favorable to both foreign and domestic businesses. The important questions are, what changes may be expected in those environments, and how will those changes affect the "external face" of the MNC?

The "external face"

The processes by which MNC in China deal with China's unique institutional environments are more likely to change than are MNC internal management processes, because of likely changes in some aspects of China's institutional environments. First, however, it is necessary to discuss the crucial Chinese institution that is *not* likely to change.

What Is Not Likely to Change: the Party-State

The record of the party-state since 1949 has been thoroughly documented by foreign and Chinese observers, and has attracted widespread criticism. From the viewpoint of the citizens of the People's Republic of China, however, the period since 1949 represents the longest period of time, since the mid nineteenth century, during which China has not suffered invasion, or political domination by foreigners. The party-state has shown itself to be sufficiently flexible to promulgate and implement the Four Modernizations and the Open Policy. Together, these policies have brought enormous changes to China, and to the everyday lives of Chinese people, including a substantial increase in living standards for some segments of the Chinese population.

At the same time, the party-state's flexibility has not extended to allowing any possible challenge to its primacy. The Four Cardinal Principles, enunciated by Deng Xiaoping in 1979, still form the foundation of both the constitution of the People's Republic of China and the constitution of the Chinese Communist Party (People's Republic of China, 2005; Communist Party of the People's Republic of China, 2002). These principles – "following the socialist path," maintaining a Leninist "dictatorship of the proletariat," upholding the leadership of the Chinese Communist Party, and upholding "Marxist-Leninist-Mao Zedong-Deng Xiaoping Thought" – remain in full force and effect, and there has been no sign yet that any or all of them will be repudiated by the leadership (Shaomin Li, 2002).

The Chinese people endured the loss of life and accompanying economic and social disruption resulting from the Cultural Revolution. Also, the history of Russia since the collapse of the Soviet Union in 1991 is well known within China. There is considerable sentiment that China should avoid similar experiences in the future. Until the party-state voluntarily disclaims its primacy, that primacy will continue.

What May Change: the Party-State's Relation to the Legal System

Local protectionism presents a serious threat to Chinese economic development. This protectionism continues to exist because of the ambiguous relationship between the central government in Beijing on the one hand, and its provincial and municipal subdivisions on the other. One possible solution would be to interpose an independent judiciary that was capable of mediating conflicts between the central government and its subordinate units. The party-state, however, is unlikely to tolerate development of a legal system based on a rule *of law*. Yet rule *by law*, as a means for Beijing to exercise control over subordinate political units, may develop, as a means to further economic development as well as administrative efficiency.

The creation of a national legal system as a "branded product" superior to the current blend of local protectionism and *guanxi* is not as far-fetched as it may seem. Since enforcement of the national law would be entrusted to courts under the control of the party-state, such a development would enhance rather than challenge party-state primacy. The common law, administered by the courts of the English Crown, proved to be a more marketable product than canon law or local customs during the twelfth century, and was a centerpiece in the development of a strong central government. The certainty and relative impartiality of the common law and the courts of King Henry II proved beneficial to the largest economic units of medieval England, the landowners. This played a major role in the "marketing" success of the common law. Similarly, development of an effective national legal system in China would be beneficial to large businesses, both Chinese and foreign owned.

What Will Change

We noted in the preceding chapter Peter Drucker's observation that:

It is possible – and fruitful – to identify major events that have already happened, irrevocably, and that will have predictable effects in the next decade or two. It is possible, in other words, to identify and prepare for the future that has already happened.
(in Ireland and Hitt, 1999, 43)

Some changes in the environments in which MNC in China must operate over the next five years can reasonably be foreseen as consequences of events that have happened since 1990.

Growth in consumption and in the service sector

It may seem disingenuous to speak of growth of consumption after earlier remarks about the tendency of foreign executives to overestimate the number of Chinese consumers who might be potential customers for their products. This is not the case, however.

The party-state itself is committed to rising living standards in the words of the preamble to the Chinese constitution, as well as in the concrete economic objectives set forth in the Ninth (1996–2000) and Tenth (2001–2005) Five Year Plans (Taylor, 2003). China is well on its way to being the world's hypermarket, as well as being the world's factory.

Chinese already have more refrigerators than Americans, and almost twice as many mobile phones. Although per capita consumption still lags America's consumerist society, gross consumption numbers from China are impressive, and growing. While US per capita consumption of meat products is 279 pounds per year, compared with China's 108 pounds per year, Chinese consumed 64 million tons of meat in 2004, while US consumption was only 38 million tons (Mann, 2005). China presently has less than one-tenth of the number of automobiles as the United States. Yet, in 2003 alone an additional 1.8 million cars took to Chinese roads, and projected growth rates indicate a *doubling* of that number within four years (Becker, 2004).

To provide services to the growing number of consumers, the service sector of the Chinese economy enjoyed an annual compound growth rate of 10 percent in the period 1991–2001, and has grown to account for one-third of Chinese GNP (Ellis, Williams and Zuo, 2003). As discussed in Chapter 2, opening of the service sector to foreign competitors due to WTO accession will likely accelerate the growth of the sector.

Improvement in living standards leading to increased consumption in the relatively poorer interior of China will be driven by industrial relocation from the developed coastal cities and provinces. Industrial relocation to the interior will be driven by two factors: the relatively lower costs of manufacturing in the interior, which is especially significant for labor-intensive production, as well as pollution of the existing industrial landscape in developed areas. The relocation process will be aided by an improved internal transportation infrastructure.

Relocation of manufacturing

As discussed earlier, there is a serious gap between the "two Chinas": the relatively prosperous, industrialized coastal cities and provinces, and the poorer interior, where economic development is still dependent on agriculture and extractive industries. Both the central government through its "Go West" campaign, and provincial and local governments in the poorer provinces, have exerted considerable efforts to establish new industries and relocate existing ones to the poorer provinces. Due to a number of factors, including serious infrastructure constraints and a relative shortage of skilled workers in the interior, results of these efforts have been mixed.

Nevertheless, increased factor costs (primarily land and labor) in the developed "first tier" areas, combined with energy shortages, are encouraging both MNC and local firms to locate or relocate manufacturing facilities to so-called "second tier" interior cities. The cost differentials involved are significant. According to Ross (2004) Jiaxing, in the interior of Zhejiang Province, has average labor costs one-half of those in metropolitan Shanghai, yet Jiaxing is only one hour from Shanghai, and is served by several major new expressways. Even China's least economically developed western provinces are attracting MNC investment. Coca-Cola and Carlsberg Brewery have each established production facilities in Gansu Province, a western province which borders Inner Mongolia (Xinhua News Agency, 2005).

The serious damage to China's physical environment due to rapid industrialization has been extensively documented in both foreign and Chinese media accounts (e.g. Cody, 2004; Kahn, 2003). The extent of the damage is as remarkable as the economic development which caused it. Jasper Becker (2004) provides several examples. Almost two-thirds of the Chinese cities in which air quality is monitored have air which does not meet Chinese national standards, which are below those of the World Health Organization (WHO). Shortages of drinkable water affect two-thirds of China's major cities, and 700 million Chinese drink water contaminated with waste at levels that exceed those allowed under Chinese standards, which again are lower than comparable WHO standards.

As documented in Chapter 2, the central government has had a mixed record of success in enforcing nationwide regulatory standards at the provincial and municipal levels. Further, provincial and municipal governments have significant economic development objectives that, up until now, have generally taken precedence over protecting the environment. Thus it is unlikely, in the short term, that environmental remediation will be achieved in China through rigorous enforcement of the extensive existing body of environmental laws. China's governments are considering industrial relocation as an alternative.

Industrial relocation, as exemplified in Dalien's successful program, aims to relocate polluting industries from city centers to outlying suburbs (Bai, 2002). This is feasible so long as there is sufficient open land near industrial cities that is relatively unpolluted, and that can be obtained at a cost that makes relocation financially practical. These two conditions cannot always be met in the already industrialized coastal areas, making it necessary to relocate further into the interior.

Environmental pollution and remediation particularly affect MNC. Both case studies and large scale surveys show that MNC implement rigorous global standards, such as the ISO 14000 series, within their China operations and thus engage in a high degree of environmental self-regulation (Gelb and Hulme, 2002; Christmann and Taylor, 2001). It is correct that MNC have less ability to control the actions of Chinese subcontractors (Kahn, 2003). Yet, the MNC themselves are highly visible both in China and in their home countries and, in the case of US multinationals, face potential legal liabilities in the home country regarding environmental activities in China.

Enhancement of China's transportation infrastructure

While local protectionism will continue to retard full development of the transportation infrastructure, the physical infrastructure itself is undergoing substantial enhancement.

As described in Chapter 2, completion of the Three Gorges dam along the Yangtze River will open the river to navigation by large, self-propelled vessels as far inland as Chongqing, which is 1,900 kilometers (1,180 miles) from the port of Shanghai. The Yangtze carries about 30 percent of all cargo that moves on China's inland and intercoastal waterways, and improvement in the river's navigability promises to accelerate the economic development of the interior (Trunick, 2003). The effects are already being seen in Chongqing itself, where Ford Motor Company is expanding its factory to produce 150,000 vehicles per year, using the Yangtze to ship components upstream from Shanghai, and finished vehicles downstream. Because Chongqing wage and land costs are estimated to be only one-half of those in Shanghai, there is a strong incentive to move labor-intensive manufacturing from the coastal areas to cities along the Yangtze that are accessible to water transportation (Simons, 2005).

Improvements to the highway infrastructure are being pushed by all levels of government as well as by private investors. Construction of the National Trunk Highway System (NTHS) began in 1990 and is expected to be completed between 2015 and 2020. The NTHS consists of both north–south and east–west toll expressways, built by private companies under contract with provincial authorities. Total length of the NTHS when completed will be over 35,000 kilometers (22,000 miles), of which almost two-thirds is expected to be completed by the end of 2005 (Field, 2004; Trunick, 2003). Governments at all levels are also going forward with expansion of the publicly developed highway network, which, it is estimated, will consist of almost one million miles (1.6 million kilometers) of highways by the end of 2005, with almost 13 percent of that total being completed in 2005 (Trunick, 2003). Finally, the central government's Ministry of Railroads has budgeted more than US$42 billion in spending to improve rail infrastructure (Sowinski, 2004).

Changes in the competitive structure of the business environment in China

The Open Policy was intended to encourage foreign direct investment that would bring foreign technology and management skills to China, both to promote economic development and to enhance the competitive abilities of Chinese enterprises. This policy has been successful in both respects (Buckley, Clegg and Wang, 2004). From the beginning of FDI, however, there has been a bifurcation in the objectives of FDI on the part of foreign investors.

Foreign direct investment by overseas Chinese enterprises initially involved moving manufacture of relatively low-value products from Hong Kong and Taiwan into the coastal provinces of the mainland. Local Chinese companies became part of this production system, as both suppliers and partners. Much of the production from these factories was intended for export.

On the other hand, investments from Western and then Japanese MNC were concentrated in producing higher-value, technologically intensive products, initially for sale within China, both to other MNC and within Chinese markets. As documented in the case studies and cross-case comparisons, once MNC were able to implement global manufacturing standards, such as Six Sigma and ISO 9000, within China, they began to integrate Chinese manufacturing into their global production systems. MNC now focus on producing high-value technologically intensive finished products and components both for export and for China's expanding internal markets.

As Chen (2005) points out, Chinese companies are now interested in moving from lower-value, labor-intensive production for export to manufacturing higher-value, technologically intensive products for export, as well as for Chinese markets. Chen and other academic as well as management observers have expressed skepticism over the abilities of most Chinese enterprises, even privately owned, to make this transition in the near future. That said, some Chinese enterprises clearly have the present ability and the capital to do so. Chen also highlights the ability of successful China-based MNC such as Lenovo and TLC to acquire high-technology businesses from long-established MNC such as IBM and Thomson.

The growing competitive abilities of Chinese domestic companies to compete with MNC both within China and globally will challenge MNC in China to retain and expand their existing positions in Chinese markets. The global expansion of Chinese MNC has already had another consequence that, in the short term, poses a major threat to the competitive position of MNC in China.

Changes in home country versus host country policies towards multinational corporations

The proliferation of products "made in China" on garment racks and store shelves throughout the developed world has made citizens of developed nations increasingly aware of China's impact on their national economies. Sharp reductions in manufacturing employment in the United States, attributed to outsourcing of production to China, have produced a serious political backlash in America, including proposed legislation imposing penal tariffs against Chinese imports and restrictions on Chinese companies' acquisition of American companies. Fear of possible similar reductions in employment within the member states of the European Union has been identified as one cause of French and Dutch voters' recent rejection of a new EU constitution. "China bashing," especially within the legislative and executive branches of the US government, has attracted increasingly hostile comments from officials of the party-state in response.

First introduced by Raymond Vernon (1971), the obsolescing bargain theory has been supported by qualitative and quantitative studies (e.g. Vachani, 1995). Simply put, the theory posits a decline in the bargaining position of an MNC versus the host country over time. It is entirely possible that MNC in China are likely to see a further validation of this theory.

Encouraged to do so by the party-state, MNC have enormous sums of money invested in China. Now that investment is, in a very real sense, "captive" to the policies of the party-state. Shaomin Li's (2004) case studies of expropriation of foreign investments in China during the last decade provide further amplification of the points raised in this work regarding the absence of the rule of law and the absence of respect for property rights in contemporary China. Ironically, changes in China's laws may pose a more serious threat.

China is presently planning to enact a national Anti Monopoly Law. Among the expressed targets of the law will be what has been referred to here as "administrative monopolies," that is, government units at all levels that act to protect favored businesses from competition. Given the general failure of the party-state's past efforts against administrative monopoly, it is difficult to be optimistic about the effect of the new Anti Monopoly Law on this type of monopoly.

There is, however, another stated target of the new law: multinational corporations operating in China. Already, in 2004 the State Administration of Industry and Commerce (SAIC) issued a report alleging that leading MNC in China were exploiting their financial and technological capabilities in an anticompetitive manner (Bush, 2005). As Bush notes, many of China's market leaders, and thus most promising targets for the Anti Monopoly Law, are MNC. If the party-state follows through on the SAIC's threat, the competitive strengths of foreign multinationals within China may be converted into liabilities.

The Summing Up

In written Chinese, the ideogram representing "crisis" (*wei ji*) is made up of one of the characters that comprise the ideogram for "danger" (*wei*, part of *wei xian*) and one of the characters that comprise the ideogram for "opportunity" (*ji*, part of *ji hwei*). This observation has been repeated so often in works about China that it has become a cliché. Like most clichés, however, it reflects an underlying truth. This book has shown how multinational corporations in China have so far been largely successful in coping with this truth. Their success has brought many benefits for them and for the People's Republic of China. Their success or failure in the future will have momentous consequences for them, for China and for the rest of the world.

Notes

Introduction

1 As used in this book, a multinational corporation (MNC) is a business enterprise that conducts operations in one or more countries in addition to its home country (Rudman, 2000). MNC is the abbreviation used here to indicate a single MNC as well more than one MNC; single or plural is denoted by the accompanying pronoun, or by context.

2 The English translation of the Chinese phrase referring to wholly owned subsidiaries of foreign companies is wholly foreign-owned enterprises (WFOE).

3 The IJV studied here are classified by the Chinese government as "equity joint ventures" to distinguish them from contractual joint ventures, another form of joint venture provided for in Chinese law.

Chapter 1

4 Barnard uses "control" in a narrower sense, to refer to the part of the communication process through which supervision is exercised (Barnard, 1938, 223).

5 Social science literature draws a distinction between "taxonomies," that is, empirically based classification systems, such as that of Linnaeus, and "typologies" that are theoretically based (Jary and Jary, 1991, 514, 531). The two terms are often used interchangeably or without definition throughout management research. As closely as possible, I will use the same phrase that is used by the author(s) of the work being discussed. When that is not possible I will use the term "typification" which can be used for either empirically or theoretically derived classification schemes.

6 A more extensive catalog of "control mechanism" studies is presented in Harzing (1999, 18–19). The above list does not include works that simply restate taxonomies first presented in the listed works, for example, works restating Ouchi's taxonomy of "input" versus "output" controls.

7 As noted above, Bartlett and Ghoshal (1989) use "control" and "coordination" throughout their work, without defining either term. The use at their p. 70, cited above, is an instance where, through the context of use, it is possible to understand

that the two words are intended to represent different concepts. Bartlett and Ghoshal do not provide additional explanations of those concepts.

8   As discussed in the previous chapter, challenges to the authority of the parent of a wholly owned affiliate to manage that affiliate are external in nature, coming from host governments. Those challenges are not the subject of this book.

Chapter 2

9   For business practitioners and students, learning more about China poses a challenge in itself. The breadth and depth of contemporary literature on China is vast. A scholarly and readable one volume study of contemporary China, with historical background, is Starr (2001). A very brief treatment of Chinese history and culture, included within a guide for business travelers, is Flower (2003).

10   There are hundreds of scholarly and popular works treating the changes in China since the death of Mao Zedong. Among the most readable general accounts are Starr (2001, 54–234), Goldman (in Fairbank and Goldman, 1998, 406–55), and Van Kamenade (1998, *passim*).

11   There is a continuing debate over the degree of precision of Chinese government economic statistics (cf. Davies, 2003 with Kynge, 2004). Nonetheless, it is possible to measure the physical and monetary volume of China's exports and imports by reference to non-Chinese statistics, and the impact of China on the world's markets is readily observable.

12   According to Jenner (1994, 54–5, 80–2), nationwide markets did exist at various times in Imperial Chinese history in regards to trade in different individual products and commodities, although these national markets developed and functioned in the absence of large, non-governmental business firms operating nationally. There is no dispute that, whether or not an integrated national market or markets existed in the Chinese past, there were no large private businesses operating on a national scale.

13   As used here, the PLA refers collectively to the Army as well as its separate maritime and aerospace components.

14   The IJV discussed in the book are classified in Chinese law as "equity joint ventures." This is an entity that is legally separate from the joint venture partners and is operated as a Chinese limited liability company. Chinese and foreign investors contribute capital and share profits, or incur losses in proportion to their respective capital contributions.

15   WFOE were legalized by statute in 1986, but implementing regulations were not adopted for quite some time (Barale, 1990).

16   The definition of "socialist market economy" is open to interpretation. China's present economic structure is characterized by an interventionist, authoritarian government exercising certain central planning functions, coupled with market-based pricing and exchange and four different business ownership structures: SOE, cooperative enterprises (primarily TVE), foreign private companies, and Chinese private companies.

17   The "Big Four" banks are the Bank of China, China Construction Bank, Industrial and Commercial Bank of China, and Agricultural Bank of China. In 2003 the first two banks issued shares for public trading, and in mid 2005 Bank of America, the

US-based multinational bank, announced plans to acquire a 19 percent interest in the China Construction Bank. The Swiss-based UBS bank previously acquired a minority interest in the Bank of China.

18 In 1994 the party-state created the State Development Bank of China, the Export-Import Credit Bank of China and the Agricultural Development Bank of China to replace the Big Four in making policy loans. Although these three banks are collectively known as the "policy banks," the Big Four have continued to make many policy loans.

19 Foreign and Chinese estimates of the extent of non-performing loans in the banking system differ substantially. Standard & Poor's, the American financial ratings organization, estimates non-performing loans at around 45 percent of total outstanding loans, while the official Chinese estimate is one-half of that (Bradsher, 2004b).

20 A *single* Big Four bank may have around 300,000 employees. Nonetheless, 58,000 out of a two-bank total of around 600,000 still indicates a significant corruption problem.

21 Although several very large Chinese SOE now have shares listed on foreign stock exchanges, the shares represent small minority interests in these companies. The right of a Chinese company to list its shares on a Chinese stock exchange is strictly controlled by the party-state at national, provincial and local levels (Gu, 2005).

22 The first use of this term to refer to contemporary China that I have found is in the work of Professor Dali Yang, of the University of Chicago (Yang, 1999).

23 Some "dialects" such as Cantonese or Fukienese are not mutually understandable and therefore may be considered to be separate spoken languages, at least by Western standards (De Mente, 1994).

24 Originally, four Special Economic Zones (SEZ) were created, three in Guangdong and one in Fujian. FIE locating in the SEZ were given substantial concessions with regard to income and property taxes, customs regulations and other incentives to encourage export-oriented industries to locate in SEZ.

25 Product, pricing, promotion and place. The last includes where sold and by whom (Koch, 1994, 221).

26 The completion of the Three Gorges Dam will open ports along the Yangtze as far inland as Chongqing to navigation by large self-propelled cargo vessels.

27 In the early 1990s an arm of the central government, the Coordinating Office of the State Planning Commission, set up several sub-offices to deal with intragovernmental disputes, but these organizations were ineffective (Stoever, 1994).

28 These refer to Chinese requirements that condition approval of investments to establish IJV or WFOE on the foreign investors' commitment to transferring technology to Chinese partners, and further commitment to allocating for export specified quantities of goods manufactured by the IJV or WFOE.

29 These are also referred to as *hongtou wenjian* or "red-heading" documents (Lai, 2003).

30 Trade in intellectual property services; footnote supplied in original.

Chapter 3

31 All corporate and individual identities have been disguised, pursuant to agreement with the host company.

Chapter 4

32   All corporate and individual identities have been disguised, pursuant to agreement with the host company.

33   In 2003 IMIGIS announced a reorganization which effectively eliminated the worldwide business function groups portion of its organizational structure in favor of a product management structure, based on three worldwide product groups. The change did not affect the management structure within the Greater Asia and Greater China geographic organizations, however.

34   In 2004 John Victors was promoted and relocated back to a new position at IMIGIS' US headquarters.

35   In 2004 a Chinese-born American IMIGIS executive was appointed to head Greater China, within the Greater Asia organization.

Chapter 5

36   ELECTRONS' identity and the identities of its executives have been disguised, pursuant to agreement with the host company.

37   The ELECTRONS abbreviation for "best known methods."

38   This is the reason given by Yu (1998, 142–3) for its use.

39   ETCL, however, does not produce a profit and loss statement. As explained by Jim Liu, his performance is measured by the output of the two factories that are administratively part of ETCL. ETCL charges the other ELECTRONS businesses that are its customers on the basis of negotiated costs for its manufacturing services. Therefore ETCL as a unit does not report profit or loss.

40   Before being broken up as part of settlement of a lawsuit brought under American competition laws, AT&T operated the largest non-governmental research facility in the US as part of its Western Electric manufacturing subsidiary. This facility was known simply as "Bell Labs." Western Electric eventually became Lucent Corporation.

41   The company does spend over US$100,000,000 annually to support basic research at leading US and foreign universities. In 1998 it established a small laboratory devoted to basic research at its California headquarters. Significantly, the laboratory is run by the head of the Microprocessor Products Group (Chesbrough, 2001; Buderi, 1998).

42   Shanghai is an exception to this statement. The ELECTRONS lab is located in central Shanghai while ETCL is located in a distant part of Pudong.

43   Although the company has made a concerted effort to establish a global consumer brand for its premium microprocessors, the great majority of sales and marketing efforts are still focused on the original equipment manufacturer (OEM) market; that is, winning acceptance of ELECTRONS products by manufacturers of computers and mobile communications devices.

44   Much of the technical information dealing with the manufacture of silicon wafers and their processing into microprocessors comes from documents supplied by ELECTRONS, as does information about the "Copy Exactly" process.

45   As will be explained by Jim Liu in a quotation from his interview, as far as ELECTRONS is concerned, ETCL is organized as a subsidiary to meet Chinese legal

requirements, but it is considered by the company to be a part of ELECTRONS, and it is not regarded in any way as a separate entity.

46   According to the company, ELECTRONS "fabs" are roughly twice as large as the semiconductor industry's average "fab."

47   Several ELECTRONS executives with whom I spoke preferred to use the term "Copy Intelligently," but this is simply their nomenclature for the same process, and does not accurately explain the process. This chapter uses the company's term "Copy Exactly" which accurately describes the process.

48   As previously noted, ETCL is a wholly foreign-owned enterprise (WFOE) as are all ELECTRONS operating companies and laboratories within China.

49   The mention of "local cultures" refers principally to ELECTRONS' extensive Malaysian manufacturing operations, in which recognition and respect is given to the requirements of Islamic law, especially with regard to diet and what types of products can be physically handled.

50   This group, headed by Gene Ma, is responsible for sustaining high-volume manufacturing through preventive and restorative equipment maintenance, reviewing manufacturing operations to determine how to improve them, and general manufacturing "troubleshooting." Gene says that he reports directly both to Jim and to the factory managers.

Chapter 6

51   One of the contributors to a prominent encyclopedic dictionary of organizational behavior, who is also a leading organizational culture scholar, observes that the dissension among culture researchers about fundamental questions such as what culture is, how it should be studied, and whether particular cultures affect firm performance makes it difficult to define culture (Martin, in Nicholson, Schuler and Van de Ven, 1998, 376). When the term is used in this chapter, it is used in the context of WORLDWIDE executives describing what I refer to as a corporate "routine."

52   Management literature is replete with discussions of the term "evolution" used in its primary meaning, that is, gradual and progressive change. Recent works (for example, Collins and Porras, 1994) have attempted to draw analogies that the authors assert are specifically based on Darwin's theory of evolution. On close examination, however, the analogies are fundamentally based on the concept of "evolution" in its primary meaning, or on misinterpretation of Darwinian theory to fit the models being proposed.

53   The identity of WORLDWIDE and individual identities of WORLDWIDE executives with one exception have been disguised, pursuant to agreement with WORLDWIDE.

54   The organizational "routines" in the Nelson and Winter conceptualization.

55   This section draws heavily on Pascale (1990, 175–219) and Vaghefi and Huellmantel (1998).

56   In WORLDWIDE terminology "businesses."

57   Other companies, as well as WORLDWIDE itself, had previously established technical training institutes to train and retrain company engineers; the General Motors Technical Institute is one example. None of these institutes had the primary mission of educating managers, however.

58   This discussion of WORLDWIDE management training draws heavily on Noel and
      Charan (1992).

59   This section draws heavily on my interviews and correspondence with Mr Robert
      Garvin the former head of Aircraft Components' China operation, who worked for
      Aircraft Components throughout the period under discussion, and from his book
      (Garvin, 1998). He also participated in the formation and operation of the WORLD-
      WIDE joint venture with a leading European company, also discussed here.

60   The story of this joint venture was recounted in several issues of *Far Eastern Economic
      Review* and summarized in Yatsko (2001, 237–41).

61   As with the earlier section on Aircraft Components, this section draws on my interview
      and correspondence with the retired head of AC's China business, and his book.

62   ME operates three Chinese factories; two are part of the joint venture discussed
      here. The third, in Wuxi, was originally part of a joint venture in which ME held
      65 percent interest and local partners the remainder. ME then bought out its partners.

63   Computerized axial tomography, also known in the US as "CAT" scanners.

Chapter 7

64   The major works reflecting the different approaches are identified in Tahib (2000, 115).

65   By "market" or "markets" I *do not* mean the bloodless abstraction proposed in
      neoclassical economics. Rather, I mean "the market" as viewed by businesses, that is,
      as a collection of selling opportunities (Bannock, Baxter and Davis, 1998, 262).

66   Barnard noted that "a sense of a situation as a whole can usually only be acquired by
      intimate and habitual association with it, and involves many elements that either have
      not been or are not practically susceptible quickly to verbal expression by those who
      understand them" (1938, 239, n. 4).

67   The text of the law is found in Title 15 United States Code, Section 78dd-1, *et seq.*

68   This does not mean that IMIGIS has no shared routines or practices. Its China
      executives confirmed that IMIGIS manages its China affiliates in much the same way
      that it manages affiliates around the world, that is, by allowing local executives
      substantial discretion to run their businesses. The worldwide Six Sigma quality
      initiative has been implemented in China and, as explained in the case, Chinese
      factories were the first in IMIGIS' worldwide organization to reach ISO 9000 and
      14000 certifications. IMIGIS also uses standardized financial and accounting systems
      worldwide.

69   In WORLDWIDE terminology referred to as its "operating system" or "learning
      culture in action" (2000 Annual Report).

70   "Incorporated" is used here to reflect the American legal concept that each division
      is a legally separate corporate entity, although each is wholly owned by MOTORS.

71   Although MBO originated in America its employment is not confined to US MNC.
      For example, see Agthe (1990) for a description of MBO as an "important component"
      of ABB's global organization.

72   As noted in the case analysis, "management by plan" was originally referred to within
      ELECTRONS as "ELECTRONS management by objectives."

73   At the moment IMIGIS does not have a global corporate culture, but, as discussed in
      the case analysis and further discussed within the following chapters, IMIGIS globally

deploys certain management processes, such as Six Sigma, that have also successfully been implemented in China.

Chapter 8

74　Child's (1996, 11) earlier research reports only a modest statistical association between the equity share held by nine US MNC in joint ventures in China and their ability to influence the management of the respective joint venture.

75　MNC executives take a somewhat different approach to the issue of joint venture longevity as an indication of relative success or failure of the venture. Although MOTORS has used joint ventures extensively throughout the world, as noted in Chapter 3 its CEO observed that "not all of our ventures last. About half of the joint ventures we have closed down were intended to be closed down. Short-term transfer of technology is one example of the hundreds of reasons why joint ventures end. 'Ending' is not necessarily 'failure'" (Bonsignore, Houghton and Knight, 1994).

Chapter 9

76　There are, however, practices that vary from ELECTRONS' normal procedures due to Chinese law. ELECTRONS' practice is to award options to purchase ELECTRONS common shares as part of the compensation of both executive and certain non-executive employees. Until such shares are listed on a Chinese securities exchange, however, the literal terms of current Chinese law would appear to prohibit Chinese citizens from exercising such options, at least while residing within China.

77　Based on company documents that I reviewed, these can be summarized as: (1) open and informed communication, both formal and informal, to provide employees with the knowledge and insight into the company so that they can do their jobs; (2) treat every employee with dignity and respect, and protect them with sound HRM practices and policies, fairly and consistently administered; (3) any variation from the previous standard will be admitted and corrective action taken; (4) pay fair wages and benefits; (5) maintain safe workplaces; and (6) obey all applicable laws and regulations of the US and of the host country. Chinese language signs bearing these principles may be found throughout MOTORS' affiliates factories and offices that I visited in China.

78　Although atypical for a US MNC, Gillette follows this policy (Deal and Kennedy, 2000, 167–8).

79　Philips' migratory "Dutch Mafia" is an often cited example (Bartlett and Ghoshal, 1987).

80　The executive in question happens to be politically very conservative and, in my opinion, unlikely to use words like "racism" indiscriminately.

81　ISO 9000 and ISO 14000 are standards established and maintained by the International Organization for Standardization (IOS). ISO 9000 refers to quality management standards in business-to-business transactions, and ISO 14000 refers to standards for environmental management (International Organization for Standardization, 2004).

82　Rodrigues' (1996, 244) textbook does mention the issue, but misunderstands the difference between US law and the laws of other nations regarding taxation of expatriates.

83   For expository purposes the following discussion oversimplifies the tax calculations by disregarding the fact that each individual US state has its own tax system, and most states have taxes on personal income. It also disregards the restrictions on the amount of money employees may contribute to pension and profit-sharing plans resulting from full use of the $70,000 exclusion.

84   A 1997 study estimated the total cost of a typical annual compensation package for North American and European expatriates in China at between US$250,000 and US$300,000 (Melvin and Sylvester, 1997).

85   Tahib (1998) provides an illuminating case study of HRM at a US manufacturer's wholly owned subsidiary in Scotland.

Chapter 10

86   According to American lawyers working in China, for many years the only means available to FIE for factoring accounts receivable in China was to sell the accounts to Chinese law firms who specialized in debt collection (Lehman and Scott, 1999).

Conclusion

87   The concept of simultaneous integration and differentiation is at the heart of the work of Lawrence and Lorsch (1967; 1970, 8), as well as that of Bartlett and Ghoshal (1988). There is at least one earlier study that recognizes that simultaneous integration and differentiation are both achievable and desirable within an MNC (Aharoni, 1996). Nohria and Ghoshal (1994) reach the same conclusion, phrased in terms of simultaneous "differentiated fit" and "shared values."

88   By "market" or "markets," I am *not* referring to the abstraction proposed in neoclassical economics. Rather, I mean "the market" as viewed by businesses, that is, as a collection of selling opportunities (Bannock, Baxter and Davis, 1998, 262).

References

Agence France-Press (AFP), 2004, China Overtakes United States as top destination for foreign investment, September 22, accessed on October 4, 2004 from http://story. news.yahoo.com/news?tmpl=story&cid=1518&e=13&u=/afp/20040922.

Aharoni, Yair, 1996, The Organization of Global Service MNEs, *International Studies of Management and Organization*, 26 (2): 6–20.

Ahmed, Pervez and Xiaokai Li, 1996, Chinese Culture and its Implications for Sino-Western Joint Venture Management, *Strategic Change*, 5: 275–86.

AmChat, 2004, Imports Could Exceed US$500 Billion, *AmChat, Journal of the American Chamber of Commerce in Shanghai*, November: 6.

American Chambers of Commerce, 2004, *2004 White Paper, American Business in China*, The American Chamber of Commerce–People's Republic of China (Beijing) and The American Chamber of Commerce in Shanghai.

Anand, J. and Andrew Delios, 1996, Competing Globally: How Japanese MNCs Have Matched Goals and Strategies in India and China, *Columbia Journal of World Business*, 31 (3): 50–63.

Anderson, Alistair R., Jin-Hai Li, Richard T. Harrison and Paul J.A. Robson, 2003, The Increasing Role of Small Business in the Chinese Economy, *Journal of Small Business Management*, 41 (3): 310–16.

Anderson, Paul F., 1982, Marketing, Strategic Planning and the Theory of the Firm, *Journal of Marketing*, 46: 15–26.

Bai, Xuemei, 2002, Industrial Relocation in Asia: A Sound Environmental Strategy?, *Environment*, 44 (5): 8–22.

Baliga, B.R. and Alfred M. Jaeger, 1984, Multinational Corporations: Control Systems and Delegation Issues, *Journal of International Business Studies*, Fall: 25–40.

Bannock, G., R.E. Baxter and Evan Davis, 1998, *The Penguin Dictionary of Economics*, 6th edn, London: Penguin.

Barale, Lucille A. 1990, Wholly Foreign Owned Enterprises, *China Business Review*, 17 (1): 30–5.

Baran, Roger, Y. Pan and E. Kaynak, 1996, Research on International Joint Ventures in East Asia: A Critical Review and Future Directions, *Journal of Euromarketing*, 4 (3/4): 7–21.

Barboza, David, 2005, Wave of Corruption Tarnishes China's Extraordinary Growth, *New York Times*, March 22: C1.

Barley, Stephen and Gideon Kunda, 1992, Design and Devotion: Surges of Rational and Normative Ideologies of Control in Managerial Discourse, *Administrative Science Quarterly*, 37 (3): 363–400.

Barlow, E.R., 1953, *Management of Foreign Manufacturing Subsidiaries*, Boston: Division of Research, Harvard University Graduate School of Business Administration.

Barnard, C., 1938, *The Functions of the Executive*, Thirtieth Anniversary Edition, 1968, Cambridge, MA: Harvard University Press.

Bartlett, Christopher and Sumantra Ghoshal, 1987, Managing across Borders: New Organizational Responses, *Sloan Management Review*, 28 (Fall): 43–53.

Bartlett, Christopher and Sumantra Ghoshal, 1988, Organizing for Worldwide Effectiveness: The Transnational Solution, *California Management Review*, 31 (1): 1–21.

Bartlett, Christopher and Sumantra Ghoshal, 1989, *Managing Across Borders: The Transnational Solution*, Boston: Harvard Business School Press.

Bartlett, Christopher and Sumantra Ghoshal, 1993, Beyond the M-Form: Toward a Managerial Theory of the Firm, *Strategic Management Journal*, 14 (2): 23–46.

Beamish, Paul W. and Andrew Inkpen, 1998, Japanese Firms and the Decline of the Japanese Expatriate, *Journal of World Business*, 33 (1): 35–51.

Becker, Jasper, 2004, China's Growing Pains, *National Geographic*, March: 68–92.

Beechler, Schon, 1990, *International Management Control in Multinational Corporations: The Case of Japanese Consumer Electronics Subsidiaries in Southeast Asia*, unpublished PhD dissertation, Ann Arbor, MI, School of Business, University of Michigan.

Birkinshaw, Julian and Neil Hood, 1998, Multinational Subsidiary Evolution: Capability and Charter Change in Foreign-Owned Subsidiary Companies, *Academy of Management Review*, 23 (4): 773–96.

Birkinshaw, Julian M. and A.J. Morrison, 1995, Configurations of Strategy and Structure in Subsidiaries of Multinational Corporations, *Journal of International Business Studies*, 26 (4): 729–55.

Bjorkman, Ingmar and Mats Forsgren, 2000, Nordic International Business Research, *International Studies of Management and Organization*, 30 (1): 6–25.

Bjorkman, Ingmar and Soren Kock, 1995, Social Relationships and Business Networks: The Case of Western Companies in China, *International Business Review*, 4 (4): 519–35.

Bjorkman, Ingmar and Yuan Lu, 1999, A Corporate Perspective on the Management of Human Resources in China, *Journal of World Business*, 34 (1): 16–26.

Blackman, Carolyn, 2001, Local Governments and Foreign Business, *China Business Review*, 28 (3): 26–34.

Blake, David H., 1981, Headquarters and Subsidiary Roles in Managing Public Affairs: A Preliminary Investigation, in Lars Otterbeck, ed., *The Management of Headquarters–Subsidiary Relationships in Multinational Corporations*, Aldershot: Gower.

Bonsignore, M.R., Michael Houghton and C.F. Knight, 1994, Border Crossings, *Across the Board*, 31 (10): 41–50.

Bothamley, Jennifer, 2002, *Dictionary of Theories*, Canton, MI: Visible Ink Press.

Bradsher, Keith, 2004a, In Near Term, the News Isn't Good for China's Banks, *New York Times*, May 8: C3.

Bradsher, Keith, 2004b, Made in India vs. Made in China, *New York Times*, June 12: C1.

Bray, Marianne, 2002, China Homes In on Bad Judges, CNN.com, accessed on May 27, 2005 from http://edition.cnn.com/2002/WORLD/asiapcf/east/07/09/china.judges.

Brecher, Richard, 2000, How China Currently Figures in Motorola's Asian/Global Corporate Strategy and How This Might Change with China's Accession to the WTO, address before the National Defense University 2000 Pacific Symposium, Asian Perspectives on the Challenges of China, Washington DC, March 8.

Brooke, Michael Z., 1984, *Centralization and Autonomy: A Study in Organization Behaviour*, London: Holt, Rinehart and Winston.

Brooke, Michael Z. and H. Lee Remmers, 1978, *The Strategy of Multinational Enterprise: Organization and Finance*, London: Pitman.

Buckley, Chris, 2005, In China, Power to the Center: State Firms' Agency Still Calls the Shots, *International Herald Tribune*, June 1, accessed on June 1, 2005 from http://www.iht.com.

Buckley, Peter J., Jeremy Clegg and Hui Tan, 2001, Winning by Learning: An In-Depth Analysis of Two Foreign Invested Firms in China's Telecommunications Manufacturing Industry, presented at the LVMH Conference "Change in Management Practice in Asia", Fontainebleau, INSEAD, February 2 and 3.

Buckley, Peter J., Jeremy Clegg and Chengqi Wang, 2004, The Relationship between Inward Foreign Direct Investment and the Performance of Domestically-Owned Chinese Manufacturing Industry, *Multinational Business Review*, 12 (3): 23–41.

Buckman, Rebecca, 2005, New Regulations Hamper Global Investors in China, *The Wall Street Journal* (European Edition), June 29, M4.

Buderi, Robert, 1998, Researchers Aim to Think Big While Staying Close to Development, *Research Technology Management*, 41 (2): 3–4.

Burgelman, R.A., Dennis Carter and Raymond S. Bamford, 1999, *Intel Corporation: The Evolution of an Adaptive Organization*, Case No. SM-65, Stanford, CA: Stanford University Graduate School of Business.

Bush, Nathan, 2005, Chinese Competition Policy, *China Business Review*, 32 (3): 30–5.

Cabestan, Jean-Pierre, 2001, The Relationship between the National People's Congress and the State Council in the People's Republic of China: A Few Checks But No Balances, *American Asian Review*, 19 (3): 35–74.

Cambridge University Press, 2002, *Cambridge Dictionaries Online*, http://dictionary.cambridge.org.

Campbell, Andrew, 1999, Tailored, Not Benchmarked: A Fresh Look at Corporate Planning, *Harvard Business Review*, March–April: 41–50.

Carver, Anne, 1996, Open and Secret Regulations in China and Their Implication for Foreign Investment, in John Child and Yuan Lu, eds, *Management Issues in China: International Enterprises*, London: Routledge.

Chakravarty, S.N. and Amy Feldman, 1993, The Road Not Taken, *Forbes*, August 30: 40–2.

Chan, Gerald, 2004, China and the WTO: The Theory and Practice of Compliance, *International Relations of the Asia Pacific*, 4 (1): 47–72.

Chandler, Alfred D. Jr 1962, *Strategy and Structure*, Cambridge, MA: MIT Press.

Chen, Min, 2005, Made In China, *China Business Review*, 32 (3): 42–6.

Chesbrough, Henry, 2001, The Intel Lookout, *Technology Review*, October 9, available at www.techreview.com/articles.chesbrough.100901.asp.

Child, John, 1972, Organization Structure, Environment and Performance: The Role of Strategic Choice, *Sociology*, 6: 1–22.

Child, John, 1973, Strategies of Control and Organizational Behavior, *Administrative Science Quarterly*, 18 (1): 1–18.

Child, John, 1981, Culture, Contingency and Capitalism in the Cross-National Study of Organizations, in *Research in Organizational Behavior*, Volume 3, 303–56, Westport, CT: JAI Press.

Child, John, 1996, *The Management of Joint Ventures within Multinational Corporate Networks: U.S. Companies in China*, Cambridge, Judge Institute of Management Studies, University of Cambridge.

Child, John, 2001, Trust – The Fundamental Bond in Global Collaboration, *Organizational Dynamics*, 29 (4): 274–89.

Child, John and David Faulkner, 1998, *Strategies of Cooperation: Managing Alliances, Networks and Joint Ventures*, Oxford: Oxford University Press.

Child, John and Sally Stewart, 1998, Regional Differences in China and Their Implications for Sino-Foreign Joint Ventures, *Journal of General Management*, 23 (2): 65–86.

Child, John and David K. Tse, 2001, China's Transition and its Implications for International Business, *Journal of International Business Studies*, 32 (1): 5–22.

China Business Review, 1999, Pondering Profitability, 26 (2): 4.

China Law & Governance Review, 2004, Heads of Provincial High Courts Found Guilty of Corruption, January, accessed on May 20, 2005, from http://www.chinareview.info/issue1/pages/legal/legal.htm.

Christmann, Petra and Glen Taylor, 2001, Globalization and the Environment: Determinants of Firm Self-Regulation in China, *Journal of International Business Studies*, 32 (3): 439–59.

Clissold, Tim, 2004, *Mr. China*, London: Constable & Robinson.

Cody, Edward, 2004, Chinese Newspapers Put Spotlight on Polluters: Factory Shutdowns Follow Reports, *Washington Post*, May 25: A10.

Collins, James C. and Jerry Porras, 1994, *Built To Last: Successful Habits of Visionary Companies*, New York: Harper Business.

Communist Party of the People's Republic of China, 2002, *Constitution of the Communist Party of China*, accessed on June 30, 2005, from http://www.fas.org/irp/world/china/docs/const.html.

Coy, Peter, 2004, Just How Cheap Is Chinese Labor?, *BusinessWeekOnline*, December 2, accessed on December 3, 2004 from www.businessweek.com/bwdaily/dnflash/dec2004/nf2004122_6762_db039.htm.

Cray, David, 1984, Control and Coordination in Multinational Corporations, *Journal of International Business Studies*, (Fall): 85–98.

Cresswell, J.W., 1994, *Research Designs: Qualitative and Quantitative Approaches*, Thousand Oaks, CA: Sage.

Crook, Frederick, 1990, Sources of Rural Instability, *China Business Review*, 17 (4): 12–17.

Dale, Ernest, 1960, *The Great Organizers*, New York: McGraw-Hill.

Dang, Tran Thanh, 1977, *Ownership, Control and Performance of the Multinational Corporation: A Study of U.S. Wholly-Owned Subsidiaries and Joint Ventures in the Philippines and Taiwan*, unpublished doctoral dissertation, Los Angeles, University of California at Los Angeles.

Davies, Ken, 2003, China's Economy: Still Some Way To Go, *OECD Observer*, July, 2003: 26.

Davis, Stanley M., 1976, Trends in the Organization of Multinational Corporations, *Columbia Journal of World Business*, Summer: 59–71.

Davis, T.R.V., 1996, Developing an Employee Balanced Scorecard: Linking Frontline Performance to Corporate Objectives, *Management Decision*, 34 (4): 14–19.

Day, George S., 1994, The Capabilities of Market-Driven Organizations, *Journal of Marketing*, 58, October: 37–52.

De Tocqueville, Alexis, 2002, *Democracy in America* (1835), pbk edn, New York, Bantam Dell.

De Mente, Boye Lafayette, 1994, *Chinese Etiquette and Ethics in Business*, 2nd edn, Lincolnwood, IL: NTC Business Books.

Deal, Terrence and Allan A. Kennedy, 2000, *The New Corporate Cultures*, pbk edn, Cambridge, MA: Perseus.

Dellacave, Tom, 1997, Mission Control, *Sales & Marketing Management*, March: 10–19.

Deng, Ping, 2001, WFOE: The Most Popular Entry Mode into China, *Business Horizons*, 44 (4): 63–73.

Dickson, Bruce, 2004, Beijing's Ambivalent Reformers, *Current History*, September: 249–56.

Ding, Daniel and Malcolm Warner, 1998, *Labour Law, Industrial Relations and Human Resource Management in China: An Empirical Field Study*, Research Papers in Management Studies, WP 17/98, Cambridge, Judge Institute of Management Studies, University of Cambridge.

Dolven, Ben, 2003, Hubble, Bubble, Toil and Trouble, *Far Eastern Economic Review*, February 20: 30–3.

Dorn, James A., 2001, China's New Political Economy, *Cato Journal*, 20 (3): 489–94.

Doz, Yves, 1978, Managing Manufacturing Rationalization within Multinational Companies, *Columbia Journal of World Business*, Fall: 82–94.

Doz, Yves, 1986, *Strategic Management in Multinational Companies*, Oxford: Pergamon.

Doz, Yves and C.K. Prahalad, 1984, Patterns of Strategic Control within Multinational Corporations, *Journal of International Business Studies*, Fall: 55–72.

Doz, Yves and C.K. Prahalad, 1993, Managing DMNCs: A Search for a New Paradigm, in Sumantra Ghoshal and D. Eleanor Westney, eds, *Organization Theory and the Multinational Corporation*, New York: St Martin's Press, 24–50.

Drickhamer, David, 2004, Appliance Envy, *Industry Week*, November: 24–30.

Drucker, Peter, 1954, *The Practice of Management*, New York: Harper.

Duffy, Edmund, 1996, Business Law in China: Evolutionary Revolution, *Journal of International Affairs*, 49 (2): 557–64.

Dunning, John H., 1958, *American Investment in British Manufacturing Industry*, London: Allen and Unwin.

Dyer, W.G. Jr and A. Wilkins, 1991, Better Stories Not Better Constructs, To Generate Better Theory: A Rejoinder to Eisenhardt, *Academy of Management Review*, 16 (2): 613–19.

Eckholm, Erik, 2001, Workers' Rights Suffering as China Goes Capitalist, *New York Times*, US National Edition, August 22: A1.

Edstrom, A. and J. Galbraith, 1977, Transfer of Managers as a Co-ordination and Control Strategy in Multinational Organizations, in Gunnar Hedlund, ed., 1993, *Organization of Transnational Corporations*, 6 United Nations Library on Transnational Corporations, London: Routledge, 242–261.

Ellis, John H.M., D.R. Williams and Y. Zuo, 2003, Cross-Cultural Influences on Service Quality in Chinese Retailing: A Comparative Study of Local and International Supermarkets in China, *Asian Business & Management*, 2 (2): 205–21.

Elvin, Mark, 1973, *The Pattern of the Chinese Past*, Stanford, CA: Stanford University Press.

Evans, Paul A.L., 1995, Managing Human Resources in the International Firm, in Christopher Bartlett and Sumantra Ghoshal, eds, *Transnational Management: Text, Cases and Readings in Cross-Border Management*, 2nd edn, Chicago: Irwin, 649–66.

Everatt, Donna, 1999, *Intel in China*, Case No. 99C007, London, Ontario: Richard Ivey School of Business, University of Western Ontario.

Fairbank, John K. and Merle Goldman, 1998, *China: A New History*, enlarged edition, Cambridge, MA: Belknap.

Fan, Ying, 2002, Guanxi's Consequences: Personal Gains at Social Cost, *Journal of Business Ethics*, 38 (4): 371–81.

Ferdows, Kasra, 1997, Making the Most of Foreign Factories, *Harvard Business Review*, March/April: 73–87.

Field, Alan M., 2004, Road to Riches, *Journal of Commerce*, November 15: 1.

Flower, Kathy, 2003, *China: A Quick Guide to Customs and Etiquette*, Portland, OR: Graphic Arts Center Publishing Company.

Fung, Daniel R., 2003, Constitutional Reform in China: The Case of Hong Kong, *Texas International Law Journal*, 39 (3): 467–78.

Fung, H.-G., 1999, Chinese Banking: Challenges and Opportunities in the New Millennium, *Business Forum*, 24 (3/4): 2–7.

Galbraith, Jay, 2001, Building Organizations around the Global Customer, *Ivey Business Journal*, 66 (1): 17–24.

Gamble, J., 2001, Localizing Management in Foreign-Invested Enterprises in China: Practical, Cultural and Strategic Perspectives, *International Journal of Human Resources Management*, 11 (5): 883–903.

Garnier, Gerard, 1982, Context and Decision Making Autonomy in the Foreign Affiliates of US Multinational Corporations, *Academy of Management Journal*, 25 (4): 893–908.

Garnier, Gerard, T.N. Osborn, F. Galicia and R. Lecon, 1979, Autonomy of the Mexican Affiliates of US Multinational Corporations, *Columbia Journal of World Business*, Spring: 78–90.

Garvin, Robert V., 1998, *Starting Something Big: The Commercial Emergence of GE Aircraft Engines*, Reston, VA: American Academy of Aeronautics and Astronautics.

Gelb, Catherine and Virginia Hulme, 2002, Ensuring Health and Safety in China Operations, *China Business Review*, 29 (1): 40–6.

Geringer, J. Michael and Louis Hebert, 1989, Control and Performance of International Joint Ventures, *Journal of International Business Studies*, 20 (2): 235–54.

Ghoshal, Sumantra and Nitin Nohria, 1993, Horses for Courses: Organizational Forms for Multinational Corporations, *Sloan Management Review*, Winter: 23–35.

Gilley, Bruce, 2001, Overexposed, *Far Eastern Economic Review*, June 28: 30–3.

Gittell, J.H., 2000, Paradoxes of Coordination and Control, *California Management Review*, 42 (3): 101–18.

Glaister, Keith W., 1995, Dimensions of Control in U.K. International Joint Ventures, *British Journal of Management*, 6: 77–96.

Goh, M. and Charlene Ling, 2003, Logistics Development in China, *International Journal of Physical Distribution and Logistics Management*, 33 (9/10): 886–918.

Goodman, Peter, 2004, Manufacturing Competition: Private Sector Hit Hardest in China's Effort to Slow Growth, *Washington Post*, August 4: E01.

Gordon, Scott, 1999, *Controlling the State: Constitutionalism from Ancient Athens to Today*, Cambridge, MA: Harvard University Press.

Gu, George, 2005, *Lessons of China's Stock Market*, accessed on June 30, 2005 from http://www.financialsense.com/fsu/editorials/gu/2005/0629.html.

Gupta, A. and V. Govindarajan, 1991, Knowledge Flow Patterns, Subsidiary Strategic Roles and Strategic Controls within MNCs, *1991 Proceedings of the Academy of Management*, New York: Academy of Management, 21–5.

Hakanson, Lars, 1995, Learning through Acquisitions: Management and Integration of Foreign R&D laboratories, *International Studies of Management and Organization*, 25 (1/2): 121–57.

Hambrick, Donald and James W. Fredrickson, 2001, Are You Sure You Have a Strategy?, *Academy of Management Executive*, 15 (4): 48–59.

Hamill, Jim and M. Pambos, 1996, Joint Ventures in China: "Same Bed, Different Dreams", *Asia Pacific Business Review*, 26 (2): 26–46.

Hamilton, Robert D. III, V.A. Taylor and R.J. Kashlak, 1996, Designing a Control System for a Multinational Subsidiary, *Long Range Planning*, 29 (6): 857–68.

Harding, James, 1999, The Italian Job in China Town, *Financial Times*, February 2: 16.

Harvard Business Review, 1995, Beyond Total Quality Management and Business Process Re-Engineering: Managing through Processes, September–October: 80–2.

Harvey, Charles, 1995, Introduction, in Charles Harvey, ed., *Business History: Concepts and Measurement*, London: Cass.

Harzing, Anne-Wil, 1999, *Managing the Multinational: An International Study of Control Mechanisms*, Cheltenham: Elgar.

Harzing, Anne-Wil, 2001, Of Bears, Bumble-Bees and Spiders: The Role of Expatriates in Controlling Foreign Subsidiaries, *Journal of World Business*, 36 (4): 366–80.

Henderson, Kim and James Evans, 2000, Successful Implementation of Six Sigma: Benchmarking: General Electric Company, *Benchmarking*, 7 (4): 260–81.

Henkoff, R., 1996, Growing Your Company: Five Ways To Do It Right!, *Fortune*, 134 (10): 78–88.

Hickson, D.J., C.R. Hinings, C.J. McMillan and J.P. Schweitzer, 1974, The Culture-Free Context of Organization Structure: A Tri-National Comparison, *Sociology*, 8: 59–80.

Hill, Charles W.L. and J.F. Pickering, 1986, Divisionalization, Decentralization and Performance of Large United Kingdom Companies, *Journal of Management Studies*, 23 (1): 26–50.

Hoover, Kenneth and Todd Donovan, 2001, *The Elements of Social Science Thinking*, 7th edn, Boston: Bedford/St Martin's.

Horsley, Jamie, 2004, China's Long March toward Rule of Law, *Journal of Asian Studies*, 63 (1): 162–5.

Hougan, Glen, C.L. Hung and Ron Wardell, 2000, Research Note: Product Adaptations for the Chinese, *Thunderbird International Business Review*, 42 (5): 551–69.

Hu, Yao-Su, 1992, The International Transferability of the Firm's Advantages, *California Management Review*, 37 (4): 73–88.

Huang, Ray, 1997, *China: A Macro History*, Armonk, NY: Sharpe.

Huffman, Ted, 2003, Wal-Mart in China: Challenges Facing a Foreign Retailer's Supply Chain, *China Business Review*, 30 (5): 18–23.

Hulbert, James M. and William K. Brandt, 1980, *Managing the Multinational Subsidiary*, New York: Holt, Reinhart and Winston.

Humes, S., 1993, *Managing the Multinational: Confronting the Global–Local Dilemma*, New York: Prentice Hall.

Hymer, Stephen, 1976, *The International Operations of National Firms: A Study of Direct Foreign Investment*, Cambridge, MA: MIT Press.

International Organization for Standardization, 2004, *ISO 9000 and ISO 14000 in Brief*, accessed on May 20, 2005 from http://www.iso.org/iso/en/iso9000-14000/understand/inbrief.html.

Ireland, R. Duane and Michael A. Hitt, 1999, Achieving and Maintaining Strategic Competitiveness in the 21st Century: The Role of Strategic Leadership, *Academy of Management Executive*, 1: 43–57.

Jaeger, Alfred, 1983, The Transfer of Organizational Culture Overseas: An Approach to Control in the Multinational Corporation, *Journal of International Business Studies*, Fall: 91–114.

Janssens, Maddy, 2001, Developing a Culturally Synergistic Approach to International Human Resources Management, *Journal of World Business*, 36 (4): 429–51.

Jary, David and Julia Jary, 1991, *The Harper Collins Dictionary of Sociology*, New York, Harper Perennial.

Jenner, W.J.F., 1994, *The Tyranny of History: The Roots of China's Crisis*, London: Penguin.

Jiang, Bian and Edmund Prater, 2002, Distribution and Logistics Development in China: The Revolution Has Begun, *International Journal of Physical Distribution & Logistics Management*, 32 (9/10): 783–99.

Johansen, J. and J. Vahlne, 1977, The Internationalization Process of the Firm: A Model of Knowledge Development and Increasing Foreign Market Commitments, *Journal of International Business Studies*, 8: 23–32.

Kahn, Joseph, 2003, Foul Water and Air: Part of Cost of the Boom in China's Exports, *New York Times*, November 4: A1.

Kanter, Rosabeth Moss and Thomas Dretler, 1998, "Global Strategy" and Its Impact on Local Operations: Lessons from Gillette Singapore, *Academy of Management Executive*, 12 (4): 60–8.

Kerr, John, 2002, 10 Key Challenges for the Chinese Logistics Industry, *Logistics Management*, 44 (2): S64–8.

Kessler, Michelle, 2004, US Firms: Doing Business in China Tough, but Critical, *USA Today* (international edition), August 17: 8A.

Kets de Vries, Manfred, 1995a, Making a Giant Dance, *Across the Board*, 31 (9): 27–36.

Kets de Vries, Manfred, 1995b, *Life and Death in the Executive Fast Lane: Essays on Irrational Organizations and Their Leaders*, San Francisco: Jossey-Bass.

Kim, Seung Chul, 1996, Analysis of Strategic Issues for International Joint Ventures: Case Studies of Hong Kong–China Joint Venture Manufacturing Firms, *Journal of Euromarketing*, 4 (3/4): 55–70.

Kim, Y.K. and Nigel Campbell, 1997, The Internationalization Process and Control Style of MNCs: The Case of Korean Electronic Companies, in Jim Slater and Roger Strange, eds, *Business Relationships with East Asia: The European Experience*, London: Routledge, 136–50.

Kinnear, T.C., 1999, How Do Firms Relate to Their Markets, *Journal of Marketing*, 63 (Special Issue): 112–15.

Kloot, Louise, 1997, Organizational Learning and Management Control Systems: Responding to Environmental Change, *Management Accounting Research*, 8: 47–73.

Knight, C.F., 1992, Emerson Electric: Consistent Profits, Consistently, *Harvard Business Review*, January–February, 57–70.

Kobrin, S., 1988, Expatriate Reduction and Strategic Control in American Multinational Corporations, *Human Resources Management*, 27 (1): 63–75.

Koch, Richard, 1994, *The Financial Times Guide to Management and Finance*, London: Financial Times–Pitman.

Kotter, John P. and James L. Heskett, 1992, *Corporate Culture and Performance*, New York: Free.

Kuin, Pieter, 1972, The Magic of Multinational Management, *Harvard Business Review*, November/December: 89–97.

Kynge, James, 2004, China's Economic Growth: Is It Sustainable?, *National Committee on United States–China Relations: Notes*, 32 (2): 11–15.

Lai, Harry Hongyi, 2003, Local Governments and China's WTO Entry, *American Asian Review*, 21 (3): 153–87.

Lawrence, Paul R. and Jay Lorsch, 1967, *Organizations and Environment*, Boston: Division of Research, Harvard University Graduate School of Business Administration.

Lawrence, Paul R. and Jay Lorsch, 1970, An Orientation and Introduction, in Paul Lawrence and Jay Lorsch, eds, *Studies in Organization Design*, Homewood, IL: Irwin, 1–15.

Lebas, Michel and Jane Weigenstein, 1986, Management Control: The Role of Rules, Markets and Culture, *Journal of Management Studies*, 23 (3): 259–72.

Leavy, Brian, 1994, The Craft of Case-Based Qualitative Research, *Irish Business and Administrative Research*, 15: 105–25.

Legewie, Jochen, 2002, Control and Co-ordination of Japanese Subsidiaries in China: Problems of an Expatriate-Based Management System, *International Journal of Human Resource Management,* 13 (6): 901–19.

Lehman, Edward and Brinton M. Scott, 1999, No More Excuses, *China Business Review*, 26 (2): 46–9.

Lehrer, Mark and K. Asakawa, 1999, Unbundling European Operations: Regional Management and Corporate Flexibility in American and Japanese MNCs, *Journal of World Business*, 34 (3): 267–86.

Lenz, R.T., 1981, "Determinants" of Organizational Performance: An Interdisciplinary Review, *Strategic Management Journal*, 2: 131–54.

Levitt, B. and James G. Marsh, 1988, Organizational Learning, *Annual Review of Sociology*, 14: 319–40.

Levitt, Theodore, 1983, The Globalization of Market, *Harvard Business Review*, May–June: 92–102.

Li, Cheng, 2002, *China's Leadership Succession and Its Implications*, written testimony prepared for The U.S.–China Security Review Commission public hearing, Washington, DC, September 23.

Li, Lusha and Brian Kleiner, 2001, The Legacy of Danwei and Job Performance, *Management Research News*, 24 (3/4): 57–66.

Li, Shaomin, 2002, *China's Political Reform is the Key to US–China Relations*, written testimony prepared for The U.S.–China Security Review Commission public hearing, Washington, DC, September 23.

Li, Shaomin, 2004, Why Is Property Right Protection Lacking in China?, *California Management Review*, 46 (3): 100–15.

Lieberthal, Kenneth, 1995, *Governing China: From Revolution through Reform*, New York: Norton.

Lieberthal, Kenneth, 1997, China–Domestic Issues: Economics, Energy and Security, Remarks before the White House Press Corps, Washington, DC, October 24, reprinted in *Vital Speeches of the Day*, 64 (3): 75–7.

Liao, Darlene, 1999, Leader of the Pack, *China Business Review*, 26 (6): 28–35.

Liu, Sunray, 2000, Multinationals Expand Design Presence in China, *Electronic Engineering Times*, November 20: 38.

Loeb, M., 1995, Jack Welch Lets Fly on Budgets, Bonuses, etc., *Fortune*, 131 (10): 145–8.

Lord, Michael D. and Annette Ranft, 2000, Organizational Learning about New International Markets: Exploring the Internal Transfer of Local Market Knowledge, *Journal of International Business Studies*, 31 (4): 573–89.

Love, John, 1995, *McDonald's: Behind the Arches*, rev. edn, New York: Bantam.

Lubit, Roy, 2001, Tacit Knowledge and Knowledge Management: The Keys to Sustainable Competitive Advantage, *Organizational Dynamics*, 29 (3): 164–79.

Lubman, Stanley, 2000, Bird in a Cage: Chinese Law Reform after Twenty Years, *Northwestern Journal of International Law & Business*, 20 (3): 383–424.

Lucente, Edward, 1994, *Managing a Global Enterprise*, Working Paper 94-2, Pittsburgh, Carnegie Bosch Institute for Applied Studies in International Management.

Luo, Yadong, 1997, Guanxi: Principles, Philosophies and Implications, *Human Systems Management*, 16 (1): 43–51.

Luo, Yadong, 2001, Determinants of Local Responsiveness: Perspectives from Foreign Subsidiaries in Emerging Markets, *Journal of Management*, 27 (4): 451–77.

Lyons, Thomas P., 1991, Interprovincial Disparities in China: Output and Consumption, *Economic Development and Cultural Change*, 39 (3): 471–507.

Ma, Rong Xie, 2002, Remarks before the World Affairs Council of Northern California, "The Future of Business and Technology in China", Palo Alto, CA, March 16, 2002.

Maljers, F., 1992, Inside Unilever: The Evolving Transnational Company, *Harvard Business Review*, September–October: 2–7.

Malnight, T.W., 2001, Emerging Structural Patterns within Multinational Corporations: Toward Process-Based Structures, *Academy of Management Review*, 44 (8): 1187–210.

Mann, William C., 2005, Report: China's Consumer Society in Full Bloom, *Associated Press*, accessed on February 23, 2005 from http://www.myrtlebeachonline.com/mid/myrtlebeachonline/business.

Martin, Joanne, 1998, Organizational Culture, in Nigel Nicholson, R.S. Schuler and Andrew Van de Ven, eds, *The Blackwell Encyclopedic Dictionary of Organizational Behavior*, rev. edn, Oxford: Blackwell, 376–82.

Martinez, Jon and J.C. Jarillo, 1989, The Evolution of Research on Coordination Mechanisms in Multinational Corporations, *Journal of International Business Studies*, 20 (2): 489–514.

McClenahan, J.S., 1997, Asia's Best Practices, *Industry Week*, 246 (17): 28–34.

McComb, Rebecca, 1999, "2009:" China's Human Relations Odyssey, *The China Business Review*, 26 (5): 30–3.

McDonald, John, 1950, *Strategy in Poker, Business & War*, 1996 pbk edn, New York: Norton.

McLean, Iain and Alistair McMillan, eds, 2003, *Concise Oxford Dictionary of Politics*, 2nd edn, Oxford: Oxford University Press.

Meieran, Eugene, 1998, 21st Century Semiconductor Manufacturing Capabilities, *Intel Technology Journal*, Fourth Quarter, available at www.intel.com.

Melvin, Sheila and K. Sylvester, 1997, Shipping Out, *China Business Review*, 24 (3): 30–5.

Mercer, David, 1988, *The Global IBM: Leadership in Multinational Management*, New York: Dodd, Mead.

Merrifield, D. Bruce, 2000, The Changing Nature of Competitive Advantage, *Research Technology Management*, 43 (1): 41–5.

Mieszkowski, Katherine, 1998, Get with the Program!, *Fast Company*, February: 28–30.

Miller, John, 1998, Values Scrawled in Blood, *Across the Board*, 35 (9): 12–13.

Mintzberg, Henry, 1989, *Mintzberg on Management: Inside Our Strange World of Organizations*, New York: Free.

Mische, Michael A., 2001, *Strategic Renewal: Becoming a High Performance Organization*, Saddle River, NJ: Prentice-Hall.

Moore, Gordon, 1996, Intel – Memories and the Microprocessor, *Daedalus*, 125 (2): 55–81.

Nathan, Andrew J. and Bruce Gilley, 2003, *China's New Rulers: The Secret Files*, 2nd rev. edn, New York: New York Review of Books.

Nelson, Richard R., 1991, Why Do Firms Differ and Why Does It Matter?, *Strategic Management Journal*, 12 (Special Issue): 61–74.

Nelson, Richard R. and Sidney Winter, 1982, *An Evolutionary Theory of Economic Change*, Cambridge, MA: Belknap.

Newberry, William and Yoram Zeira, 1999, Autonomy and Effectiveness of Equity International Joint Ventures, *Journal of Management Studies*, 36 (2): 263–86.

Newman, William H., 1992, "Focused" Joint Ventures in Transforming Economies, *Academy of Management Executive*, 6 (1): 66–75.

Nicholson, Nigel, R.S. Schuler and Andrew Van de Ven, eds, 1998, *The Blackwell Encyclopedic Dictionary of Organizational Behavior*, rev. edn, Oxford: Blackwell.

Noel, James and Ram Charan, 1992, GE Brings Global Thinking to Light, *Training & Development*, 46 (7): 28–33.

Nohria, N. and S. Ghoshal, 1994, Differentiated Fit and Shared Values: Alternatives for Managing Headquarters–Subsidiary Relations, *Strategic Management Journal*, 15: 491–502.

Nolan, Peter, 1995, *Joint Ventures and Economic Reform in China: A Case Study of the Coca-Cola Business System, with Particular Reference to the Tianjin Coca-Cola Plant*, Cambridge: ESRC Centre for Business Research.

O'Connor, Neal and Peter Chalos, 1999, The Challenge for Successful Joint Venture Management in China: Lessons from a Failed Joint Venture, *Multinational Business Review*, 7 (1): 50–61.

O'Donnell, Sharon Watson, 2000, Managing Foreign Subsidiaries: Agents of Headquarters or an Interdependent Network?, *Strategic Management Journal*, 21: 525–48.

Osland, Gregory E., 1993, *A Bilateral Analysis of the Performance of U.S.–China Equity Joint Ventures*, unpublished PhD thesis, East Lansing, MI, Department of Marketing and Logistics, Eli Broad School of Business, Michigan State University.

Osland, Gregory E. and I. Bjorkman, 1998, MNC–Host Government Interaction: Government Pressures on MNCs in China, *European Management Journal*, 16 (1): 91–100.

Ouchi, William, 1977, The Relationship between Organizational Structure and Organizational Control, *Administrative Science Quarterly*, 22: 95–112.

Ouchi, William, 1980, Markets, Bureaucracies and Clans, *Administrative Science Quarterly*, 25: 129–40.

Packard, David, 1996, *The HP Way: How Bill Hewlett and I Built Our Company*, pbk edn, New York: Harper Collins.

Parkhe, Arvind, 1993, "Messy Research:" Methodological Predispositions and Theory Development in International Joint Ventures, *Academy of Management Review*, 18 (2): 227–68.

Parkhe, Arvind, 1996, International Joint Ventures, in Betty Jane Punnett and Oded Shenkar, eds, *Handbook for International Management Research*, Cambridge, MA: Blackwell, 429–60.

Pascale, Richard, 1990, *Managing on the Edge: How the Smartest Companies Use Conflict to Stay Ahead*, New York: Simon & Schuster.

Paterson, Alan, 1994, Barrett Moves to Boost Intel's Asia Ties, *Electronic Engineering Times*, April 4: 8–9.

Pearson, Margaret M., 1991, *Joint Ventures in the People's Republic of China: The Control of Foreign Direct Investment under Socialism*, Princeton, NJ: Princeton University Press.

Pei, Minxin, 1999, Is China Stable?, *Asian Wall Street Journal*, July 28: 10.

Pei, Minxin, 2002, China's Split Personality, *Newsweek International*, October 28: 40–4.

Pei, Minxin, 2003, The Real Test of China's Appetite for Reform, *FT.com*, accessed on May 20, 2005 from http://proquest.umi.com/pqdweb?did=281108611.

Pei, Minxin, 2004, China Is Still Far from Being a Free-Market Economy, *Asian Wall Street Journal*, August 24: A9.

Peng, Mike, 1997, Winning Structures, *China Business Review*, 24 (1): 30–6.

Peng, Mike, 2000, Controlling the Foreign Agent: How Governments Deal with Multinationals in a Transition Economy, *Management International Review*, 40 (2): 141–65.

People's Republic of China, 2005, *Constitution of the People's Republic of China*, accessed on July 10, 2005 from http://english.peopledaily.com.cn/constitution/constitution.html.

Perlmutter, Howard A., 1969, The Tortuous Evolution of the Multinational Enterprise, in Gunnar Hedlund, ed., 1993, *Organization of Transnational Corporations*, 6 United Nations Library on Transnational Corporations, London: Routledge, 295–310.

Peterson, Richard B., Nancy Napier and Won Shul-Shim, 2000, Expatriate Management: A Comparison of MNCs across Four Parent Countries, *Thunderbird International Business Review*, 41 (2): 145–66.

Pettigrew, Andrew, Richard Woodman and Kim Cameron, 2001, Studying Organizational Change and Development: Challenges for Future Research, *Academy of Management Journal*, 44 (4): 697–713.

Pine, Ray and Pingshu Qi, 2004, Barriers to Hotel Chain Development in China, *International Journal of Contemporary Hospitality Management*, 16 (1): 37–54.

Prahalad, C.K. and Kenneth Lieberthal, 1998, The End of Corporate Imperialism, *Harvard Business Review*, July/August: 69–79.

Quelch, John and Edward Hoff, 1986, Customizing Global Marketing, *Harvard Business Review*, May/June, 59–69.

Richards, Malika, 2001, US Multinational Staffing Practices and Implications for Subsidiary Performance in the U.K. and Thailand, *Thunderbird International Business Review*, 43 (2): 225–42.

Rodrigues, Carl, 1996, *International Management*, Saint Paul, MN: West.

Rohwer, Jim, 2000, GE Digs into Asia, *Fortune*, October 2: 164–79.

Rondinelli, Dennis, B. Rosen and I. Drori, 2001, The Struggle for Strategic Alignment in Multinational Corporations: Managing Readjustment during Global Expansion, *European Management Journal*, 19 (4): 404–17.

Rosen, D.H., 1999, *Behind the Open Door: Foreign Enterprises in the Chinese Marketplace*, Washington, DC: Institute for International Economics.

Ross, Adam, 2004, Critical Eye on Jiaxing and Zhenjiang, *China Business Review*, 31 (6): 44–7.

Roth, Kendall and D. Nigh, 1992, The Effectiveness of Headquarters–Subsidiary Relationships: The Role of Coordination, Control and Conflict, *Journal of Business Research*, 25: 277–301.

Rudman, Stephen Todd, 2000, Building Blocks: How to Structure Overseas Operations, *House Counsel*, 5 (5): 16–19.

Rumelt, Richard, Dan Schendel and David Teece, 1991, Strategic Management and Economics, *Strategic Management Journal*, 12 (Special Issue): 5–29.

Saez, Lawrence, 2001, Banking Reform in India and China, *International Journal of Finance & Economics*, 6 (3): 235–44.

Salk, Jane, 1996, Partners and Other Strangers: Cultural Boundaries and Cross-Cultural Encounters in International Joint Venture Teams, *International Studies of Management and Organization* 26 (4): 48–72.

Scalapino, Robert, 1999, The American Response to A Changing Asia, address before the National Defense University 1999 Pacific Symposium "U.S. Engagement Policy in a Changing Asia: A Time for Reassessment?", Honolulu, Hawaii, March 2.

Schenk, Deborah H., 1998, Taxation, in *Fundamentals of American Law*, New York University School of Law, Alan B. Morrison general editor, pbk edn, New York: Oxford University Press.

Schwartz, Howard and Stanley M. Davis, 1981, Matching Corporate Culture and Business Strategy, *Organizational Dynamics*, 10 (1): 30–49.

Seligman, Scott, 1999, *Guanxi*, Grease for the Wheels of China, *The China Business Review*, 26 (5): 34–8.

Sender, H., 1991, Yotaro Kobayashi of Fuji Xerox: Managing a Cross-Border Joint Venture, *Institutional Investor*, 25 (10): 29–36.

Shenkar, Oded, 1990, International Joint Ventures' Problems in China: Risks and Remedies, *Long Range Planning*, 23 (3): 82–90.

Simon, Herbert, 1994, *Is International Management Different from Management?*, Working Paper 94-1, Pittsburgh, Carnegie Bosch Institute for Applied Studies in International Management.

Simons, Craig, 2005, Yangtze Highway, *Newsweek* (international edition), July 25: 42.

Sowinski, Lara, 2004, The World's "Factory Floor" has some rough spots, *World Trade*, May: 57–60.

Sparaco, Pierre, 1999, CFMI Anticipates Slower Engine Sales, *Aviation Week & Space Technology*, 150 (12): 39–42.

Starr, John Bryan, 2001, *Understanding China*, pbk edn, New York: Hill & Wang.

Stein, Charles, 2005, Small Change, *The Boston Globe*, May 31, accessed on May 31, 2005 from http://www.boston.com/business/articles/2005/05/31/small_change.

Stewart, Sally and P. de Lisle, 1994, Hong Kong Expatriates in the People's Republic of China, *International Studies of Management and Organization*, 24 (3): 105–21.

Stoever, William, 1994, Foreign Investors Caught between Central and Provincial Governments in China, *Multinational Business Review*, 2 (2): 8–18.

Stopford, J.M. and Louis T. Wells Jr, 1972, Developing an Organization for Multinational Business, in Gunnar Hedlund, ed., 1993, *Organization of Transnational Corporations*, 6 United Nations Library on Transnational Corporations, London: Routledge, 25–45.

Stopper, William G., 1998, Agility in Action: Picturing the Lessons Learned from Kodak and 23 Other Companies, *HR: Human Resources Planning*, 21 (1): 11–13.

Sun, T. and Guohua Wu, 2004, Consumption Patterns of Chinese Urban and Rural Consumers, *Journal of Consumer Marketing*, 21 (4/5): 245–54.

Sundaram, A.K. and J.S. Black, 1992, The Environment and Internal Organization of Multinational Enterprises, *Academy of Management Review*, 17 (4): 729–66.

Swasy, A., 1997, *Changing Focus: Kodak and the Battle to Save a Great American Company*, New York: Times Books.

Swift, Douglas, 2000, "Kodak in China", presentation to securities analysts, September 11, 2000, available at www.kodak.com/country./US/en/corp/pressCenter/presentations/2000Analyst/index.shtml.

Taggert, James H., 1998, Strategy and Control in Multinational Corporations: Too Many Recipes?, *Long Range Planning*, 31 (4): 571–65.

Tahib, M., 1998, Transfer of HRM Practices across Cultures: An American Company in Scotland, *International Journal of Human Resources Management*, 9 (2): 332–58.

Tahib, M., 2000, *The Management of International Enterprises: A Socio-Political View*, New York: St Martin's.

Tanzer, Andrew, 2001, Chinese Walls, *Forbes*, November 12: 74–5.

Taylor, Bill, 1999, Patterns of Control within Japanese Manufacturing Plants in China: Doubts about Japanization in Asia, *Journal of Management Studies*, 36 (6): 853–73.

Taylor, Robert, 2003, China's Consumer Revolution: Distribution Reform, Foreign Investment and the Impact of the WTO, *Asian Business & Management*, 2 (2): 187–204.

Tedlow, Richard S., 2001, *Giants of Enterprise: Seven Innovators and the Empires they Built*, New York: Harper Business.

The Economist, 2000, China's State-Owned Enterprises: The Longer March, September 30: 71–4.

The Tax Advisor, 2001, Tax Planning for Expatriates, 32 (4): 244–8.

Tichy, Noel and Ram Charan, 1989, Speed, Simplicity, Self-Confidence: An Interview with Jack Welch, *Harvard Business Review*, Sep./Oct.: 112–21.

Tindall, Robert E., 1975, *Multinational Enterprises: Legal and Management Structures and Interrelationship with Ownership, Control Antitrust, Labor, Taxation and Disclosure*, Dobbs Ferry, NY: Oceana.

Ting, Shi, 2004, Breaking down the Barriers to Progress: Taskforce Sent to 28 Jurisdictions to Inspect Efforts against Protectionism, *South China Morning Post*, November 10: 7.

Tjoa, Laetitia, Ouyang Jianyu and Like Pykstra, 2005, Complying with PRC Anti-Bribery Laws, *China Business Review*, 32 (2): 34–8.

Trianto, Oliver, 2001, Rules of Engagement: Joint Venture Law Feels WTO Effect, *China International Business*, May: 42–3.

Troiano, Peter, 1999, Sharing the Throne, *Management Review*, 88 (2): 39–44.

Trunick, Perry A., 2003, Logistics Links Are Critical in China, *Transportation & Distribution*, August: 57–60.

Tsang, Eric W.K., 1999, Internationalization as a Learning Process: Singapore MNCs in China, *Academy of Management Executive*, 13 (1): 91–101.

Underwood, Laurie, 2004, Shades of Gray, *AmChat, Journal of the American Chamber of Commerce in Shanghai*, August: 18–19.

US–China Business Council, 2005, *China's Economy 2004*, accessed on May 31, 2005 from http://www.uschina.org/statistics/2005economyforecast.html.

Usunier, Jean-Claude, 1998, *International and Cross-Cultural Management Research*, Thousand Oaks, CA: Sage.

Vachani, Sushil, 1995, Enhancing the Obsolescing Bargain Theory: A Longitudinal Study, *Journal of International Business Studies*, 26 (1): 159–81.

Vaghefi, M.R. and A.B. Huellmantel, 1998, Strategic Leadership at General Electric, *Long Range Planning*, 31 (2): 280–94.

Van Kemenade, Willem, 1998, *China, Hong Kong, Taiwan, Inc.*, New York: Vintage.

Vernon, Raymond, 1971, *Sovereignty at Bay*, New York: Basic.

Wall Street Journal, 1991, Two Asian Agencies, U.S. Group to Buy 25% of Chinese Bank, July 29: A5E.

Walsh, James and Er Ping Wang, 1999, Same Bed, Different Dreams: Working Relationships in Sino-American Joint Ventures, *Journal of World Business*, 34 (1): 69–94.

Walton, Julie, 2005, WTO – Year 4, *The China Business Review*, 32 (1): 24–9.

Warner, Malcolm, 1997, Management–Labour Relations in the New Chinese Economy, *Human Resource Management Journal*, 7 (4): 30–44.

Weber, Yaakov, 1996, Corporate Cultural Fit and Performance in Mergers and Acquisitions, *Human Relations*, 49 (4): 1181–205.

Westney, D.E., 1993, Institutional Theory and the Multinational Corporation, in Sumantra Ghoshal and D. Eleanor Westney, eds, *Organization Theory and the Multinational Corporation*, New York: St Martin's.

Wilkins, Mira, 1974, *The Maturing of Multinational Enterprise: American Business Abroad from 1914 to 1970*, Cambridge, MA: Harvard University Press.

Wilkins, Mira, 1975, Comments, in Harold F. Williamson, ed., *Evolution of International Management Structures*, Newark, DE: University of Delaware Press.

Wills, Christopher, 1989, *The Wisdom of the Genes*, New York: Basic.

Wilms, Welford W., Deone Zell, Osamu Kimura and Dennis Cuneo, 1994, *Reinventing Organizational Culture across International Boundaries*, Working Paper 94-3, Pittsburgh, Carnegie Bosch Institute for Applied Studies in International Management.

Wonacott, Peter, 2002a, China's Secret Weapon: Smart, Cheap Labor for High-Tech Goods, *Wall Street Journal*, March 14 (US Edition): A1.

Wonacott, Peter, 2002b, PetroChina Unit, After Job Cuts, Is Besieged by Protestors, *Wall Street Journal*, March 14 (US Edition): A9.

Wonacott, Peter, 2002c, Technical Barriers Keep WTO Reforms at Bay in China – Flurry of New Regulations on Trade Limit Pain of Opening Up Markets, *Wall Street Journal*, February 6: A12.

Wong, Chi-Sum and Kenneth Law, 1999, Managing Localization of Human Resources in the PRC: A Practical Model, *Journal of World Business*, 34 (1): 26–41.

Wooldridge, A., 1995, Who Wants To Be a Giant?, *The Economist*, Special Survey: Multinationals, July 24: 1–22.

World Bank, 2004, *China Data Profile*, accessed on May 26, 2005 from http://devdata. worldbank.org/external/CPProfile.asp?SelectedCountries/China.

Wright, Daniel, 1999, The Other Side of China's Prosperity, *The China Business Review*, 26 (5): 22–9.

Wright, Lorna L., 1996, Qualitative International Management Research, in B.J. Punnett and Oded Shenkar, eds, *Handbook of International Management Research*, Cambridge, MA: Blackwell Business.

Wright, Lorna L., P.W. Beamish and H.W. Lane, 1988, International Management Research: Lessons from the Field, *International Studies of Management and Organization*, 18 (3): 55–71.

Wu, Christina, 2003, *China Logistics Profile*, Washington, DC: United States Department of Agriculture, Foreign Agricultural Service, Global Agriculture Information Network (GAIN) Report No. CH3833.

Wu, Xiaoling, 2005, Develop Corporate Bond Market to Improve Financial Asset Structure, address, *Ninth Forum of China's Capital Markets*, Beijing, February 7, accessed on May 22, 2005 from http://www.pbc.gov.cn/english//detail.asp?col=6500&ID=70.

Xin, Katherine and J. Pearce, 1996, Guanxi: Connections as Substitutes for Formal Institutional Support, *Academy of Management Journal*, 39 (6): 1641–58.

Xinhua News Agency, 2001, Press Release: Foreign Enterprises Speed Up Merger with Chinese Counterparts Prior to WTO Entry, Beijing: November 7.

Yan, Aimin, 1998, Structural Stability and Reconfiguration in International Joint Ventures, *Journal of International Business Studies*, 29 (4): 773–95.

Yan, Aimin and Barbara Gray, 1994, Bargaining Power, Management Control and Performance in United States–China Joint Ventures: A Comparative Case Study, *Academy of Management Journal*, 37 (6): 1478–1517.

Yan, Yanni, John Child and Yuan Lu, 1995, *Ownership and Control in International Business: An Examination of Sino-Foreign Joint Ventures*, Series 1994–1995, no. 6, Cambridge, Judge Institute of Management Studies, University of Cambridge.

Yang, Dali, 1999, Can China Overcome Legal Balkanization?, *Chinaonline.com*, November 2, accessed on May 28, 2005 from http://www.pnl.gov/china/balkaniz.htm.

Yang, Dali, 2002, Can the Chinese State Meet Its WTO obligations? Government Reforms, Regulatory Capacity and WTO Membership, *American Asian Review*, 20 (2): 191–220.

Yang, Jijian, 2002, Market Power in China: Manifestations, Effects and Legislation, *Review of Industrial Organizations*, 21 (2): 167–83.

Yang, Keming, 2002, Double Entrepreneurship in China's Economic Reform: An Analytic Framework, *Journal of Political and Military Sociology*, 30 (1): 134–49.

Yang, Mayfair Mei-hui, 1994, *Gifts, Favors and Banquets: The Art of Social Relationships in China*, Ithaca, NY: Cornell University Press.

Yatsko, Pamela, 2001, *New Shanghai: The Rocky Rebirth of China's Legendary City*, Singapore: Wiley.

Yeung, Henry Wai-chung, 1997, Cooperative Strategies and Chinese Business Networks, in Paul W. Beamish and J.P. Killing, eds, *Cooperative Strategies: Asian Pacific Perspectives*, San Francisco: New Lexington.

Yi, L.M. and Paul Ellis, 1999, Guanxi: A Comparison of Mainland and Overseas Chinese Perspectives, presented at the 1999 Annual Meeting of the Academy of International Business, November 20, Charleston, South Carolina, USA.

Yin, Robert K., 1994, *Case Study Research: Design and Methods*, 2nd edn, Thousand Oaks, CA: Sage.

Yu, Albert, 1998, *Creating the Digital Future: The Secrets of Innovation at Intel*, New York: Free.

Zakreskie, Judy and Fred He, 2001, Reaching China's Middle Class through Retail Pharmacies, *China Business Review*, 28 (5): 60–5.

Zhang, Wei, 2001, Rethinking Regional Disparity in China, *Economics of Planning*, 34 (1/2): 113–34.

Zou, Keyuan, 2000, Judicial Reform versus Judicial Corruption: Recent Developments in China, *Criminal Law Forum*, 11 (3): 323–53.

Index

Note: page numbers in **bold** refer to tables.